Cambridge Historical Essays.   No. XIX

THE

THEORY OF TOLERATION

UNDER THE LATER STUARTS

THE
THEORY OF TOLERATION
UNDER THE LATER STUARTS

BY

A. A. SEATON, M.A.
FELLOW OF PEMBROKE COLLEGE, CAMBRIDGE

THE PRINCE CONSORT PRIZE, 1910

" Coffined thoughts of coffined men."

Cambridge :
at the University Press
1911

CAMBRIDGE
UNIVERSITY PRESS

University Printing House, Cambridge CB2 8BS, United Kingdom

Cambridge University Press is part of the University of Cambridge.

It furthers the University's mission by disseminating knowledge in the pursuit of education, learning and research at the highest international levels of excellence.

www.cambridge.org
Information on this title: www.cambridge.org/9781316603680

© Cambridge University Press 1911

First published 1911
First paperback edition 2016

A catalogue record for this publication is available from the British Library

ISBN 978-1-316-60368-0 Paperback

PREFACE

THE following essay is one of two to which the Prince Consort Prize was awarded in 1910, and is now published in accordance with the prescribed regulations. With the permission of the examiners I have made certain alterations in preparing it for the press, considerably expanding the first chapter, and adding a final chapter of recapitulation and summary. Also a large number of minor alterations and additions have been made. Thus the essay is somewhat increased in bulk, but it has undergone no essential change in substance or structure.

In dealing with the actual controversy between the years 1660 and 1714, as distinct from the intellectual tendencies which led up to it, I have presented the views of writers as far as possible in their own words, and have as a rule tried to bring forward all the main arguments for toleration used in the particular work under consideration, whether they had been employed in an earlier work or not. Such a method necessarily involves a good deal of repetition of arguments, but I have conceived of my task not as that of pointing out what fresh contribution (if any) each writer made to the discussion—indeed, if originality were the test, perhaps few writers in this period would have deserved mention at all—but rather

as that of following the course of the controversy as it
actually took place, and of setting forth, with as few
considerable omissions as possible, the contemporary views
upon the subject. In a word I have tried, not so much to
speak for the age, as to let the age speak for itself. With
this object in view I have devoted no small share of my
attention to the writers upon the intolerant side. This
was necessary, I think, from two points of view. In the
first place, it is clear that we are insufficiently provided
with means of understanding the attitude of the tolerationists, unless we know what were the views which they
attacked, and on what grounds resistance was made to
their attack. Secondly, the anti-tolerationists were in our
period fighting, so to speak, a rearguard action, and a
knowledge of the position they took up from time to time
is a valuable indication of the point to which the tolerant
forces had advanced.

If, however, I have taken a comprehensive view of my
duties in this respect, I have confined my efforts rather
strictly in another. The question of toleration was closely
connected with the kindred questions of comprehension,
of the tests, and of occasional conformity. While references now and then to these questions, and to the ideas
entertained upon them, are of value as throwing light
upon the matter with which we are more immediately
concerned, I have not felt it part of my task to deal at all
with these questions for their own sake.

More open to criticism, perhaps, is my omission of all
reference to the freedom of the press. But the inclusion
of this question would, I think, militate against unity of
treatment, while adding little to the theory of toleration
as set forth in its bearings upon religion, to which aspect

I have confined myself (save for a few references) for reasons set forth in the first chapter.

In certain cases I have suggested an earlier date for a book than that found on its title-page, because a reply to it appeared bearing the date of the previous year. Thus Parker's *Ecclesiastical Polity* is dated 1670, but Owen's reply to it is dated 1669. Presumably Parker's book was published actually in 1669 bearing the date of the following year—an example of a practice which seems to have been not uncommon.

I have tried to make the index full enough to be of use for purposes of study: for any inconsistencies of method it may show I plead the excuse that it was compiled amidst great pressure of other work.

It is unlikely that I have in all cases succeeded in acknowledging, where acknowledgment is due, my debts to the authors of books I have consulted: for all such omissions (which I trust are few) I apologise.

It remains for me to express my thanks to Professor Gwatkin, to Mr T. R. Glover, Fellow of S. John's College, and to the Rev. J. K. Mozley, Fellow and Dean of Pembroke College, for the help they have given me. To Mr Glover I am especially indebted, not only for valuable advice given while the essay was still in manuscript, but also for a very helpful revision of the proofs.

A. A. S.

Pembroke College,
  Cambridge.
      January 18*th*, 1911.

CONTENTS

CHAPTER I

THE THEORIES OF PERSECUTION AND TOLERATION

TOLERATION is the practical recognition of the *The question of toleration* right of the individual to form and to act upon his own opinions on the great issues of life generally, as against the claim of external authority to prescribe limits to thought and practice. As a matter of fact the battle for toleration has been fought and won *contested mainly in relation to religion,* (so far as it has been won) mainly in relation to one of those issues, religion. And it is not difficult to see why this should have been so. In the absence of systematized scientific knowledge, theology usurped *because of (1) usurpations of theology,* dominion over departments of thought to which it had no just claim ; and consequently the progress of thought in these departments has been quite irrelevantly challenged on theological grounds, and the new opinions have been treated as a matter of religion. And in the proper sphere of religion, which affords *(2) activity of, and limitations on, theological speculation,* the widest field for speculation, the prescribed limits of speculation have been most jealously guarded. But while the limits themselves have been specially insisted upon, within those limits considerable activity of thought has generally prevailed; it is not surprising, therefore, that speculative minds have frequently overrun the mark and come into collision with authority. Besides this, decisions in religious matters being generally regarded as of the highest import, there is the strongest impulse on the one side for a man to decide for himself and to maintain his decision, and on the other for authority to enforce the decisions already received. Hence arises a struggle from a divergence of opinion which in affairs of less moment might have been avoided or disregarded. Decisions in religious matters, again, tend more than those in some other departments of thought[1] to show themselves in practice. If I come to dissent from the established religion, I am likely to show my dissent by attending the worship of some other religious body, if there is one to suit my views, or by abstaining from public worship altogether; but a change in opinion from the theory of the divine right of kings to a belief in republicanism, or from the corpuscular to the undulatory theory of light, does not lead me to any such overt act, unless indeed I feel impelled to join or found some society for the propagation of republicanism or the undulatory theory of light. It is possible of course that even though I dissent from the established religion I may take no action which gives indication of the fact, but the probability that I shall do so is much greater than in either of the alternative cases

(3) importance of religious decisions, and

(4) their tendency to show themselves in practice.

---

[1] Not necessarily than in any other. That a man is, for instance, a vegetarian may be much more conspicuous than that he is an agnostic or a Plymouth Brother.

mentioned, because religion by its very nature claims to govern a man's practice, which politics and physics do not[1]. Here we touch the crucial point in the question of toleration. The clash of the individual with authority is naturally most severe and finds its most ample justification in cases where the former feels himself impelled not merely by intellectual interest or emotion or wilfulness, but by conscience, to a course which the latter has forbidden. And though nowadays we are learning to distinguish between religion and morality, in the period to which the main body of this essay is devoted religion was practically the invariable ultimate background of conscience[2].

These considerations, then, explain why the question of toleration is so intimately bound up with religion. Further, there is no motive to persecution in matters not directly bearing on religion, which does not operate in religious persecution, but there are motives to the latter which do not operate in the former; if, then, we can make clear the reasons for which men have come to tolerate even divergent forms of religion, we shall

[1] Men's practice no doubt largely conforms to their political and physical theories, but this is not simply because they hold those theories, but because of some sanction (e.g. altruism or self-interest) external to them. That a man's practice should accord with his beliefs is not a political or physical principle, but a moral one.

[2] Apparently the first attempt to construct a system of morals without the aid of theology was that of Cumberland, afterwards Bishop of Peterborough, in his *De Legibus Naturae*, 1672. Buckle, *History of Civilization in England*, I. 425 and n. (Longmans' Silver Library, 3 vols. 1908).

necessarily include those for which differences on other subjects are tolerated.

Toleration represents, as we have seen, the with-drawal of external authority from control of certain regions of human activity; hence it is essentially *Complete* negative[1]. It also follows from its nature that it *toleration* *impossible.* can in any case be but partial. The ages of perse-cution were not completely intolerant; complete toleration is impossible even in our own. It is immediately obvious that, human nature being what it is, an organized state must be prepared to punish actions even for which the dictates of conscience may be pleaded. Otherwise the individual would be given a free hand ; for the excuse, if allowed, might be raised to cover any action whatever, and the state cannot discriminate between genuine and counterfeit pleas of conscience. And even though the plea be genuine, it may be put forward in defence of actions

[1] 'Toleration' and 'tolerance' are also used in a more re-stricted and positive sense. Thus tolerance—the mental attitude which finds its outward expression in toleration—has been de-scribed as "an allowance of that which is disapproved. The subject-matter is man's attitude towards the opinions of his fellow-men. It is therefore the mean or middle state in which virtue consists—*persecution* being the excess, *indifference* the defect of this quality. The attitude of the persecutor is clear—he wishes to impose his own opinions on his fellow-men. The attitude of the indifferent man is also clear—he has no opinions and there-fore is heedless….The virtue of the tolerant man lies in having opinions, but not wishing to impose them by any external pres-sure, or to enforce them by any means save temperate argument " (J. O. Bevan, *Birth and Growth of Toleration and Other Essays*, 3). This sense is no doubt convenient for ethical classification, but is only with difficulty, if at all, applicable to politics : the negative sense, therefore, is to be understood in this essay.

which the government owes to its subjects in general to repress. Some control, then, irrespective of conscience, the state must claim. The question, therefore, is one of properly adjusting the boundary between the sphere in which the individual's activity may be determined by himself without liability to punishment, and the sphere in which the state claims control. During the last few centuries there has taken place a great extension of the former at the expense of the latter, and a definite principle has been recognized for the determination of the boundary between them.

We may more clearly understand this process of evolution if we examine it with respect to religion, and divide it for purposes of thought into three successive stages. The first stage is that in which the mere holding of certain views—the mere adherence to a certain religion as such—is in itself a punishable offence. It may be held that a certain religion, as a religion, is bad; that it will involve serious consequences after death to those who believe in it, or that it is an insult to the Almighty[1]. Persecution of this type of course implies that the authority enacting the persecuting laws either is itself competent to pronounce upon theological questions, or is acting under the advice of those who are so competent; and arises, not indeed only, but most naturally, in cases where the authority believes itself to be in possession of the one true religion.

STAGES IN THE EVOLUTION OF TOLERATION.

(1) Persecution of a religion as itself a crime.

The second stage is entered upon when punish-

[1] And possibly therefore it may be regarded as likely to bring disaster upon the whole community.

(2) *Perse-cution of a religion as connoting a crime.* ment is inflicted upon the adherents of a certain religion, not because of the supposed vicious character of the religion itself, but because adherence to it is supposed necessarily to connote enmity to the established order, ecclesiastical, political, or social. An obvious instance of this type of persecution is given by the penal laws enacted in England against the Roman Catholics from the reign of Elizabeth onwards[1]. The idea of persecuting them simply because they adhered to the Roman Catholic Church was officially disavowed; they were punished not simply because they were Roman Catholics, but because it was assumed that a Roman Catholic must necessarily be disloyal. Thus the priests executed under Elizabeth were not burnt as heretics, but hanged as traitors. This stage shows a very distinct advance on the previous one; the persecuting authority no longer takes upon itself to condemn a religion upon the ground of its effects outside this present world, but confines its attention to the effects likely to be produced on contemporary politics, of which it is, no doubt, more competent to judge. But even so it runs a great risk of being unnecessarily severe. The system is based upon the false assumption that men follow out principles to their logical conclusions, and sometimes also upon another false assumption as to what those conclusions are. To return to our instance; supposing that Roman Catholicism logically connoted disloyalty to Queen Elizabeth and her government (and there was a very great deal to be said for the

---

[1] The persecution of the early Christians by the Roman government is another case in point.

view), it would not necessarily follow—as a matter of fact we know that it did not follow—that Roman Catholics were generally disloyal.

The third stage is that which is generally described as religious toleration. In this, no religion is punishable, either as being in itself a crime or as connoting any crime, and no act performed as part of a religion is punishable unless it is punishable apart from religious considerations. The state may especially countenance some particular form of religion by retaining an established church, but, so far as the use of force or persuasion is concerned, the attitude of the state to religion has become purely negative, promoting nothing, and prohibiting nothing but what is supposed to be harmful to society from a temporal point of view. *(3) The state takes no cognizance of religious motives.*

The first stage, as we have seen, is most natural to a society in which the one true religion is understood to be unquestionably and exactly known. In such a case the government is supposed to take up a positive attitude, and to maintain the welfare of society by upholding and promoting this one true religion to the extirpation of all other, and therefore false, religions.

In the intermediate stage it does not necessarily take it upon itself to decide that a certain religion is true, but it does decide that some religions are false, or rather politically or socially harmful, and therefore to be suppressed. We still believe that certain forms of religion are harmful to society— Mormonism for instance and the religion of the Thugs—but we do not regard as a crime mere

adherence to those religions, but only such anti-
social acts—to wit, polygamy and strangling—as
may be performed under their sanction. If a man
holds the belief that community of goods is divinely
ordained and that he is obliged in conscience to do
all he can to make it general, and if he acts upon
it so far as to treat other people's property as his
own, he must suffer for it quite irrespective of his
conscientious convictions. Similarly, if a Christian
Scientist, disbelieving in the reality of pain and
disease, allows his child to die from want of medical
attendance and general neglect, he must undergo the
same penalties prescribed by law for such cases as
an Anglican or a Mohammedan, who have no religious reason to plead and may have acted from
mere callousness or brutality. The fact that an act
is performed for reasons of religion neither invests it
with guilt if it is otherwise innocent, nor makes it
innocent if it is otherwise an offence against the
law : of such reasons the state takes no cognizance.
Religion as such has been entirely abandoned to the
extended sphere of internal control.

*Develop-
ment of
toleration
partly
moral,
partly in-
tellectual.*

The process of extension of that sphere—in other
words the development of toleration—exhibits two
aspects, which, though not entirely separable in fact,
it is convenient to distinguish for purposes of thought.
From some points of view it is primarily a moral
movement, from others it is primarily intellectual ;
from others again both characteristics are to be observed in close combination. We shall prepare the
way for a better understanding of the nature and
relation of these aspects, if we consider the motives

which have led men to persecute, and the way in which they have been neutralized partly by moral, and partly by intellectual, development[1]. These motives *MOTIVES TO PERSECUTION:* may perhaps best be classified under five heads[2].

If a religion be conceived of as having been *(1) religious,* directly revealed by God, it is not unnatural to hold that the honour of God is impugned by the denial of any doctrine supposed to be essential to

---

[1] Buckle (*History of Civilization in England*, I. 174–190) attempts to prove that progress in general and toleration in particular result not from moral but from intellectual causes. His argument is as follows:—Progress is twofold, moral and intellectual: moral systems have not changed; but intellectual systems are constantly changing : therefore the causes of progress are intellectual. But even if his assertion that "in reference to our moral conduct, there is not a single principle now known to the most cultivated Europeans, which was not likewise known to the ancients" (p. 181) were true, it would not be relevant. The question is not one of formulating a principle, it is one of applying it in its full meaning and carrying it into practice. Buckle strangely confuses morality itself with the intellectual apprehension of its principles. If his theory were sound we must regard our professors of moral philosophy as our greatest saints. Dealing with toleration in particular, he lays stress on the disinterested character of persecution and on the exalted motives from which persecutors have acted ; but this is merely to prove that ignorance combined with power is dangerous, and that good intentions are no adequate substitute for, or equivalent of, intelligence—propositions which no one, presumably, is concerned to deny. Further he seems to confound religion or religious fanaticism with morality, and to take no account of the common phenomenon of the moral sense being excluded from one particular department of life, e.g. religious or commercial affairs. Intellect may be the liberator, but it cannot be the driving power of morality. Modern humanitarianism, for instance, is not in its essence an intellectual product. But the subject is more suited for a volume than for a footnote.

[2] For the argument of pp. 9—33 briefly set out in tabular form, see Appendix I.

that religion, or by the conception of God in any other manner than that which is—rightly or wrongly—supposed to be prescribed; and zeal naturally dictates a persecution, which, as it is undertaken on behalf of the divine honour, is presumed to meet with the divine approval; nor is it difficult for the persecutor to discover or invent divine commands to be the warrant of his action and a spur to greater efforts. Thus we have what may perhaps be called the religious motive for persecution.

(2) theological,

Our duty to God being thus properly performed, our duty to our neighbour must not be forgotten, and supplies us with a motive equally strong. If our religion be the one true religion, and the only way to salvation, it is not cruelty to persecute a man in order to make him embrace it; rather is it merciful to expose him to the most excruciating tortures, if it is only so that we may win him to that eternal happiness, which he cannot enter save through conversion from his errors. The doctrine of exclusive salvation, then, provides us with a motive which for purposes of convenience we will label as theological[1].

The third, fourth and fifth motives are supplied by the conservatism inherent in the natural man. Applied to religious affairs this quality has a distinct bearing both upon doctrine and upon ecclesiastical organization. With regard to the former it exhibits itself in the attempt to suppress any views supposed

(3) doctrinal,

[1] This not altogether satisfactory name I take from Sir Frederick Pollock's *The Theory of Persecution* in his *Essays in Jurisprudence and Ethics*, whose system of classification suggested that adopted here, though differing considerably from it.

to corrupt or to be likely to corrupt the purity of
the church's doctrine, which it is surely worth while to
keep uncontaminated at the cost of some temporal
suffering inflicted on the innovators; in the latter (4) *ecclesiastical*,
case it finds the objects of its attack in any new-
fangled notions calculated to disturb the ecclesiastical
status quo by causing divisions or lack of discipline in
the church, if not her actual overthrow.

But a religion may embody opinions directly (5) *politico-social*.
inimical to the state in which they are propagated,
or to society in general. Or though not directly
inimical to the state or to society they may be considered to be so indirectly, because inimical to the
existing order in the church. For when church and
state are intimately bound together, a serious disturbance in the ecclesiastical organization cannot
but have a momentous effect upon the whole politico-
social structure; and hence conservatism, applied to
purely temporal affairs, can afford a strong motive
for the persecution of a religion on politico-social
grounds. It need not be supposed that men who
felt concern for society generally distinguished as to
whether it was in its ecclesiastical or its temporal
aspects that it was primarily threatened, but once
again it is convenient to make a distinction in
thought between ideas which presumably in practice
men often did not disentangle. It is worth noticing
in passing, that those who are in a position to
organize or direct persecution are usually persons
who would lose seriously in a material sense by the
disturbance of the existing order of things; it is
likely, in consequence, that there will often be an

element of pure selfishness, conscious or unconscious, in persecution undertaken in the interests of the ecclesiastical or civil *status quo*.

The motives considered in their mutual relations. These five motives fall naturally into three divisions. The first two—the religious and the theological—are based on supposed occurrences, present or future, in the unseen world, namely, in the one case the experience of satisfaction or the reverse on the part of the Deity, and in the other the salvation or damnation of the misbeliever according as he does or does not ultimately embrace orthodoxy. The last two—the ecclesiastical and the politico-social—on the other hand, arise from the wish to maintain actual organizations existing in this world, namely the respective constitutions of church and state. The third—the doctrinal—occupies, as it were, a middle position : it is connected with the last pair in that it arises proximately from the wish to maintain something actually existing in this world, namely, a body of doctrine; while it is connected also with the first pair in that it looks ultimately to the salvation of souls in the next—in this case the souls of the faithful, while the theological motive applies to the case of the misbeliever.

From another point of view it may be noticed that there is a sense in which the first and the last— the religious and the politico-social—alone are not concerned with the salvation of souls; for the one is solely concerned with the supposed preferences of the Deity, while the other is solely concerned with temporal affairs. The third and fourth, however, as well as the second—that is, the doctrinal and the ecclesiastical, as well as the theological—are concerned ultimately with the salvation of souls, that being the end for which the doctrine of the church and the ecclesiastical organization for propagating and pre-serving it alike ultimately exist. But, while the theological motive is concerned with that and nothing else—a matter transacted entirely beyond the range of human cognizance—, in the case of the doctrinal motive there intervenes a proximate concernment with the maintenance of a body of doctrine—a matter by no means beyond the range of human cognizance—which absorbs a considerable share of the attention otherwise directed solely to ultimate considerations. Similarly in the case of the eccle-siastical motive there intervenes a proximate con-cernment with the maintenance of a certain form of organization in the church—a matter conspicuous before the eyes of all its members, and touching the material interests of many—which absorbs so great a share of attention as to make men in no small measure oblivious of the purpose for which that organization ultimately exists.

Though these three motives, then, can all claim justification as different manifestations of the desire to save souls, yet the idea of salvation is in the case of the doctrinal motive partially, and in the case of the ecclesiastical motive almost wholly, obscured by intervening considerations, which in the nature of the case must receive attention, and on which at-tention tends (especially in the latter case) to be wholly concentrated. Indeed—a point which we have already noticed, and to which we shall have occasion to recur—the ecclesiastical motive can be so far removed from considerations of the next world as to fade insensibly into the politico-social motive, which is concerned solely with this.

THE CASE FOR TOLER-ATION. Having now, it is hoped, formed, at the risk of tedium, a fairly clear idea of the meaning of our terms[1], let us proceed to consider the ways in which these various motives to persecution may be met in the cause of toleration. As the motives themselves tend to fade into one another, so the application of the considerations which may be advanced from the tolerant side cannot always be confined to one particular motive; we will try, however, to deal with each in connection with that to which it applies, if not solely, at least most directly.

We have seen that the religious and theological motives look to the unseen world. It follows that they have this important element in common, that the soundness or unsoundness of the assumptions on which they rest are incapable of demonstration, and consequently those who persecute on these grounds are more than usually beyond the reach of argument. We have no practical test of what is pleasing to the Almighty, or of what tends to the ultimate welfare *Effect of the de-velopment of the moral sense.* of the misbeliever beyond the grave. It is in opposi-tion to these two motives that the moral aspect of toleration is brought most into prominence; for they largely depend upon the conception formed of God, and in that conception the moral sense of the subject is an all-important factor, informing as it does his

[1] If this has not been done, reference is recommended to Appendix I.

intellectual outlook. "Thou thoughtest that I was altogether such an one as thyself[1]"—the moral sense of the various ages and divisions of humanity tends to be reflected in their respective conceptions of the divine[2]. Hence the development of the moral sense involves modification in the view taken of the divine nature and of the eschatology consistent with it, and thus strikes at the root of the religious and theological motives to persecution respectively. In Western Europe a movement in this direction was an outcome of the great intellectual and religious movements of the fifteenth and following centuries. In the midst of the mutual attrition of conflicting views, ecclesiastical and theological prejudice could no longer lay so great an incubus as before upon the moral sense; and as men applied their partially liberated moral sense more freely to religious matters, they could not but raise the moral standard conceived of as attributable to the Almighty. The process was slow and partial. Persecutors, both Catholic and Protestant, still under the domination of the ecclesiastical spirit, had no difficulty in quoting Scripture to their purpose, and continued to read into and justify from the New Testament their own perverted morality. But the gradual liberation of the moral sense slowly made it possible to read a higher, because freer, morality into the New Testament. The discovery was made, now

The religious motive undermined (1) morally, owing to the liberation of the moral sense

(a) modifying the conception of God,

(b) revealing the tolerance of the New Testament:

---

[1] Ps. l. 21.

[2] Allowance of course must be made for the fact that doctrines are professed in some cases before their full implication is realized, and in some after they have become obsolete and their implications are virtually discarded. See *Lux Mundi*, pp. 68 f. (Moore's essay on *The Christian Doctrine of God*).

in one quarter, now in another, that in it persecution was so far from being enjoined as to stand manifestly condemned, and it became possible to credit the Creator with feelings at least of ordinary humanity.

(2) intellectually, by Protestant disclaimers of infallibility.

Moreover, in Protestant countries the ecclesiastical power, practically compelled in justification of its own existence to disown the theory of an infallible church, cut away the ground from under its own feet. The civil ruler, indeed, might be exalted as head or governor of the church, he might be regarded as the vicegerent of God, but the fallen mantle of the pope could impart to his substitute only a half-portion of the papal spirit. It gradually dawned on men's minds that it was no longer possible to advance with the same plausibility as Rome confident pretensions to intimacy with the divine point of view; and that persecution was capable of being regarded not as a vindication of God's honour, but as an invasion of His rights, Whose prerogative alone it is to "see in secret."

The theological motive undermined owing to destruction of belief in exclusive salvation, (1) morally, by higher moralization of the conception of God:

Not only the religious motive, but also the doctrine of exclusive salvation, and therefore the theological motive, is undermined by the liberation of the moral sense and the consequent change in the conception of God. For the latter involves an increasing recognition that moral rectitude is more acceptable to God than merely intellectual rectitude, while the former cannot but cause men of reflection to realize that the lines of intellectual and moral cleavage among their kind are neither identical nor coincident. Hence follows the overthrow of the fundamentally immoral belief in the damnation of all Jews, Turks, infidels and heretics—of all, that is, who disagree with us— as being inconsistent with the higher justice, which finds a place among the divine attributes when narrow ecclesiastical prepossessions are shaken off. Thus is struck away the main prop of the theological motive.

Intellectual enlightenment, which, as we have seen, coöperates with moral enlightenment in the cause of toleration in general, must also be considered as a factor in the opposition to the doctrine of exclusive salvation. The persecutor always runs the risk of being wrong. His faith may not be the true faith ; or it may not be absolutely necessary to salvation. To Isabella and Philip II and to the generality of Roman Catholic princes and clergy down to a much later time, doubtless it never even occurred that such a risk existed[1]. But the narrowness of mind, with which a man believes that those alone can be saved who hold the same body of doctrine as himself, is hardly compatible with the growth of a spirit of inquiry which tends to question what has before been implicitly received. Not by any means that at the first stirrings of the questioning impulse the formula "*extra ecclesiam nulla salus*" and parallel doctrines will necessarily be repudiated, for words long survive the actual realization of the doctrines which they express. The beliefs which men realize are but a small part, as a rule, of the beliefs which they profess, and it is possible for them to retain among the latter, doctrines to which they

(2) intellectually, by the growth of the spirit of inquiry.

---

[1] Sir F. Pollock, *Theory of Persecution (Essays in Jurisprudence and Ethics)*, 155.

give a formal assent, carrying with it no influence over their practice, and from the full realization of which they would shrink with horror.

So it has been, to a great extent, with the doctrine of exclusive salvation. It was only when men had abandoned or had ceased to realize this belief that toleration became possible. For, indeed, if we once grant that one faith is known not only to be true but also to be absolutely necessary to salvation, the case for persecution on theological grounds admits of no answer. For the answer that truth will in any case prevail of itself does not meet the case. Whether or no truth prevails, surely it is a matter of experience that it prevails but slowly. And in the meantime souls are perishing. To say nothing of the fact that the bonds of charity, sympathy, and mutual understanding, of which the tolerant spirit so largely consists, are unlikely to be strongly developed between men or societies of men who whole-heartedly, (perhaps even exultantly), believe in one another's damnation[1].

Separation of the ideas of intellectual and of moral error. For the overthrow of the doctrine of exclusive salvation, then, the moral and the intellectual movements contributing to the extension of toleration combined. The moral sense and the sceptical[2] spirit

[1] A thorough examination of the exact reason why A, who hates B for being a heretic and would rejoice at his damnation, yet spends time and trouble in a desperate effort to save his soul by persecution, would be an interesting study in the psychology of religious fanaticism.

[2] It is unfortunate that the word 'sceptic' and its derivatives, implying as they do merely an attitude of inquiry, should usually be taken as implying disbelief, or a measure of doubt bordering

alike led the way to the recognition that difference of opinion is due to intellectual fallibility rather than to moral error, and is therefore inevitable, and, because inevitable, blameless. As long as the holding of particular opinions is regarded as a direct proof of wilful perversity or as the result of intellectual blindness caused by moral obliquity, the heretic differs in guilt from the drunkard and the murderer only in that his crime is fraught with more terrible consequences; but when the fallibility of mankind is recognized to the point of believing that the heretic is guilty of no more than an intellectual misapprehension, still more when it is recognized to the point of believing that orthodoxy itself may be in some points a misinterpretation or misconception of the truth, a great obstacle to toleration is cleared away. But the extrication from one another of the ideas of intellectual and moral error is a process as slow as its results have been momentous, nor is it yet by any means completed in the minds of the generality of men.

We have seen that when one faith is held to be true and absolutely necessary to salvation the persecutor is possessed of an invincible argument, which scepticism alone can meet. Some measure of scepticism, therefore, is an indispensable foundation of the case for toleration without which all other arguments fall to the ground. Or, to change the metaphor, *But the sceptical argument merely negative,*

upon disbelief; the more so because there is no satisfactory set of synonyms. The words are to be understood in this essay in their strictly etymological sense as implying a questioning spirit and nothing more.

scepticism alone can break the spell of invulnerability with which the case for persecution is otherwise invested, and lay it open to attack. But it does not touch the root principle of persecution itself, which is ingrained more deeply in human nature than any theological theories[1]. The sceptical argument for toleration is purely a negative argument: it dissuades from persecution as involving a risk of terrible error; it does nothing to show that toleration has any positive merits.

and not practically adequate. And so long as the matter is regarded merely from the point of view that there is always a risk that suffering is being inflicted without bringing about the end to which it is directed, because it cannot be absolutely known that the faith thus propagated is true and necessary to salvation, the reply to the theological argument for persecution is not in practice a really powerful one. For if a man

---

[1] Persecution is sometimes spoken of as though it had been introduced into the world by Christianity. This of course is not so. It was in the world long before Christianity, and is the heritage not distinctively of the Christian, but of the natural man. "It [the spirit of persecution] comes from the universal sense of inconvenience when we do not at once get our own way. Then follows impatience, irritation and resentment. Then reason is called in to help passion, and clothe the feelings with the semblance of deliberate action founded on policy and expediency. The love of power comes next, suggesting the future good to be obtained from a prompt display of resoluteness. Power supplies its own justification; for would it be there if it were not meant to be used? And who can blame it when it has succeeded? Then comes 'that last infirmity of noble minds,' the hope for fame, the gratification that attends success, the proud consciousness of having cleared a difficulty out of the way." Creighton, *Persecution and Tolerance*, 43.

earnestly holds that a certain form of belief is either indispensable to eternal welfare or even merely of great spiritual benefit, it is not by any means an insuperable obstacle to point out that his belief, however high a degree of assurance it attains, is not absolute knowledge. This merely reduces the matter to a question of balancing the possibility, which to him is hardly more than academic, of the suffering inflicted being unnecessary, against the probability, amounting to complete conviction, that it is conducive to the eternal welfare of such sufferers as may be convinced by it or by the fear of it. And if we add to this side of the balance the expected advantages to generations of descendants, gained without any further suffering, the total sum of supposed benefit becomes so great compared with the suffering actually inflicted, that there may well seem an overwhelming case for taking the risk of error to one who upon the same grounds of faith may be prepared, if necessary, to sacrifice—perhaps has actually sacrificed—the pleasures and rewards of this world, and is in any case staking without misgiving his hopes for eternity. The sceptical argument from human fallibility only shows that there is a risk; it does not necessarily show that the risk is not worth taking. And it does not follow that the risk is not worth taking, even if the persecutor has given up the doctrine of exclusive salvation. The theological motive to persecution can still find refuge on the impregnable ground that certain beliefs are more favourable to moral and spiritual development than others, that is, more conducive to salvation, even though a man may perhaps be saved without them. Something more than mere negative scepticism is necessary to meet the case.

Need of positive belief in intellectual freedom which arose from the revival of the sense of truth.

But the intellectual side of the case for toleration includes other than merely destructive elements; it appeals in the spirit of the Renaissance to the dignity of the individual man, and in the spirit of the Reformation to the claims of truth upon him. The revival of the sense of truth from its mediaeval sleep brought into view the natural right of man to judge for himself and the obligation upon him to follow his own judgment. In the long gap between the belief that one particular form of religion is indispensable to salvation and the belief that all religions are indifferent, there is room for beliefs in infinitesimal gradations; and, considerations of secular expediency apart, men will tend to persecute or to tolerate, according to the value they set upon the holding of certain views as compared with intellectual freedom. It is only a strong realization of the positive claims of intellectual freedom as an actual good, that can effectively curb the theological motive[1]; and an indispensable preliminary to this realization was the revival of the sense of truth which inspired the Reformation.

Necessity of persecution questioned.

From the same source—the revival of the sense of truth—arose questionings as to the value of persecution. Were fire and sword necessary to the defence and propagation of truth? Surely truth had prevailed by its own intrinsic merit in the early

[1] Positive disbelief cannot be said to do so, because in that case the theological motive does not exist

days of Christianity, and presumably could do so still. Moreover, persecution, whether necessary or not, was palpably clumsy and inefficient. It began to be seen that a faith, propagated by barbaric methods, gains less than may at first sight appear by forced conversions; for physical penalties are not a means proper to produce intellectual conviction, and only succeed as a rule in producing verbal assent and outward conformity, the valuelessness of which a juster appreciation of the essence of religion tends to expose. On the other hand, however, it should be noticed that owing to the ability which men frequently show to arrive at such convictions in speculative matters as conduce to their comfort, penalties have a considerably greater power of producing actual conviction, however irrational, than they are usually credited with at the present day. To say, with William Penn, "The Tower is to me the worst argument in the world," and to act upon the words, a depth of conviction is necessary which many minds do not reach; and invariably to challenge the sincerity of changes of views under pressure argues alike a lack of charity and a misunderstanding of human nature. Moreover, though persecution may produce mere conformity in those to whom it is applied, their children, born in the faith to which the parents were compelled, are likely to grow up its sincere adherents, and the suffering of two generations[1] may produce the honest unconstrained conviction of an indefinite number.

Persecution inefficient,

failing, as a rule, to produce conviction,

(though its power in this direction is usually underrated),

[1] Persecution at any time must fall upon persons differing too widely in age to be classed together as a single generation.

*or (fre-
quently)
con-
formity ;*

But as a matter of fact persecution has frequently failed to produce even outward conformity, and tends to defeat its own object by still further alienating the minds of those whom it is intended to bring into the fold, and disgusting the fair-minded of all persuasions. It has been, and still is, often said that persecution always fails; this is, of course, untrue; but it has failed often enough to give the statement an air of plausibility[1].

*while it
damages
the morals
of both
persecuted*

A far more serious objection to persecution than its inefficiency, arises from its direct effect upon the morality of both parties concerned. Wherever persecution fails to produce conviction but succeeds in producing conformity on a considerable scale, it produces a mass of hypocrisy involving a total moral loss to the community difficult to estimate. But

*and per-
secutors.*

this is by no means the only moral damage done. Whatever be the effect of persecution upon its victims, its effect upon the persecutors can hardly fail in the long run to be extremely bad. If to persecute does not tend to distort a man's morality, it can only be because his morality is already distorted. The force of this contention, however, the persecutor himself can hardly be expected to appreciate.

[1] The plausibility is the greater owing to the fact that successful persecution by its very success reduces itself to inactivity. "No tree is withered by the frost of the polar regions; or by the scorching winds of the Arabian deserts ; because none can exist in those regions. And no Protestant is now [1830] brought to the stake in Spain, because, there, persecution has done its work." The persecuting spirit acts as a *preventive*, and thus renders unnecessary recourse to actual persecution as a cure. Whately, *Errors of Romanism*, 242–3.

In view of these several considerations the *Theo-*
theological motive to persecution must be judged *logical motive in-*
inadequate. It has attracted more attention than *adequate.*
any other motive—probably a good deal more than
it really deserves; indeed it would seem to be
generally regarded as the great outstanding motive
to persecution. Its appeal is at once striking and
insidious, disguising, as it is capable of doing for
persecutor and spectator alike, the most revolting
cruelty under a mask of charity to its victims, and
contaminating the highest of human ambitions, by
giving full scope in its service to the lowest of human
instincts.

There remain the three motives arising from *The con-*
innate conservatism, which we have named, from *servative motives.*
the spheres to which they apply, the doctrinal, the
ecclesiastical, and the politico-social motives.

We have seen that the moral element in the
case for toleration—the quickening of the moral
sense involving a modification in men's conception
of God—is the main force rebutting the religious
motive, and a powerful factor in the downfall of the
theological motive. The conservative motives, which
we are now to consider, being mainly the outcome
of intellectual narrowness, are to be met mainly by
intellectual considerations; they are, however, as we
have already noticed, not entirely without the moral
element; for when a particular set of men hold
influential positions and other advantages, pride and
selfishness can do much to increase the numbers of
those who sincerely believe that the established
order which serves their interest so well is just and

reasonable, conducive to the best interests of religion and the state, and therefore to be defended by penal laws.   They do not, that is, act exactly immorally, but they do act as they would not, were they morally more enlightened.   Moral development, then—the growth of human sympathy and of the sense of responsibility—here also plays its part.

Doctrinal motive   Doctrinal conservatism, which attempts to preserve the teaching of the church unchanged, and so to protect its members from the fatal infection of new doctrines, is in one aspect, as we have seen, closely allied to the theological motive, both being concerned with spiritual welfare; the latter with that of the misbeliever, the former with that of those who as yet remain faithful.   It would seem to be generally supposed that the persecution practised in the middle ages was inspired by the theological motive: but the mediaeval church was less concerned for the one lost sheep than for the ninety and nine that went not astray, and it seems that we must look to the doctrinal and ecclesiastical motives for the driving power of her unchristian deeds.   Doctrinal conservatism caused persecution to be regarded rather "as a surgical operation, as cutting out plague spots that the health of the body politic might be preserved[1]"; and, as in the case of theological persecution, once granted the infallibility of the church and the supreme eternal importance of the church's *met by* doctrine, the argument is unanswerable.   When, *considera-* however, it is grasped that we have not the total *tion of the* *vastness of* sum of truth as a treasure to be guarded with fire *truth.*

[1] Creighton, *Persecution and Tolerance*, 3–6.

and sword, but an infinitesimal portion of it to be increased, if possible, by zealous and humble search, the question assumes a different aspect; and it is recognized that, though persecution may preserve what we have, yet, by suppressing theological discussion, it chokes, so far as it is successful, one of the main channels through which our little store may be increased[1]. For the doctrine suppressed may either itself contain an element of truth, or be fitted to bring out by contrast some as yet unsuspected or only half-realized aspect of the truth which we already hold. There can hardly be a nobler motive to toleration than the conception of the multitudinous religions of mankind as contributing each its quota —infinitesimal, it may be, but precious—to some vast synthesis of religious thought, aspiration, and experience at present beyond the limits of our narrow intellectual range.

From the vastness and many-sidedness of truth, then, it follows that unanimity is undesirable, lest one custom, be it bad or good, should corrupt the world into stagnation; a proper appreciation of the sadly fallible nature of the human mind shows that, desirable or not, unanimity is impossible. Nor is it to be supposed that while no attempt is made to secure unanimity in general, some few points can safely be excepted from those open to general discussion; not only because there is no question of which we may safely say that it cannot be exhibited in a new aspect or may not receive fresh light from

[1] This consideration bears, of course, upon the theological motive also.

being canvassed anew, but also because such exception may tend to make belief in the points excepted a merely formal thing for the unintelligent and bring it into suspicion with the active-minded. "If your religion," said Archbishop Tillotson pertinently, "be too good to be examined, I doubt it is too bad to be believed[1]."

Ecclesiastical motive.

We come next to the ecclesiastical motive—fears for the organic structure of the church, which lead to the persecution of doctrines, not, primarily at any rate, because they are regarded as being themselves pernicious, but because it is thought that to tolerate them is to expose the church as a society to imminent danger of dissolution. "The immediate motive of the persecutions of later days," wrote Sir Leslie Stephen of the mediaeval church, "was not the love of men's souls, but the desire to support the great institution against which the heretic was rebelling.... If it were possible to admit that the heretic was a well-meaning person avowing what he believed to be true, he was not the less a rebel against an essential part of the social order, who may rightly be put to death as we should now put to death the most sincere anarchist who applied his principles by assassination[2]." Persecution of this type is likely to arise in controversies over church government; an episcopal church might persecute the preachers of presbyterianism, or a presbyterian church those of congregationalism, merely to protect their respective organizations. The

[1] Sermon lviii., Works, iv. 84, 10 vols., London, 1820.
[2] *Encyclopaedia Britannica*, vol. xxviii., Prefatory Essay, p. viii.

most obvious method of procedure in such a case *Expulsion* would seem to be the simple expulsion of the mal- *instead of* contents without resort to persecuting measures; *persecu-* *tion the* but it may be held that it is of the essence of the *obvious* *method,* church that it be co-extensive with the state; from *but for the* which it follows that the toleration within the limits *ecclesias-* *tico-poli-* of the state of any ecclesiastical bodies standing *tical* outside the organization of the established church, *theory of* *the state,* involves *ipso facto* the break-up of the church. And in cases where church and state have never been dissociated it is not unnatural that the state should be looked upon as the ultimate power which holds the national church together, as supplying the chief bond of unity deprived of which the church would split into disunited atoms. - Conversely, it is not unnatural that the church should be looked upon as one of the great bonds of unity in the state, alongside of such bonds as community of blood and community of language.

Thus, " to make toleration practicable in the early days, men had not only to point out the immorality of persecution, but to show how the political and ecclesiastical constitution could be reorganized[1]." For *the main* from this conception of the state as an ecclesiastico- *source of* *the eccle-* political society mainly arises not only the eccle- *siastical* siastical motive, but also the politico-social motive. *and politi-* *co-social* These are likely to survive at any rate the vigour *motives;* of the religious and theological motives; for as long *which,* *though* as these latter flourish the former are supported by *likely to* *survive* them and sheltered by them from attack, and it is *the re-* natural that men should still claim the right to *ligious and* *theological* *motives,*

[1] *Ibid.*, p. viii.

decide what beliefs are advantageous or the reverse
to organizations in this life, even after they have set
aside the future life as a subject unfit for legislation.
For unlike the religious and theological motives, as
we have already seen, these do not deal directly with
realities beyond the grave, but with visible organizations of which the cohesion can be observed and
tested.   But from this very fact it also follows that,
unlike the other motives, they are capable of practical
are seen to refutation; indeed, their unsoundness may be clearly
be unsound suggested without the actual repeal of the persecuting laws, if it is seen that the lax administration
of those laws shows no tendency to let loose the
catastrophic forces prophesied as the inevitable
outcome of toleration.   Hence with the growth of
as political political philosophy they were gradually consigned
philosophy to the limbo of outworn fallacies.   When the re-
develops. ligious and theological arguments have been already
discredited, these motives, deprived of such powerful
support, form the least plausible and lasting basis
for a policy of persecution, because of their fatal
capacity of being demonstrated to be unsound.   On
(Case of the other hand, there may be cases where the course
the Roman of events would seem, by showing that some religious
Catholics belief is hostile to the peace and quiet of the nation,
in Eng- to justify the continuance of persecution; and thus,
land.) if the course of events be sufficiently unfortunate,
a persecution on political grounds may be extensively
prolonged.   The persecution of the Roman Catholics
in England is a case in point, largely owing to the
favour with which their cause was regarded at foreign
courts.   The plots in favour of Mary Queen of Scots,

the Spanish Armada, Gunpowder Plot, the supposed Romanizing policy of Laud and the activity of Roman Catholicism at the court of Charles I, the same phenomenon at the courts of both his sons, Charles II's attempts to secure toleration for the Roman Catholics, his intrigues with aggressive Roman Catholicism on the continent, the Popish Plot, James II's undisguised and flagrantly illegal attempt to reduce England to the papal supremacy, and finally the Jacobite intrigues and rebellions— all these, following one another at intervals too short for the apprehensions aroused ever to be quite allayed, seemed fully to demonstrate that Roman Catholicism by plots, rebellions, foreign invasion, or the more subtle methods of conversion was a dangerous and irreconcilable enemy of the Church of England, and of English liberty, if not of English independence.

In spite, however, of such cases, the opportunity of an appeal to facts is on the whole unfavourable to the continuance of persecution, and constitutes a weak spot in the armour of the persecutor who is inspired by fears for the continued existence and welfare of the church or the state.

Thus far we have seen that the idea that Church and State are two names for the same social organism according as it is ecclesiastically or politically considered gives rise to persecution on both ecclesiastical and political grounds. If we now set aside ecclesiastical considerations and confine our attention to the political implications of the theory, it would seem to support persecution from two points of view. *Political implications of the ecclesiastico-political theory of the state,*

In the first place, it sanctions the insidious but apparently harmless and praiseworthy proposition that it is the duty of every man in his particular station to promote the true religion, and therefore of the magistrate, as magistrate, to promote it by attaching penalties to divergence from it[1]. Secondly, —a point we have already noted,—if church and state be the same organism considered in two different aspects, the toleration of dissent, that is, the dissolution of the unity of the organism ecclesiastically considered, may reasonably be supposed inevitably to involve serious disturbances in the same organism in its political aspect, if not its actual dissolution.

which has the sanction of history, Now this theory of the state, if applied to highly civilized modern communities, shows a failure to appreciate what are the actually effective bonds of a political society; but as applied to states in an earlier period of evolution it has abundant historical sanction. In western Europe the state had no choice as to whether it would be allied with the church or not, for the Catholic Church was at once more extensive and better disciplined than any state or alliance of states[2]: and, to extend our view beyond our own civilization, it would seem that, in any primitive society, community of religion is a bond without which cohesion is impossible. And the

---

[1] Persecution inspired by this idea of course will not necessarily be undertaken on politico-social grounds; the magistrate may act from any or all of the five motives. But I have thought it more convenient to mention it here, arising as it does from the ecclesiastico-political conception of the state.

[2] Sir F. Pollock, *op. cit.*, 170.

development of the state to a point at which it is able to stand by its own strength without support from community of religion among its members is a slow process. In the case of Christian states it would be more correct to describe it as development to a point at which the state was strong enough to resist the disintegrating force of the disorders which diversity in religious matters generated. And just as the national states were gathering strength, the upheaval of the sixteenth century spread religious diversity over western Europe. But the natural course of social development, which slowly asserted itself, gives increasing relative efficiency to the secular bonds,—community of civil government, of blood, of language, of history,—and decreasing relative efficiency to community of religion. But such a development is carried on unseen and for the most part unsuspected till it is already far advanced; men's perceptions naturally lag behind the facts; but at length the discovery was slowly reached that ecclesiastical ties had ceased to exert anything like their previous power, and that consequently the ecclesiastical and political aspects of society might be separated without serious damage arising to either church or state. *but is decreasingly applicable as social evolution proceeds.*

The growth of this separation in practice consisted in the gradual appropriation of the state to purely political, and of the church to purely religious, functions. In England affairs followed the logical course of evolution through successive stages, from one in which intolerance was the result of regarding the state not only as a political but also *Separation of ecclesiastical and political aspects of society: course of affairs in England* as a semi-religious organization under the tutelage of the church, towards one in which it resulted rather from regarding the church not only as a religious, but also as a semi-political organization under the tutelage of the state. In the first stage the church managed to lay upon the state religious duties, and the bond of union between the two was primarily religious; but as the power of the state increased, it managed to lay upon the church political duties, and the bond between the two was primarily political; hence it was mainly by political considerations that the rupture was caused. It is not implied that historical facts uniformly conform to this plan; it certainly would not be true to imply that the stages indicated were chronologically successive in the sense that a clear line of demarcation can be drawn marking the end of one and the beginning of the other. It is however the logical course of the secularization of politics; and in England the Reformation—on its political side the self-assertion of the increasingly powerful state in the ecclesiastical sphere—may be taken roughly as the division. Henceforward to support the monarchy was an especial care of the Church of England, which acted as an organization for the propagation of an illiberal political creed; and the alliance was drawn closer by the community in suffering of Cavaliers and clergy during the interregnum. The divinity of kingship as preached from the Restoration onwards was a last attempt to find the religious element in the state (but now rather in its origin than its ends), and also to cast the glamour of religious obligation over the political duties thrust upon the Church.

The Church took over police duties from the state and the state endorsed the intolerance of the Church, both falsely assuming that political and ecclesiastical unity were bound up together. This confusion of thought, it should be noticed, was not merely in the minds of the rulers, but also in those of the ruled; and hence, up to a certain stage in evolution, had toleration been granted, religious disagreement would, not improbably, have formed parties, which, regarding one another as heretical and traitorous, might have seriously imperilled the established politico-social order. Hence we may find on civil grounds a possible justification for religious intolerance. After all, the discovery of the separability of the ecclesiastical and political aspects of society was not the discovery of an eternal law like that of gravitation. The compatibility of religious diversity with social order was not, indeed, given much opportunity of being demonstrated till social evolution had already passed the point at which it became possible; it does not follow that it had always been possible.

However this may be, belief in toleration is not *Principles* new; the execution of the Priscillianists for their *of tolera-* opinions in the fourth century aroused a vehement *tion not* *new,* protest; and the main principles of legal toleration, namely that no ecclesiastical organization has a right to enforce temporal punishments, and that the magistrate has no right to punish for mere opinions, were clearly enunciated by Marsiglio of Padua in 1327[1].

but it is now more fully recognized that persecution Lapse of time has driven home what were then unaccustomed propositions. Not only has an immense diffusion of intelligence brought about a general recognition that such repressive measures may be

(1) may be mistaken in its object, mistaken, in that they may repress what should be encouraged and encourage what should be repressed; but modern experience has shown that it is not true

(2) is more dangerous than heterodoxy, that all heterodoxy is necessarily dangerous to society either as dividing a kingdom against itself or as sapping the foundations of morality; and that whether any particular form of heterodoxy be dangerous to society or not, it is likely to inflict less moral and intellectual damage than the persecuting of it. Another fact gleaned by modern experience is that

(3) is largely inoperative, owing to the attitude of public opinion, repressive measures are inoperative save so far as they are endorsed by public opinion. Thus at the present day in England, anyone who has been educated in or made profession of Christianity in England and who, by " writing, printing, teaching or advised speaking[2]," denies the truth of Christianity or the authority of the Scriptures, commits a criminal offence rendering him liable to very severe penalties[3]. But this law is never enforced simply because public opinion does not allow it. But, should public opinion allow persecution to be tried, the limit of severity which from the point of view of secular expediency

[1] See Creighton, *Persecution and Tolerance*, 73–5, 93–8.

[2] 9 Will. III, c. 35.

[3] A. V. Dicey, *The Law of the Constitution*, 241, 6th ed., 1902.

can be made to appear reasonable is soon reached; and while severe persecution cannot be employed because to our age it is morally intolerable, moderate persecution would be likely (if the persecuted were really animated by conscientious convictions) to be futile.

Thus in so far as persecution is successful it is in danger of checking intellectual progress, and therefore is from the point of view of society (though not perhaps from that of the persecuting party) inexpedient; while in so far as it is unsuccessful it causes disturbance and suffering to no end whatever, and therefore again is inexpedient. In fact, the theory of persecution in the secular interests of society can be weighed in the balances of experience, and has been found wanting. Persecuting measures need in a democratic country the support of public opinion if they are to be enforced, and public opinion will not support them. "Laws of this kind do not work, and no harm appears to come of their not working[1]." But there was a time when laws of this *which has* kind did work, and when it is quite conceivable that *changed.* harm would have come of their not working. Their present ineffectiveness is due to a change in that anything but constant quantity, public opinion, the ultimate court of appeal. Similarly though heterodoxy may be now less dangerous to society than persecution, it does not necessarily follow that there have been no occasions when persecution was less dangerous than heterodoxy.

[1] Sir F. Pollock's *Essays in Jurisprudence and Ethics*, 166, to which (163–6) I am indebted for much of the substance of the paragraph up to this point

Modern toleration, however, is due not only to expediency but also to recognition of abstract right,

In view of this change in modern conditions it has been urged that general arguments, concerning the sanctity of individual opinions as such, or of religious opinions above others, are of little use; for the various theories of persecution deny the premises on which these arguments are founded: it is not the demonstration of abstract right but the experience of inutility which has made governments leave off persecuting[1]. This is no doubt true if we confine our attention to immediate causes; but surely the belief in abstract right has had a great influence upon the question, in that this very inutility which has caused persecution to cease is largely due to the incorporation of that belief in public opinion. It is closely connected both with the recognition of the serious intellectual and moral effects of successful persecution, and also with its frequent futility owing to general unwillingness to enforce the laws. Opinion has changed not only as to the things which can be safely repressed by force and the methods which it is expedient to use, but also as to the things which ought to be so repressed and the methods which it is right to use[2].

which offered a new basis for political philosophy.

The ecclesiastico-political conception of the state cannot, indeed, be confuted by theories of natural right or social contract. All alike are really fundamental assumptions not reached by inductive reasoning. It is only possible to offer them as alternatives and let each man choose what commends itself to him. But the ecclesiastico-political conception of

[1] Sir F. Pollock's *Essays in Jurisprudence and Ethics*, 175.

[2] D. G. Ritchie, *Natural Rights*, 161.

the state was breaking down in England at the
time of the Restoration, and the theories of natural
right and social contract had come to sufficient
maturity to offer a new basis for a political philosophy recognizing the separability of the ecclesiastical
and the political aspects of society. Thus the slow
and laborious processes of social evolution gradually
brought about circumstances favourable to the practical application of this discovery, and a generation
willing at least in some measure to apply it.

Since then persecution in the sense of the in- *The spirit*
fliction of legal penalties has disappeared, but the *of persecu-*
tion still
spirit of persecution survives. Indeed, it could *survives,*
hardly be otherwise, for that spirit, if not actually
a constituent element of human nature, falls but
little short of being one. Hence people are still
intolerant, though they manifest their intolerance *but mani-*
with less violence and brutality than in former days. *fests itself*
differently,
Giving a rather wide interpretation to the term,
Lecky has pointed out that there are four lessening
stages of persecution—burning, penal laws, exclusion
from office, and social excommunication[1]. Though
the last two cannot perhaps properly be described as
persecution, the four stages do represent a descending series of manifestations of the intolerant spirit,
to which may be added a fifth in which it shows
itself, as it most commonly does, in abuse, scorn,
uncharitableness or impatience. When we call
people intolerant nowadays we mean that they are
impatient of differing views, not that they use
violence towards the holders of them. The change

[1] *History of Rationalism*, II. 89, (2 vols. 1877–8).

is a creditable one, but we must be careful to give the credit where it is due; and it is by no means all due to the individuals concerned. Among the few people who feel violently on any particular point a considerable proportion exhibit exactly the same spirit as that which set up the Inquisition, and in the seventeenth century embodied itself in the *owing to changed circumstances.* Clarendon Code. The difference in its manifestation is due to a difference in the circumstances under which it is manifested: the government and public opinion (which are little more than two aspects of the same thing) are now tolerant. And public opinion is tolerant not only because of the more or less partial appreciation of the case for toleration which has already been outlined, but for another reason which makes it more tolerant than the average of the individual opinions of which it is *Diffusion of interest.* the composite. A characteristic of modern times is the diffusion of men's interests. A far greater variety of subjects is offered for men to work at, to study, to amuse themselves with, and each claims chief attention from a large or small number of votaries. The result is that there has been a relative decline in the numbers of persons who take a genuine interest in those questions on which earlier centuries concentrated their attention; and that there are not enough people of influence, thinking violently enough and with enough agreement on any matter, to set a persecution on foot; for in order to do so they must persuade the indifferent majority, and indifference is on the side of toleration. In the middle ages and long afterwards religious persecution could be practised because interest was concentrated on religion ; and therefore those who felt most violently on religious matters were not hampered by the deadweight of general indifference. It has been said that "a disposition is to its appropriate behaviour as a man is to his shadow. The shadow represents the man, but it often misrepresents him. It is larger than he is, or smaller[1]." So the spirit of the age has tended at times to translate the intolerant disposition of men into exaggerated action, as it now tends to translate it into comparatively modest action supplemented by much frothy talk. But, be the shadow larger or smaller, the intolerant disposition is still there, and some shadow it must cast.

And it would be rash to assert that the mani- *Intoler-* festations of the intolerant spirit have been and are *ance not* necessarily in all cases bad. The very fact that *sarily* intolerance is so deeply set in human nature would *always* seem to show that it must have been at least in *bad.* some early stage of social evolution a valuable cohesive force. And this, practically beyond question, it was. From this consideration arises the question whether it is now merely an awkward and baneful survival of man's earlier struggles, or still serves some useful purpose. It has been vigorously argued by Sir James Fitzjames Stephen that the latter is the case, and that intolerance in its modern form is still entitled to respect as a preservative of society. He justifies intolerance (working not through legal penalties but through social pressure) on the grounds

[1] Phillips Brooks, quoted by J. O. Bevan, *Birth and Growth of Toleration and Other Essays*, 2.

that " to attack opinions on which the framework of
society rests both is and ought to be dangerous,"
and that till a man " has formed opinions " on morals
and religion " for which he is prepared to fight, there
is no hardship in his being compelled by social
intolerance to keep them to himself and to those
who sympathise with him[1]."   But to examine this
extremely interesting question at any length would
be to digress from the purpose of this chapter,
which is to consider the theories of persecution and
toleration in general as a preliminary to a more
detailed study of them as set forth under the Stuarts.

*Is perse-
cution in
England
absolutely
dead?*
Another question that can only be suggested
here is whether even in England actual persecution
is dead and buried for all time.   To those for whom
the course of progress may be formulated like a proportion sum in which our descendants will be to us
as we are to our ancestors, an affirmative answer is
so obvious that the question is hardly worth the
asking; but to others it may not be altogether
incredible that a line of cleavage could still so arise
as to cut off a minority from the rest of society on
a question on which passion might run high enough
to lead to active repression by " the state—that is
to say, a number of influential people sufficient to
dispose of the public force[2]."

*The sanc-
tions of
legal tole-
ration.*
As a general result of our examination it may
be said that there are at present three sanctions of
the policy of legal toleration.   The first is morality—

[1] *Liberty, Equality, Fraternity*, 77–9.
[2] *Ibid.* 67.   See also Sir Leslie Stephen in *Encyclopaedia
Britannica*, vol. xxviii., Prefatory Essay, pp. xii, xiii.

the recognition that persecuting laws are wrong: the second is expediency—the recognition that persecuting laws do not pay: and the third is necessity—the recognition that persecuting laws will not work. Now persecuting laws will not work, not only because of what may be termed diffusion of interest or, more bluntly (from the point of view of any particular subject such as religion) indifference, but also because of the general recognition that they are immoral and inexpedient: in other words the third sanction partly depends upon the first and second. And persecuting laws are inexpedient not only because of the material and intellectual loss which they may inflict on the community, but also because of the indignation which they may cause among others than the sufferers,—that is, the general recognition that they are wrong: in other words the second sanction partly depends upon the first. And if the first be examined it will be found that here too a distinction appears. Morality may be appealed to on the ground that it is a duty to allow to every man scope to think for himself, and, as far as possible, to act according to his conscience, quite apart from considerations of the truth or falsity of his views: this is a direct appeal to morality. Or on the other hand morality may be appealed to on the ground that the individual should be allowed this freedom, not apart from considerations of the truth or falsity of his views, but because we cannot infallibly know whether his views are true or false: this is an indirect appeal to morality through the intellect; it finds persecution immoral because it is liable to be mistaken.

The strengths of these sanctions as compared with one another will be estimated differently by different types of mind: but the highest form of tolerance is that exhibited by those who, while fully believing in the importance of the subject under discussion, and holding firm convictions upon it, yet have no desire to enforce their views by any means save temperate argument and living example. In the last three hundred years it has come about that belief (or at any rate fully realized belief) in the vitally serious consequences of purely intellectual error on religious matters has largely disappeared; and hence the whole-hearted adherent of a creed has, generally speaking, no such spur to intolerance as his less enlightened ancestors. But in the face of strong convictions arguments based on politico-social expedience or human fallibility are inadequate. It is not enough to show that toleration is a negative good in that it wards off the evils attendant on persecution. It can be firmly based only on those reasons which show it to be a positive good—the belief in the dignity and prerogatives of the intellect and moral sense of the individual man, the recognition of the varying forms of religion as setting forth diverse aspects of the one truth, and, in the Christian world, the perception of the true spirit of the religion so long and so grossly distorted into a justification of inhumanity.

CHAPTER II

TOLERANT TENDENCIES IN ENGLISH THOUGHT IN THE SEVENTEENTH CENTURY

IN the seventeenth century arose a spirit of *Spirit of inquiry in the 17th century* inquiry which spread itself with far-reaching effects into all departments of thought. To it must be ascribed the dawning of modern science upon the darkness of mediaeval magic and superstition: in the political sphere it played an important part in stimulating the intellectual activity which formed the background of the Great Rebellion: in religion it manifested itself in a growing freedom of theological thought, which, in the reaction from the pressure of the Laudian ecclesiastical system, ran riot among the ephemeral sects, and carried with it the proclamation of the right of private judgment. This great impulse was implicit in the Reformation *implicit in the Reformation* movement of the preceding century, which on its intellectual side was an assertion of the instinct for truth—an assertion the corollaries of which in logical sequence were the recognition of the rights of the intellect to come to its own decisions, and the recognition of the rights of the conscience to make those decisions guides to practice. The Reformation, indeed, by substituting an infallible Bible for an infallible church, still maintained very definite limits within which alone the intellect was free; but emancipation from the control of the Papal see gave a consciousness of freedom which servitude to the letter of Scripture did not counterbalance. The fact of emancipation was at the same time more prominent and of greater moment than the fact that the emancipation was limited.

in spite of Protestant dogmatism, But those who raise the cry for liberty usually mean liberty for themselves, and it is only after bitter experience and much searching of heart that they realize (if they realize at all) that the term, if it is to have any ethical value, must be used in a sense of general application, including even those who differ from them. The Reformation was no exception to the rule; the less so because, though the force of a great intellectual revival lay behind it and worked through it, it was not distinctively an intellectual movement aiming at rational liberty. It was mainly a religious movement aiming at spiritual salvation; and hence the reformed churches, having modelled themselves more appropriately, as they supposed, to that end, settled down into that spirit of dogmatism against which their very existence was a semi-conscious protest. "The inevitable consequence was that doctrinal correctness became divorced as in pre-Reformation times from true faith and moral sincerity. Men subjected themselves to the ideas of theologians, as formerly to the guidance

of priests[1]." Usually, the less rational the grounds
upon which belief is based, the greater is the stress
laid upon the importance of mere belief, and thus
for a time the element of free intellectual inquiry
in the reforming movement—to which alone Protestantism could rationally appeal for self-justifica-
tion—was obscured in the Protestant churches. But
Protestant dogmatism could not but be in a condition
of unstable equilibrium. It lacked the firm basis upon *which had*
which Roman Catholic dogmatism stood. The voice *no firm*
of the Church was a living voice to which appeal *basis.*
could be made, and which had given and still could
give a decisive answer upon definite problems as
they arose: the voice of the Bible needed an interpreter; and infallible though the Bible might be,
unless the interpreter too was infallible there was
no means of discovering for purposes of general
application what the decision of the Bible was. The
efforts of the Protestants virtually to claim the
substance of infallibility, while disclaiming the word,
were bound to fail so soon as a discussion of some
point as yet unsettled should lead the way to a controversy involving important issues, and inspire the
spirit of inquiry with fresh vigour.

This work was accomplished by the Arminian con- *The Ar-*
troversy which formally broke out in the University *minians.*
of Leyden in 1603. No Protestant confession disputed the supremacy of Scripture, and no Protestant

---

[1] J. K. Mozley, *Ritschlianism*, 121: q.v. pp. 114–22, 150–1, for
the difference between Roman Catholic and the Protestant conceptions of the relations of faith and dogma, and the corruption
of the Protestant conception.

communion claimed infallibility for its confession. The confession, then, could not finally determine the sense in which alone Scripture must be understood. The Arminians saw that in consequence the supremacy of Scripture must mean the supremacy of Scripture as interpreted by the individual. This view brought them inevitably into opposition to the whole system of confessions and Church authority by which that supremacy was, as a matter of fact, impeded and obscured. They raised, moreover, the momentous distinction between fundamental and non-fundamental doctrines—a distinction fraught with possibilities as yet undreamed of.

With the fortunes of the Dutch Arminians and their condemnation at the Synod of Dort in 1619[1] we are not now directly concerned, but the doctrines that they taught were transported to English soil and there took root and fructified.

Liberalizing tendencies in the Church of England: The Church of England had not avoided the prevailing dogmatism, but was fortunate in this, that her comprehensive character had enabled her to develop two different and opposing types of dogmatism, the one Puritan, the other Anglo-Catholic. But these two parties did not together include the whole of the English Church. Whether a survival of the undifferentiated Anglicanism of the Reforma-

---

[1] The Synod opened late in 1618 and broke up on Jan. 14, 1619. Tulloch, *Rational Theology and Christian Philosophy in England in the 17th Century*, I. 184 n., 186. I take this opportunity of saying that my indebtedness to Tulloch in the portions of this chapter dealing with the Arminians, the liberal churchmen, and the Cambridge Platonists, is far greater than I can acknowledge piecemeal in the footnotes.

tion, or the offspring of a search for a mean between the two extreme and more prominent sections of the Church, there were minds in which the strife of (1)*reaction from theological strife,* Puritan and Anglo-Catholic generated aspirations after a basis of religion more profound than the dogmatism of either.

To the Puritans the Arminian tenets were here- (2) *Arminian influence,* tical, and their progress in the English Church was made a matter of complaint in Parliament. But, fostered by the first two Stuart kings[1], Arminianism " passed into the Anglo-Catholic movement as its theological background, and gave to it a party meaning and consistency which it had not hitherto possessed....The High Church and Puritan parties were henceforth divided theologically as well as ecclesiastically[2]." In spite of their Arminianism, however, the High Churchmen abated nothing of their ecclesiastical dogmatism, which rather took a more aggressive form with the rise of Laud: it was in the liberal minds, which were identified with neither party, that the liberalizing doctrines of Arminianism found a favourable nidus for their reception and development.

There was another force at work calculated to (3) *aggressions of Rome.* evoke the rationalistic tendencies inherent in Pro-

[1] James I never definitely adopted Arminianism, but the Arminian clergy, supporting the royal prerogative, received preferment at his hands towards the end of his reign (which gave currency to a rumour that he had renounced Calvinism) ; for " much as he loved Calvinism, he loved servility and the principle of passive obedience still more," Tulloch, I. 73 ; Hunt, *Religious Thought in England from the Reformation to the End of the Last Century,* I. 148.

[2] Tulloch, I. 73.

testantism. From the latter part of the reign of
James I onwards the aggressions of Roman Catholicism caused serious alarm, and the need was felt of
a restatement of the current Protestant theories
upon the question of authority in religion. When
to the infallible Church the Protestant controversialist opposed the infallible Bible, there came the
formidable question, "Who is to decide what the
infallible Bible says?" and, if the true spirit of
Protestantism was adhered to, eventually must be
wrung out the answer, "The individual for himself."

These three forces, then,—revulsion from the opposing dogmatisms of Puritan and High Churchman,
the spread of Arminianism, and the necessity of
finding an answer to the pertinent questions of the
Rise of a Roman Catholics—combined to bring about the rise
LIBERAL of a liberal school of thought within the Church of
ANGLICAN England, pleading for the religious freedom implicit
SCHOOL. in the principles of the Reformation. A prejudice
centuries old is not easily overthrown, and to the
average seventeenth century mind—especially when
rendered pugnacious by party strife—religious freedom was outside the pale of comprehensible ideas.
" Neither High Churchmen nor Puritans understood
it—or, so far as they understood it, they hated it.
Their essential conception, both of a national and
ecclesiastical polity, implied dogmatic as well as external uniformity.   In opposition to this our Rational
Theologians announced as a *principle* that dogmatic
uniformity is unattainable, and that the prosperity
both of the Church and the country are to be sought

in toleration and latitude of religious opinion. They proclaimed, in other words, that religious questions can only be settled by being left to free discussion[1]."

Lucius Cary, the second Lord Falkland, who played a prominent part in the early days of the Long Parliament, was the centre of this school, and his residence at Great Tew near Oxford its rendezvous. Its greatest name is that of Chillingworth. Himself a convert to the Roman Church, who had returned to the Church of England, he came to a thorough knowledge of the points at issue between the two churches; and his "The Religion of Protestants a Safe Way to Salvation," published in 1637, was the first full exposition in English theological literature of the inner meaning of the Reformation, and of the fact that religious latitude was the logical corollary of Protestantism. Following the Arminians he objected to the principle of articles in general "as an imposition on men's consciences, much like that authority which the Church of Rome assumes[2]." "The Bible, I say, the Bible only," he asserted, "is the religion of Protestants[3]," and the essential teaching of the Bible, which is clear to all honest minds, and which all Protestant churches have acknowledged, is contained in the Apostles' Creed: to the minute definition and the damnatory clauses of the Athanasian Creed he ob-

Chillingworth.

---

[1] Tulloch, I. 457.

[2] Des Maizeaux, *Historical and Critical Account of the Life and Writings of William Chillingworth*, 101.

[3] *Religion of Protestants*, ch. VI. 56, Works, II. 410 (3 vols. Oxford, 1838).

jected. But if all essentials are contained in the Apostles' Creed it follows that the questions on which Protestants are separated refer to matters not necessary to salvation—matters upon which it is possible to hold different opinions without breach of unity. Chillingworth vigorously, almost passionately, insisted on a truth which was as yet but rarely understood—the innocence of those who fall into error provided that an honest search has been made for the truth. "If they suffer themselves neither to be betrayed into their errors, nor to be kept in them by any sin of their will; if they do their best to endeavour to free themselves from all errors, and yet fail of it through human frailty, so well am I persuaded of the goodness of God, that if in me alone should meet a confluence of all such errors of all the Protestants of the world that were thus qualified, I should not be so much afraid of them all as I should be to ask pardon for them[1]." Thus toleration was with Chillingworth not the product of indifference but the logical outcome of an enlightened rational view of religious questions, and of the right of the individual to examine them for himself and come to his own conclusions; and as such it was elevated into a positive principle of ecclesiastical government.

Chillingworth's friends, Falkland and Hales, must not be passed over. Their views upon toleration practically coincided with his; but it is worth notice *Falkland* that Falkland appears to have remained a militant *and Hales.* Calvinist, and Hales, though he "bid John Calvin

[1] *Answer to Preface*, § 26, Works, I. 81.

good-night" at the Synod of Dort, never took up a line of definite opposition to Calvinism. It was the Roman controversy which, if it did not generate, at any rate called forth, Falkland's liberal views upon religious questions. He pointed out that in the search for truth we must ultimately depend upon our reason, for even if we accept the infallibility of the Church, yet we must employ our reason to decide that the Church is infallible. Rational inquiry, then, which is the sound basis for religion, is itself at least as meritorious as unquestioning belief; and intolerance can never be justified on grounds of difference upon questions of dogma.

Similar in tone was the protest of "the ever memorable Mr. John Hales of Eton College," an older contemporary of Chillingworth and Falkland[1]. He approached the question from the point of view that religion is a thing deeper than theological dogma, differences in which are not really religious, and should not be an obstacle to joining in common faith and worship. Nor should the right of private judgment be regarded by the Church as a necessary evil, but rather should the Church educate it and make allowance for it in her organization.

The distinction between fundamental and non-fundamental doctrines, raised by the Arminians, adopted by Chillingworth, and so made a permanent possession of English religious thought, formed the usual basis for toleration in the latitudinarian school which now arose in the English Church. The prin-

[1] The dates of their births were—Hales 1584, Chillingworth 1602, Falkland 1610.

ciple was one of widely variable application, and the body of fundamental doctrines might be almost indefinitely expanded or contracted according to the inroads which the spirit of inquiry in any particular case had made upon dogmatic prejudice, from the unyielding sternness of the Westminster Confession to the bare assertion that Jesus is the Messiah of Taylor, Hobbes, and Locke.

Doctrine of exclusive salvation shown to be not only unreasonable but immoral. On purely rational grounds the doctrine of exclusive salvation was no longer tenable as a realized belief by minds open to reason[1]. But the rational school did more than show its unreasonableness, they exposed its repulsive immorality. Speaking of things as to which the divine testimony is not clear, Chillingworth writes, "to say that God will damn men for errors as to such things, who are lovers of him and lovers of the truth, is to rob man of his comfort and God of his goodness; is to make man desperate and God a tyrant[2]." To the same effect Falkland declares that where God has not so revealed His will as to put it beyond doubt "it will not stand with his goodness to damn man for not following it[3]"; while Hales, according to Clarendon, "would often say that he would renounce the religion of the Church of England to-morrow, if it obliged him to believe that any other Christian should be

[1] Which perhaps most minds were not. Chillingworth's admission that even a Papist might be saved was denounced by a Presbyterian divine as "a miserable weakness." See Tulloch, I. 297–304 for the story of an amazing exhibition of religious intolerance and moral blindness.

[2] *Answer to Preface*, § 26, Works, I. 80.

[3] *Discourse of the Infallibility of the Church of Rome*, 5, quoted by Tulloch, I. 161.

damned; and that nobody would conclude another
man to be damned who did not wish him so[1]."

Thus the doctrine of exclusive salvation broke
down under the combined attack of rationalism and
the liberated moral sense, and a great step was
taken towards the unfolding of the far-reaching consequences implicit in the Reformation, but unrealized
by the reformers, which slowly amid the clash of
theological warfare were winning their way to recognition. But when we speak of rationalism in this *Ration-*
connection, we must remember that judged by the *alism of*
our theo-
standard of what bears that name at the present *logians re-*
day it was a very restricted rationalism. Our rational *stricted.*
theologians never dreamed of making the human
reason take the place of divine revelation as the
sole ultimate criterion of religious truth: reason was
not to excogitate truth for itself, it was merely to
discover it in the infallible Bible. "Propose to me
anything," wrote Chillingworth, "out of the Bible,
and require whether I believe it or no, and seem it
never so incomprehensible to human reason, I will
subscribe it with hand and heart, as knowing no
demonstration can be stronger than this: God hath
said so, therefore it is true[2]." Reason, in fact, was
to test not the evidences of revelation but only its
content. The great point however was gained that *Its valu-*
intellectual fallibility was recognized as the cause of *able re-*
sults.
difference of opinion, and therefore that the holding
of opinions supposed to be erroneous need not be
regarded as tantamount to, if not actually, a moral
fault. Apart from the increase of charity rendered

[1] Quoted by Tulloch, I. 258.
[2] *Religion of Protestants*, ch. VI. § 56, Works, II. 411.

possible by this change of view, morality, thus separated out from its confusion with the intellect, afforded a new criterion of religion. A great step was taken towards bridging the gulf of intellectual divergence by community of moral aspiration on a Christian basis, which might even be put forward as a sounder principle of church unity than either intellectual agreement (consisting in a common assent to a certain body of doctrine or to a particular form of church government), or the purely external test of conformity to particular ritual or discipline. The seventeenth century had not succeeded in shaking off the Roman conception of dogmatic and ceremonial uniformity in favour of the charitable unity to which the spirit of Protestantism pointed the way; and the attempt to maintain, or rather, amid the war of hostile confessions, to realize rigid uniformity stood as an insuperable obstacle in the way of the realization of unity. The essential service done by the rational theologians was this, that they showed the incompatibility of the former with Protestant principles, and suggested the possibility of the latter—a possibility still only too far from being realized.

Jeremy Taylor.

In the way in which Hales and Chillingworth in the days of prosperity had led, Jeremy Taylor, under the stimulus of persecution, followed. His "Liberty of Prophesying" was published in 1647, later, that is, than Chillingworth's "Religion of Protestants" by ten years during which the cause of episcopacy had suffered severely. His general position closely resembles that of Chillingworth, both the rational and the moral sides of whose teaching reappear.

But while Chillingworth's advocacy of comprehensiveness and tolerance was incidental to his task of
championing Protestantism against Rome, Taylor's
plea was put forward in direct relation to the now
pressing problem of the ecclesiastical settlement.
Taylor insists upon the likelihood of error in the
persecutors, and asserts that he is not a heretic,
in spite of intellectual error, whose life is good.
Following Hales who had defined heresy as wilful
error[1] he argues that heresy does not consist in the
holding of certain views—no view honestly held is
heretical—but depends upon the motive causing
them to be held. This mere playing with words
reduces heresy to little more than a superfluous
synonym for the sinful motive, and is interesting as
showing the moralizing drift of the age. Moreover
as heresy lost its distinctive meaning, it tended to
lose also its distinctive horror, and thus even loose-
ness of language did service in the cause of religious
liberty[2]. Nor was Taylor's test of orthodoxy exact-
ing. "The article upon the confession of which
Christ built his church" is "no more but this simple
enunciation, 'We believe and are sure that thou
art Christ the son of the living God': and to this
salvation is particularly promised[3]." Thus all sects
are to be tolerated, save such as injure the state.
Unanimity is impossible, therefore it cannot be
necessary, and the lack of it need not cause a breach

---

[1] Tulloch, i. 237. Similarly, Hales having described heresy
and schism as "two theological Μορμώς, or scarecrows," Taylor
called the name heretic a "terriculamentum" to frighten people
from their belief. *Ibid.* i. 231 ; Hunt, i. 336.

[2] Sir J. F. Stephen, *Horae Sabbaticae*, i. 221-2.

[3] Works, vii. 444 (ed. Heber, 15 vols. London, 1822).

in the unity of faith.   It is not diversity of thought
that causes trouble, but want of charity and breadth
of mind.

Taylor might plead for charity, but charity was
not likely to be stimulated by the animosities of the
civil wars.   The course of the wars, however, indirectly served the cause of toleration by eventually
bringing the Independents into power, and thus an
undercurrent of thought long making for toleration
was at length thrown up to the surface.

INDEPEND-
ENCY.

The appli-
cation of
democracy
to religion:
compared
with
liberal
Angli-
canism.

Independency consisted in the application of
democracy to religion, and was another form in
which the individualistic spirit of the Reformation
struggled into self-expression.   The rational theologians had given expression to that spirit by aiming
at liberty of thought, and showing that diversity
of opinion is not incompatible with religious unity,
because dogma is merely the shell within which the
kernel of religion is concealed.   It was natural that
the tolerant attitude of Churchmen should find its
characteristic expression in the aim at greater comprehensiveness of communion, rather than at the
recognition of bodies outside the Church of England.
The distinction between fundamental and non-fundamental articles of belief and the idea of allowing
latitude of belief without breach of communion were
not systematically expounded in the seventeenth
century save in the writings of liberal Churchmen,
in whose eyes toleration was good, but comprehension better.   The Independents on the other hand,
to whom the idea of organic unity did not appeal,
found the solution of the religious problem in
agreeing not merely to differ on dogmatic questions

but to separate congregation from congregation, each following its own bent in creed and worship: for comprehensive liberty of thought they substituted the liberty of exclusive sectarian association. The Churchmen proposed to solve the question from the side of doctrine, the Independents from that of church-government. Their theory of the Church as "a voluntary concourse of like-minded atoms[1]" was in itself an implicit recognition of the compulsory power of the individual conscience; hence it is not surprising to find that the logical outcome of that theory, the full principle of liberty of conscience was first discovered and enunciated in a church formed on Independent lines. Before the end of the sixteenth century, Robert Browne, the founder of Congregationalism, taught that magistrates "have no ecclesiastical authority at all, but only as any other Christians, if so they be Christians[2]"; and in 1611 a congregation of English *The Anglo-Dutch Baptists.* Baptists in Holland, an offshoot from the Brownists who had taken refuge in Amsterdam, put forth a confession of faith denying the right of the magistrate to interfere in religion. This is believed to be the first unqualified expression of the principle in the public articles of a Christian body; and the Independents generally were so far from carrying their principles to their logical conclusion as to disapprove of this doctrine. Shortly afterwards, Helwisse or Helwys, the pastor of this congregation, returned to England with his followers and formed

[1] Masson, *Life of Milton*, III. 99.
[2] *Treatise of Reformation*, published 1582, Def. 4, quoted by Scherger, *Evolution of Modern Liberty*, 123.

a congregation of Baptists in London, of which it has been conjectured that Leonard Busher, the author of a pamphlet published in 1614 entitled "Religion's Peace, or a Plea for Liberty of Conscience," was a member[1]. The pamphlet was addressed to King James and the Parliament, and asserted that true religion could not be propagated by fire or sword, and that Christianity could only be received by those who were convinced of its truth. It was the first of a series of pamphlets from Baptist sources, some of which will come under our notice later.

The tolerant principles of the Independents received vigorous exposition in 1644 by the publication *Roger Williams.* of Roger Williams' "The Bloody Tenent of Persecution" declaring that the people cannot trust the magistrate with any spiritual power, and advocating absolute liberty of conscience without a national church or state-interference of any kind in religion[2]. This was in strong contrast with the views of the Presbyterians, a party surpassing in rigid intolerance Archbishop Laud himself[3], who in the following year expiated on the scaffold his zeal for "the beauty of holiness." The short-lived Presbyterian

[1] Masson, *Life of Milton*, III. 101–2. For this and other Baptist pamphlets on the same subject, see *Tracts on Liberty of Conscience and Persecution* 1614–1661, edited for the Hanserd Knollys Society by E. B. Underhill, 1846.

[2] Masson, III. 112–7, 122–4. Scherger, 169. Williams' book has been edited by E. B. Underhill and published by the Hanserd Knollys Society.

[3] Hence Milton's famous comment, "New Presbyter is but old Priest writ large." But while Laud's intolerance was shown in matters of discipline and ceremonial, the Presbyterians showed theirs in matters of discipline and dogma, as to the latter of which Laud was fairly liberal.

tyranny was not yet overpast, but the Independents were already the rising power. The formation of the New Model army, the rapid spread of Independent principles in it, its quarrel with the Presbyterian parliament, and consequent usurpation of the supreme power, were all steps in the advance of the cause of religious liberty as interpreted by the Independents.

Their views found their fullest expression in Milton's passionate advocacy of freedom.   " Give me *Milton.* liberty," he cried, " to know, to utter, and to argue freely according to conscience above all liberties[1]." " Who knows not that truth is strong next to the Almighty ? She needs no policies, no stratagems, nor licensings to make her victorious ; those are the shifts and defences that error uses against her power[2]." "Let her and falsehood grapple; who ever knew truth put to the worse in a free and open encounter ? Her confuting is the best and surest suppressing[3]." " Methinks I see in my mind a noble and puissant nation rousing herself like a strong man after sleep, and shaking her invincible locks.   Methinks I see her as an eagle mewing her mighty youth, and kindling her undazzled eyes at the full midday beam, purging and unscaling her long-abused sight at the fountain itself of heavenly radiance, while the whole noise of timorous and flocking birds, with those also that love the twilight, flutter about, amazed at what she means, and in their envious gabble prognosticate a year of sects and schisms[4]."

[1] *Areopagitica*, Works (8 vols. London, 1851), IV. 442.
[2] *Ibid.* IV. 444.   [3] *Ibid.* IV. 443.   [4] *Ibid.* IV. 441.

"Under these fantastic terrors of sect and schism, we wrong the earnest and zealous thirst after knowledge and understanding which God hath stirred up in this city. What some lament of, we rather should rejoice at, should rather praise this pious forwardness among men to reassume the ill deputed care of their religion into their own hands again[1]." "We do not see that, while we still affect by all means a rigid external formality, we may as soon fall again into a gross conforming stupidity, a stark and dead congealment of wood and hay and stubble forced and frozen together, which is more to the sudden degenerating of the Church than many subdichotomies of petty schisms. Not that I can think well of every light separation…yet if all cannot be of one mind—as who looks they should be?—this doubtless is more wholesome, more prudent, and more Christian; that many be tolerated rather than all compelled[2]." From this toleration he excepted Papists ("for just reason of state more than of religion"), the intolerant and idolaters[3]. He pointed out that persecution in Protestants is worse than in Papists, for toleration is of the essence of Protestantism, since all Protestants agree in following Scripture; and since Scripture is the only divine rule or authority from without us, "no man or body of men in these times can be the infallible judges or determiners in matters of religion to any other men's

---

[1] *Areopagitica*, Works, IV. 438.

[2] *Ibid.* IV. 445.

[3] *Treatise of Civil Power in Ecclesiastical Causes*, Works, V. 317–8.

consciences but their own[1]." "They who would
seem more knowing, confess that there are things
indifferent, but for that very cause by the magistrate
may be commanded. As if God of his special grace
in the gospel had to this end freed us from his own
commandments in these things, that our freedom
should subject us to a more grievous yoke, the commandments of men[2]." "The settlement of religion
belongs only to each particular church by persuasive
and spiritual means within itself, and...the defence
only of the church belongs to the magistrate[3]."

The Independents failed, indeed, to put their
principles completely into practice; but it must be
remembered that the period of their supremacy was
one of exceptional disturbance in both political and
religious affairs; the attachment of the Episcopalians
to the monarchy, on the one hand, and the extravagances of the sects on the other, made toleration
appear more formidable in practice than in theory[4],
and certainly the experiment would have been fraught
with greater risk to the established order than in
the days of Laud.

The theory of the Independents did not wholly *Individual*
consist in the application of democracy to religion, *enlighten-*
but also contained an element of more thorough- *ment.*
going individualism, which went beyond mere individual immunity from interference and extended to
a belief in special individual enlightenment. "For
such," wrote Milton, "is the order of God's enlighten-
ing his Church, to dispense and deal out by degrees

[1] *Ibid.* v. 306.   [2] *Ibid.* v. 326-7.   [3] *Ibid.* v. 335.
[4] Masson, *Life of Milton,* iii. 136.

his beam, so as our earthly eyes may best sustain it.
Neither is God appointed and confined, where and
out of what place these his chosen shall be first
heard to speak[1]." Thus Independency and the sects
which grew up under its wing found a further basis
for toleration in the religious enthusiasm which
The
Quakers.
developed, in an extreme form, into the Quaker
doctrine of the inner light, and by which the rights
of conscience were indefinitely emphasized. Presbyterianism was dogmatically scriptural in a narrow
sense: the liberal Churchmen gave rein to the
reason only within the limits of scriptural infallibility, their difference from the Presbyterians being
as to the interpreter of Scripture: the doctrine of
the inner light carried the individualization of the
basis of faith to its furthest limit[2,3].

The Quaker movement originated as a reaction
from the narrow dogmatism and discipline of the
Solemn League and Covenant[3,4]; and, like most
violent reactions, it tended to discredit itself (and
unfortunately in this case also the cause of toleration
for which it pleaded) by the extravagances with
which it was associated[4,5], and so provoked another

[1] *Areopagitica*, Works, IV. 446.

[2] See *Essays and Reviews* (7th ed. 1861), 290. (Pattison on
Religious Thought in England, 1688–1750.)

[3] Gardiner, *Cromwell's Place in History*, 110.

[4] Henson, *English Religion in the Seventeenth Century*, 252–3.

[5] The Presbyterian description of them is worth repeating:—
"The very dregs and spawn of old accursed heresies, which had
been already condemned, dead, buried and rotten in their graves
long ago." "Abominable errors, damnable heresies, and horrid
blasphemies, to be lamented, if it were possible with tears of blood."
A Testimony of the ministers of the province of Essex; also *A*

reaction in the opposite direction. The pendulum, once violently disturbed, must make many journeys to and fro before its swing settles down within a moderate compass. And the Quakers were only one among other sects, the views of some of which were more extravagant, though their practice may have been less noticeably eccentric. This outburst of what came to be known as "enthusiasm," produced two widely different reactions. In the first place it *Reactions* filled the more sober sections of the nation with *from "en-thusiasm.* a horror of anything approaching religious eccentricity, and a consequent determination to allow no deviation from the established worship: this showed itself chiefly after the Restoration, and will form a subject for consideration later. In the second place it gave an impetus to a philosophical movement which was itself, indirectly indeed, but essentially, tolerant. The contemplation of the *differentiae* of the sects could not fail to raise in thinking minds serious questionings as to the true nature of religion. Impartial observers could hardly avoid being struck by the parallel between the position of the sects with regard to the established order[1], and that of the sixteenth century reformers with regard to the Roman Catholics. On what principle were the latter to be justified and the former to be con-

Testimony subscribed by the ministers within the province of London, against the errors, heresies, and blasphemies of these times. London, 1647–1648, quoted by Tulloch, II. 9 and 10 n.

[1] Presbyterianism was theoretically established from 1646 to 1660, but the system was never carried into operation save locally, and with the triumph of the army was practically superseded by Independency.

demned ? Was it impossible, then, after all, to cast off the yoke of the infallible church and yet to find a substantial basis for a sane religion ? Was there no faculty in man capable of discovering a body of central doctrines which might form a common nucleus of personal religion ?

THE CAM-BRIDGE PLATO-NISTS. These, and other questions such as these, the second great school of English latitudinarians, centring round the Cambridge Platonists, set themselves to answer. Of the Cambridge Platonists the most notable were Benjamin Whichcote, Ralph Cudworth, John Smith, and Henry More. The first three of these all passed their undergraduate days at the great Puritan college of Emmanuel, "that zealous house," as Evelyn calls it[1]; but in 1644, when the Parliament was remodelling the Universities, Whichcote and Cudworth were respectively appointed Provost of King's College, and Master of Clare Hall. In the same year Smith was elected Fellow of Queens' College, but eight years later he died at the age of thirty-four, leaving behind him ten Discourses, posthumously published in 1660, and the memory of "a living, a doing and an obeying Christian[2]." At the Restoration Whichcote was deprived of the Provostship of King's, but remained in the Church of England and held a succession of benefices. Cudworth, on the other hand, was undisturbed in the Mastership of Christ's College, to which he had been appointed from that of Clare Hall in 1654, and retained it till his death in 1688. Less than a year before had died Henry More, successively

[1] *Diary*, Aug. 31st, 1654.   [2] Tulloch, II. 126.

undergraduate and Fellow of the same college, in the chapel of which the two Christian philosophers are buried.

The Cambridge Platonists have the distinction, rare among clergymen, of unstinted praise from Burnet. "Whichcote," he wrote, "was a man of rare temper, very mild and obliging. He had great credit with some that had been eminent in the late times[1]; but made all the use he could of it to protect good men of all persuasions. He was much for liberty of conscience; and being disgusted with the dry systematical way of those times, he studied to raise those who conversed with him to a nobler set of thoughts, and to consider religion as a seed of a deiform nature (to use one of his own phrases). In order to do this he set young students much on reading the ancient philosophers, chiefly Plato, Tully, and Plotin, and on considering the Christian religion as a doctrine sent from God, both to elevate and sweeten human nature, in which he was a great example as well as a wise and kind instructor. Cudworth carried this on with a great strength of genius and a vast compass of learning....More was an open-hearted and sincere Christian philosopher, who studied to establish men in the great principles of religion against atheism, that was then beginning to gain ground, chiefly by reason of the hypocrisy of some, and the fantastical conceits of the more sincere enthusiasts[2]."

Burnet on the Platonists.

---

[1] I.e. the Commonwealth and Protectorate. Burnet is dealing with the years immediately following the Restoration.

[2] *History of My Own Time* (6 vols. Oxford, 1823), I. 321-2.

*Charac-
teristics
of the
school.*

Earlier in the seventeenth century the urgent
question had been that of church organization and
its relation to the individual; and the inner reality
of religion had been searched for in the form of the
essentials of church-communion and the nature of
the bond of common church-membership. But the
disturbance of the twenty years which followed the
assembling of the Long Parliament, shifted the
centre of discussion from church politics to religious
truth itself and man's means of attaining to it.
Chillingworth and his friends had approached theology from the ecclesiastical side: the Cambridge
men approached it from the philosophical. The
philosophical liberalism of the Platonists took over
and carried forward all that was best in the ecclesiastical liberalism of the earlier movement, though
we have no evidence to show that they drew their
inspiration from it: according to Burnet, however,
"they read Episcopius much[1]," so that probably
they, like Chillingworth, were indebted to the
Arminians. This also they had in common with
their predecessors, that their movement was largely
a reaction against dogmatism. "The sense of
schism between theory and practice—between divinity and morals—was painfully brought home
to them. It was no wonder if they began to ask
themselves whether there was not a more excellent
way, and whether reason and morality were not
essential elements of all religious dogma....Especially

[1] *History of My Own Time*, I. 324. Episcopius was the
spokesman of the Arminians at the Synod of Dort, and con-
tributed much to the development and influence of Arminianism.

they tried to find a common centre of thought and action in certain universal principles of religious sentiment rather than in the more abstruse conclusions of polemical theology. They became, in short, eclectics against the theological dogmatism and narrowness of their time, very much as Hales and Chillingworth became advocates of comprehension against the ecclesiastical dogmatism and narrowness of theirs[1]." " The maintenance of truth," wrote Whichcote, " is rather God's charge, and the continuance of charity ours[2]." And Cudworth insisted in a sermon preached before the House of Commons in 1647 that the object of religion is not to propagate opinions, " but only to persuade men to the life of Christ[3]."

Thus a consideration merely of the religious phenomena of the time gave rise to a felt need that " enthusiasm " and dogmatism should yield place to reason and morality, but it was not only from religious sources that the Cambridge movement drew its strength. Rather was it a manifestation in the ethical and theological spheres of a phase common to other departments of speculation. We *Scientific* have already referred[4] to the effect of the spirit of *and philo-sophical* inquiry in the seventeenth century in bringing *spirit* about the genesis of modern science, which gave especially vigorous signs of life in the period immediately following the Restoration. This rise of science was related to the growth of the tolerant

[1] Tulloch, II. 12–13.
[2] *Letters*, p. 118, quoted by Tulloch, II. 79.
[3] Tulloch, II. 235–6.   [4] p. 45.

spirit not only as a collateral product, but also as an
additional cause, both because the exercise of the
reason in scientific matters may act in the long run
as a corrective of theological prejudice, and because
absorption in a new interest is calculated to produce
an indifference to theological minutiae,which, though
it may not be an exalted reason, is yet a very effective
one for the fall of the persecuting spirit.   The foundation of the Royal Society was by no means un-
connected with the Toleration Act.   This revival
of the sense of truth as against credulity, to which
modern science wholly, and toleration partly, owe
their birth, is clearly marked in the writings of the
great secular philosophers of the century[1]—Bacon,
Descartes, Spinoza, and Locke.   The seventeenth
century was preeminently one in which tradition
was (compared with its position in preceding ages)
at a discount, and the disregard of it, shown by
Bacon in philosophy, we have seen manifested in
theology by Chillingworth and Hales: the same
spirit is seen in the metaphysics of Hobbes and
Glanvill, and in the political speculations of Hobbes
and Harrington[2].   "There is an infinite desire of
knowledge broken forth in the world," wrote a
Restoration pamphleteer, "and men may as well
hope to stop the tide, or bind the ocean with chains,
as hinder free philosophy from overflowing[3]."

[1] Lecky, *History of Rise and Influence of Rationalism*, i. 402-8
(2 vols. 1877-8).
[2] See Buckle, *History of Civilization in England*, i. 363 (3 vols.
Longmans' Silver Library, 1908).
[3] "S. P. of Cambridge," *A Brief Account of the New Sect
of Latitude-Men : Together with some Reflections upon the New*

Bacon, indeed, basing his system exclusively upon physical experimentation "consistently placed the united provinces of ethics and theology beyond the *and re-* pale of his new unity of the sciences. He appears *ligion.* to have held his own creed by an effort of the will or as a legacy from the past rather than as the result of conscious conviction and the crowning triumph of the intellect[1]." But it was impossible that this arbitrary and unnatural division should be maintained, and that the secular and theological manifestations of the same spirit should proceed contemporaneously but separately upon lines indefinitely parallel : it was in the Cambridge school that the two lines converged. The development of scientific and philosophical inquiry was a call to a restatement of the relation of religion to the other departments of human knowledge, and "in their writings we pass into a higher, if not more bracing, atmosphere than that in which we have been dwelling in the pages of Hales and Chillingworth. They discussed larger questions and principles of a more fundamental and far-reaching character. They sought in a word to marry philosophy to religion, and to confirm the union on the indestructible basis of reason and the essential elements of our higher humanity[2]." Especially did they set

Philosophy. 1662. This tract will be found in *The Phenix : or a Revival of Scarce and Valuable Pieces* (2 vols. 1707–8), ii. 499–519. The quotation is from p. 503. The identification of S. P. with Simon Patrick, afterwards Bishop of Ely, is rejected by Alex. Taylor in his preface to Patrick's Works, pp. xlv, xlvi.

[1] Alex. Taylor, Preface to Patrick's Works, p. xx, q.v. for an excellent criticism of the Cambridge Platonists.

[2] Tulloch, ii. 13–14.

themselves in strong reaction from the materialistic views of Hobbes to vindicate the eternity of morality, the essential importance of morality in religion, and the capacity of the human spirit or reason for direct intuition of God[1].

Effect upon the question of toleration. The influence of men engaged on such a task naturally made for toleration, not so much directly through the discussion of the question as indirectly by the lifting of the whole matter of religion into a higher sphere. From the altitudes of thought in which they moved the petty shibboleths of party strife were dwarfed into meaninglessness[2]; and though the highest impulse given by the Cambridge theologians passed away with them, yet something of their spirit remained in the later Latitudinarians, who, mixing more in ecclesiastical politics than their teachers, not only imparted greater breadth of mind to English Churchmanship, but gave a firmer and deeper basis to English Christianity[3].

The search for the one true religion, stimulated

[1] Three sayings of Whichcote: "Morals are owned as soon as spoken, and they are nineteen parts in twenty of all religion," *Aphorisms*, 586, quoted by Tulloch, II. 107: "Gallantly doth the poet tell us, *Remember to reverence thyself.* There is much of God in every man. If a man do justly value himself, he will not do that which is base, though it be in the dark": "The spirit of man is the candle of the Lord, lighted by God, and calling men to God": quoted by Hunt, I. 432 n.

[2] "I am above all sects whatsoever as sects; for I am a true and free Christian; and what I write and speak is for the interest of Christ, and in behalf of the Life of the Lamb." Henry More, Pref. to Reply to Eugenius Philalethes, sect. 11; quoted by Tulloch, II. 339.

[3] Abbey and Overton, *English Church in the Eighteenth Century*, I. 337.

by the diversity of the sects, and natural to the speculative spirit which was abroad, by no means always led men, as it led the Cambridge Platonists, to orthodox conclusions. John Biddle, in 1644 *Biddle.* master of Crisp's Grammar School, Gloucester, fell foul of the Assembly of Divines and the Long Parliament for his unsoundness on the doctrine of the Trinity; and only escaped execution through the rise of the Independents[1]. He is generally regarded as the first of the English Unitarians, though the name itself did not appear for another forty years[2]; and it was from him that Thomas Firmin, afterwards the most prominent Unitarian in England, imbibed heterodoxy on the Trinity and deeper convictions on religious toleration[3].

A third movement[4] which subsequently played a larger part in English religious controversy than the Unitarianism of Biddle, was already in progress. Its origin can be traced back to Hooker's declaration *NATURAL* that the doctrines of religion were founded in nature, *RELIGION.* and that natural reason teaches the main principles *Hooker.* of religion and morality. From the point of view of Christian apologetic this was a double-edged weapon. No doubt it was a valuable defence to Christianity to show that reason gave independent support to revelation; but if the testimony of reason was to the

[1] Hunt, I. 245.

[2] It seems to have been first used in *A Brief History of the Unitarians, called also Socinians,* published in 1687.

[3] *Dictionary of National Biography,* article on Thomas Firmin.

[4] The correlation of these three movements I have derived from Professor Gwatkin's chapter (XI.) in the fifth volume of the *Cambridge Modern History.*

same effect as that of revelation, the latter would tend to be regarded as merely confirmatory of the former. Hooker, indeed, asserted that with regard to matters of faith we may have a " certainty of adherence " which is greater than the " certainty of evidence " in the case of a thing manifest to us; but from this point it would be no great step to the view that if revelation had less evident certainty than the conclusions of reason, it was of no value for purposes of confirming them, and was therefore unnecessary. This line of argument is open to exception, but has considerable plausibility; and the step indicated had *Herbert.* already been taken by Edward Lord Herbert of Cherbury, whose " De Veritate " was published in Paris in 1624[1]. A swashbuckler of childlike vanity, Herbert was also an independent explorer in the realms of metaphysics and theology, and may be regarded as the forerunner both of Deism and of the study of comparative religion. It was primarily for the moral reasons which we have already seen exemplified in Falkland and Chillingworth (writing some years later)[2], that he found himself at variance with contemporary orthodoxy. Revolted by the doctrine of exclusive salvation as propounded by both the sacerdotal and puritanical parties of his day, he laid it down as a first principle that it was not consistent with God's goodness not to have given to all mankind the opportunity of salvation, which therefore could not depend either upon predestination or upon the proper administration of certain rites by properly

[1] It was not published in London till 1645.
[2] p. 54

ordained ministers. He did not deny the truth of revealed religion or of Christianity, but he attached little authority to any revelation not made directly to the individual[1]. He claimed that he had greater certainty that the intuitions of his own mind were a word from God, than that the Scriptures were the word of God[2], and that God's self-revelation to all men was to be found in "the only true catholic religion," which is natural to man, and consists of five *notitiae communes*, or innate ideas, in the soul to which the universal reason testifies[3]. In his "De Religione Gentilium," published posthumously at Amsterdam in 1663[4], he set himself to show that these five articles were universally received in the heathen world,—a fact the discovery of which, (after much labour as he confesses), made him " more happy than Archimedes" in his consequent ability to vindicate the moral character of God[5]. It is worth noticing how often the moral sense appears as the driving power in new speculations: in the seventeenth century morality was outrunning what was still received as religious orthodoxy. Noticeable also is the affinity in some respects between the speculations of Herbert and those of the Cambridge

[1] Hunt, i. 443, 450.

[2] Hunt, ii. 334.

[3] These are : (1) That there is a God. (2) That he ought to be worshipped. (3) That virtue and piety are the chief parts of worship. (4) That we are to repent and turn from our sins. (5) That there are rewards and punishments in another life. Hunt, i. 444-5.

[4] A second edition appeared in 1700, and an English translation in 1705. Herbert died in 1648.

[5] Hunt, i. 449.

Platonists[1], both vehemently upholding the doctrine of direct intuitive knowledge of God, and both inspired by the belief (itself the natural development of Protestantism), that the prevalent differences of opinion were superficial and that a common ground might be discoverable on which all could agree.

The extravagances of the sects no doubt were not responsible for Biddle's heresy, nor for the rise of the Platonist doctrine, (though they may have exerted some influence upon the evolution of the latter), and Herbert's system had been thought out long before; but the sects accomplished this, that the reaction from sectarianism prepared a favourable soil for the reception of all these theories. Natural religion was not without affinity to the "enthusiasm" of the sects, and especially to the Quaker doctrine of the inner light, but it was possessed of a sober stability which removed it a whole heaven from the eccentricities which brought the sects into discredit. Here was another line of thought making for toleration, for a religion with its roots in common humanity must of necessity be of a tolerant tendency; but it was only slowly that it worked its way into the circle of customary ideas.

POLITICAL PHILOSOPHY. Natural Law. Parallel to the idea of Natural Religion was the idea of Natural Law. While the former made for toleration on the grounds that the matters of quarrel between different communions were non-essentials, and that the essentials were implanted in the natural

[1] Especially in *The Light of Nature* by Nathaniel Culverwel, a member of the Cambridge school, who refers with approval to Herbert's writings. See Tulloch, II. 415–26.

reason of all men, the latter, as interpreted by some
of its exponents, made in the same direction by
claiming for the individual the right to keep his
conscience free from external control. Natural
Religion emphasized the value of the individual's
religious perceptions, Natural Law emphasized his
right not to be molested on account of them. Not
that this was the necessary result of the belief in
Natural Law, the content of which varied according
to the personal equation of the various theorists, but
its general tendency was to make for liberty by
making possible an appeal in the interest of the
individual to obligations and rights antecedent to
those of social and political life; and though the
greatest effects of the doctrine were not seen till
towards the end of the eighteenth century in the
American Bills of Rights, and the French Declarations of the Rights of Man, it must take its place
among the forces which in the period under consideration were making for individual liberty and
therefore for toleration. Especially did the ultra-
republican sect known as the Levellers appeal to the *The*
Law of Nature; by which, they said, all men were *Levellers.*
equal, and in contravention of which no laws were
valid. They demanded toleration for all except
Roman Catholics (who were to be excluded not upon
religious, but upon political, grounds) as a part and
branch of the subject's birthright. Toleration was
with them the outcome of a consistent theory of
human equality based upon the conception of
Natural Law; with which we have passed into the
sphere of political speculation.

Thought on political subjects had naturally received a great impetus from the constitutional conflict, the Great Rebellion, and the subsequent efforts to build up the constitution afresh. Deep questions were raised as to the origin, nature, and extent of political authority: in whom was it vested? by whom should it be exercised? Here, too, the spirit of inquiry was abroad. And in the movement towards the elaboration of a political philosophy the religious question was found to be a difficulty, to surmount which the most diverse methods were *Harring-* propounded. James Harrington came to conclusions *ton.* very similar to those of the Independents, but from a very different standpoint. So marked indeed in his work is the secular spirit, shortly afterwards[1] to triumph at the Restoration, that Burnet supposed he was a Deist. The fact is important for the reason that the separation of political philosophy from theology is naturally followed by the separation of politics from religion. Harrington advocated liberty of conscience as the logical corollary of democracy. " Where civil liberty is entire it includes liberty of conscience. Where liberty of conscience is entire it includes civil liberty[2]." " Democracy," he said, " pretends not to infallibility, but it is in matters of religion no more than a seeker[3] "—a notable application of the sceptical spirit. He saw too that religious liberty implies not merely tolera-

[1] Harrington's *Oceana* was published in 1656, and was followed by various minor works in 1659–60.

[2] *Political Aphorisms*, 23–4, Works (ed. Toland, 1746), 516.

[3] *A System of Politics*, ch. VI. § 21, Works, p. 507.

tion, but a total abolition of religious disqualifications.
These views, however, he did not find incompatible
with the support of some form of establishment.
"Where there is no national religion, there can
neither be any government, nor any liberty of
conscience[1]."

Very different was the scheme worked out by
Harrington's older contemporary, Thomas Hobbes, *Hobbes.*
of Malmesbury. He solved the knotty problem of
the conflict between obligation in temporal matters
and obligation in spiritual matters by making the
former the source of the latter: he resolved the
discord between the two by practically asserting that
ultimately there was but one[2]. This startling
doctrine arose from the turn which he gave to the
theory of the social contract. According to Hobbes,
when men entered into society they gave up the
right of self-government to the sovereign whom they
set up and who was henceforth their representative
and "bore their person." Against him the people
could have no rights; he *was* the people and his
acts were their acts: hence his authority was in all
matters absolute[3]. He could establish any form of
religion, and to that religion his subjects must

[1] *Certain Maxims calculated unto the present State of England*,
Works, 613.

[2] Hobbes seems to have wavered as to the exact position of the
clergy with regard to the sovereign, but this is what his doctrine
seems to have amounted to in effect. See Hunt, I. 388.

[3] Hobbes' doctrine was the outcome of the perception that in
the ultimate analysis of a constitution there must be an absolute
power somewhere. He recognized that the sovereignty need not
be lodged in a single person, but regarded monarchy as the best
form of government.

conform[1], while retaining freedom to think as they pleased simply because compulsion of thought is impossible. Hobbes said, indeed, that a wise sovereign would require assent only to the fewest and simplest possible dogmas, but he recognized no limit to the sovereign's right to require assent to anything he pleased save that it was not the subject's duty to obey, if called upon to blaspheme God, or to abstain from worship. Further Hobbes professed belief in Christianity and in natural and immutable laws of morality[2], but his system did to all intents and purposes find the sanction of religious and moral duties in the command of the sovereign[3].

It should be noticed that the intolerance of Hobbes was very different from the intolerance of *Character of Hobbes' intolerance.* the middle ages. It was different in its origin, being the outcome not of theological or of ecclesiastical, but of political views: and it was corre-

---

[1] The doctrine "that whatsoever a man does against his conscience is sin," Hobbes asserted to be "repugnant to civil society." Quoted by Whewell, *Lectures on the History of Moral Philosophy in England* (1852), 18.

[2] Elsewhere, however, he asserted that nothing is in its own nature good or bad, which certainly agrees better with the rest of his system.

[3] "The sovereign, whether he be a single person or an assembly, contains in himself the origin of all good and justice." "The notions of right and wrong, justice and injustice have there no place. Where there is no common power, there is no law; where no law, no injustice. Force and fraud are in war the two cardinal virtues. Justice and injustice are none of the faculties either of the body or the mind." Quoted by Whewell, *op. cit.* 18, 17. Hence, as Whewell justly observes, "we can have no right and wrong, except what positive law and consequent punishment make such. Right is the power of enforcing; Duty is the necessity of obeying," *op. cit.* 17.

spondingly different in its character, being entirely a
question of civil right, and not in the least one of
religious obligation.   Hobbes was not intolerant in
the sense of advocating the maintenance by persecution of a large and intricate body of doctrine—on the
contrary, he was an advocate of religious latitude—
but in the sense of denying to the individual the
right to freedom in religious matters, he was in
tolerant in the extreme.   Persecution had been
regarded primarily as a duty; Hobbes regarded it
primarily as a right; he thought indeed, that considerable freedom should be granted, but granted
through the wisdom and by the grace of the
sovereign; and thus, though not an advocate of
persecution, he was a champion of the right to
persecute.

Conversely, it may be said that Hobbes, in the *His in-*
very process of showing persecution to be justifiable, *fluence for*
toleration
went a long way towards showing it to be un- *through*
necessary.   Clearly if matters of religious belief *unbelief.*
and practice could be almost indefinitely modified
to suit the caprice of the sovereign, these matters
must be of far less importance than was usually
supposed: indeed it was not a very great step from
Hobbes' position to the view that all religions, as
such, are of equal value, because none are of any,
except so far as they may serve a political end.
Hence all men may without scruple profess the same
religion, whether they believe it or not, and the need
for persecution disappears.   Moreover, there seems
to have been a considerable outbreak of unbelief at
this time, a reaction, no doubt, from the high

religious tension of Puritanism: but, whether
Hobbes himself were an unbeliever or not, the truth
of the accusation that his philosophy was a contributing cause can hardly be questioned. But
unbelief consorts ill with persecution, and must be
reckoned among the tolerant forces of the time.
Thus, strangely enough, the influence of Hobbes
made in both directions at once, inspiring alike
justifications of persecution, and indifference to
which such justifications might appeal in vain.

Hobbes' theories were the extreme logical outcome in a secularized form of the conception of the
state as an ecclesiastico-political society. It was a
courageous attempt to transfer to the sovereign of
the state that combination of temporal and spiritual
power claimed by the mediaeval popes: in both cases
a unification of authority was aimed at. " How men
were to live together at all ?—how society was to be
formed and the state constituted ?—were in the
seventeenth century still identical with the questions
how men were to live together as religious beings ?
what dogmas they were to profess ? what mode of
worship they were to observe[1] ?" The decision of
both sets of questions by the same authority had at
least the advantage of simplicity. But even Hobbes,
for all his heroic methods had been forced to confess
the inability of his Leviathan to prescribe men's
thoughts, and had even indicated circumstances in
which his authority would be met and overruled
by a higher law. But the fact that Hobbes had
attempted to bring the whole field of human action

[1] Tulloch, ii. 119.

under the domination of the state, and yet had left *Effect of* a tiny corner of it free, made it clear that the an- *his views.* tagonistic claims of the state and of religion were not ultimately reconcilable by the extension of the claims of the state : the inference remained open that if a reconciliation was to be made, it must be by their abridgment.   The opposition between religious and political obligations had been brought into clear relief by Hobbes with religious obligations at their irreducible minimum, and that minimum formed a firm centre from which the boundaries of the region of inner control might be pushed forward in an ever-expanding circle till complete religious liberty compatible with public well-being was reached.

Hobbes' "Leviathan," published in 1651, provoked violent attacks from all quarters.   Its essentially irreligious character was perceived through the veil of Biblical phraseology[1].   Men confuted, ridiculed, lampooned and vilified the " Monster of Malmesbury[2] " with the energy and hatred born of fear.   Opposition to Hobbes was one of the great forces which moulded the Cambridge movement.   Especially to our purpose in the reaction which he provoked is the contribution which it made to the realization of the separability of what Hobbes had striven indissolubly to unite, and with the separation of which the cause of toleration was bound up—the political and ecclesiastical aspects of society.

[1] I make no implication with regard to the question of Hobbes sincerity.
[2] See Hunt, i. 407.

CHAPTER III

FROM THE RESTORATION TO THE
TOLERATION ACT

Tolerant tendencies at work at the Restoration. IN the last chapter we examined several intellectual movements which were making for toleration. In Falkland, Chillingworth and Hales, the forces of rising rationalism were arrayed against ecclesiastical narrowness in the interests of a comprehensive and tolerant church. The Independents cared nothing for comprehensiveness, but declared even more strongly for toleration as the guarantee of individual and congregational liberty. Individual liberty was further reinforced by the doctrines of the sects and especially by the Quaker doctrine of the inner light. Meanwhile at Cambridge the second great school of latitudinarian thought was raising religion out of the dust of controversy, and vindicating the dignity of man by emphasizing the directness of his intercourse with God. The views of this school were subverting that theological narrowness and cramped conception of religion which fostered the intolerant spirit. Natural Religion, too, as expounded by Herbert, served the same purpose of universalizing religion, and rendering dogmatic differences insignificant; while the conception of Natural Law tended to vindicate the rights of conscience as part of the inalienable rights of man.   Upon the side of political philosophy, a difficulty was felt in fixing the relations of the civil power to religion, and it was beginning to be seen that the only rational settlement was to be found in toleration.

All these tendencies were at work at the time of the Restoration; and the Restoration seemed to be giving the nation a king who would take advantage of them to bring about a peace in ecclesiastical affairs unknown since the breach with Rome. Charles in the Declaration of Breda expressly recognized the principle that liberty of conscience should be granted to all save those who caused disturbance in the state.   "And because the passion and uncharitableness of the times," he wrote, "have produced several opinions in religion, by which men are engaged in parties and animosities against each other, which when they shall hereafter unite in a freedom of conversation will be composed or better understood; We do declare a liberty to tender consciences; and that no man shall be called in question for differences of opinion in matters of religion which do not disturb the peace of the Kingdom: and that we shall be ready to consent to such an Act of Parliament as upon mature deliberation shall be offered to Us for the full granting that indulgence[1]."   Here is nothing of

Declaration of Breda, Apr. 4, 1660.

---

[1] Journals of the House of Commons, VIII. 6.

the religious, theological, doctrinal, or ecclesiastical reasons for persecution. Charles's political position was too precarious for him to venture, and his religious position probably too nebulous for him to care, to give much attention to the affairs of another world. Nor could he afford as yet, however much he may have desired to do so, to disclose any preferences he might have with regard to ecclesiastical organization. Thus there seemed a hopeful prospect of a lasting settlement satisfactory to the great mass of the nation ; but the fulfilment of this hope was to be deferred through many weary years of persecution and controversy.

Stilling-
fleet :
" Ireni-
cum."

The weightiest contribution made about this time[1] to the discussion of the ecclesiastical settlement was Edward Stillingfleet's "Irenicum, or a Weapon-salve for the Church's Wounds." The future Bishop of Worcester, who was still quite young at the time of its publication, was now rector of Sutton in Bedfordshire. In spite of having been educated at Cambridge, Stillingfleet shows little trace of distinctively Platonist influence, and is rather to be regarded as a follower of the earlier latitudinarian school of Chillingworth, which was more closely connected with Oxford. But while upon the ecclesiastical side of his thought, he maintained and carried forward the tradition of liberal Anglicanism, he shows on the political side a considerable measure of the intolerance which found its fullest expression in Hobbes. It is an easy and common mistake, in

[1] For discussion of the exact date of the *Irenicum*, see Appendix IV.

dealing with great movements of thought which stir
the common consciousness of the race, to describe
two successive manifestations of the same spirit as
standing in the relation of cause and effect, when
they are really alike effects of the same cause; and
certainly the catastrophic constitutional changes in
the twenty years which followed the meeting of the
Long Parliament, might well inspire independently
in many minds a reverence for authority expressed in
theories which could only logically lead to absolutism;
but yet it is difficult to avoid the conclusion that
Stillingfleet had studied the "Leviathan," and that
it had made a deep impression upon the cast
of his thought. His "Irenicum" is a strange com-
pound of ecclesiastical liberalism and political intolerance.

On ecclesiastical questions he follows the lead *His eccle-*
of the rational theologians. "It would be strange," *siastical*
he writes in his preface, "that the Church should *liberalism*
require more than Christ himself did; and make
other conditions of communion than our Saviour
did of discipleship. What possible reason can be
assigned or given why such things should not be
sufficient for communion with a church, which are
sufficient for eternal salvation?" And again, "The
unity of the Church is a unity of love and affection
and not a bare uniformity of practice or opinion....
The same we hope may remain as the most infallible
evidence of conformity of our Church of England
to the primitive, not so much in using the same
rites that were in use then as in not imposing
them."

In his first chapter he argues that no one form
of government was intended as the only means to
peace in the Church, for, if so, it would have been
clearly revealed, which the controversy upon the
question shows that it has not been.   This view
is developed at greater length in the second part of
the " Irenicum."   Christ, says Stillingfleet, gave no
form of government in the Church[1], and even if we
could discover what was the practice of the apostles,
this would not necessarily be binding at the present
day, because the times and circumstances have
changed[2] (152)—a manifestation of the historical
sense rare in the seventeenth century.   It is indeed
dictated by the law of nature that the Church must
have some power to keep up peace and unity within
itself, but it has " no direct immediate power over
men's opinions," for " Opinionum diversitas et
opinantium unitas non sunt ἀσύστατα"; unity of
opinion is no more to be obtained by men's endeavours than perfection is; and though the promulgation of opinions contrary to those of the
established church may be punished, "it is not
the difference of opinion formally considered that
is punishable, but the tendency to schism which
lies in the divulging of it."   Schism, however, is
not intrinsically evil, its character is determined as

[1] Part II., ch. IV.

[2] This argument is twice repeated in the second part.   The
numbers in brackets throughout the essay refer to the pages of
the particular work under consideration.   In the case of the
Irenicum the references are to the edition dated 1661, with which,
however, both issues of the edition of 1662 are practically identical
in pagination.

good or evil according to the grounds on which it is
made (105–108). But here Stillingfleet's liberalism
ends : though he admits that cases may arise in
which separation is lawful and convenient (113),
he lays down no principle which will protect the
separatists from persecution.

As to things undetermined by the Law of God, *associated*
everyone, notwithstanding his private judgment, *with in-*
is bound to submit to the determination of the *principles.*
governors of the church. The very formation of a
society implies that the members part, not indeed
with the freedom of their judgment, but with the
authority of it (124).

This vicious schism between thought and practice,
based upon a strained rendering of the contract theory
of society, and developed to its extreme limits by
Hobbes, was one of the favourite arguments of the
intolerant writers of the time, in whose hands it did
yeoman service. Stillingfleet's liberalism on ecclesiastical grounds, and intolerance on political grounds are
well exemplified in his proposition that the officers of
the church, though they should be obeyed (to avoid
scandal), unless the thing commanded is unlawful, have
no authority given them by divine law to make new
laws to bind the church : yet they have a power based
on mutual compact to bind all included under the
compact (45–6). Indifferent matters may be determined and Christian liberty restrained therein, because
lawful authority may command anything that may be
lawfully done, and nothing can exempt from obedience
to the lawful magistrate except the unlawfulness of
the thing commanded. Christian liberty is con-

sistent with the restraint of the exercise of it, because it is founded upon freedom of judgment, and not of practice (53–6).

As standards by which the lawfulness or the reverse of the commands of the lawful authority may be judged, Stillingfleet recognizes the law of nature (of which his book is full) and divine positive law ; in cases predetermined by these, no human law can bind the conscience (69). Otherwise, what is determined by lawful authority binds the consciences of men, subject to that authority, to obedience to those determinations[1]. The authority of the magistrate, indeed, only extends to outward actions : he "hath no proper power over religion in itself": he cannot dissolve the obligation of worship nor force the consciences of men. But he must restrain public action tending to subvert religion as publicly owned and professed. "So that the plea for liberty of conscience as it tends to restrain the magistrate's power is both irrational and impertinent; because liberty of conscience is liberty of men's judgments, which the magistrate cannot deprive them of." It is the open expression of opinion to the restraint of which the magistrate's power extends. Liberty of all opinions subverts peace ; the magistrate, therefore, cannot discharge his office unless he has power to restrain such a liberty (39–40).

The "Irenicum," upon its political side—and its exaltation of the civil power over the ecclesiastical[2]

[1] Ch. II.

[2] Though the magistrate may not by his own will constitute what laws he please for the worship of God, but must consult and

gives the political side the greater practical importance
—is little more than somewhat mitigated Hobbism.
It advises, indeed, religious latitude; Hobbes did as
much: but its principles by no means involve the
carrying of that advice into practice, and would
justify the establishment of an oppressive ecclesiastical *régime*.   Indeed such a result could hardly be
avoided save in the event of a general, precise, and
final agreement being arrived at between the civil
power and all its subjects as to exactly what matters
were "indifferent," what were "determined by the
law of God," what were "corruptions in doctrine
and practice," and so forth.   But it was the impossibility of anything approaching such an agreement which had been the very cause of the prevalent chaos.   Stillingfleet's remedy contains the
very germ of the disease which he proposes to cure.
In a sense indeed, he recognizes liberty of conscience; but it is a sense which deprives it of all its
meaning by limiting it to mere liberty of intellect.
To describe as liberty of conscience the liberty of
the intellect to come to its own conclusions with
impunity (which cannot well be denied save by
revolting inquisitorial methods) without the right
of divulging those conclusions or acting upon them
is a pitiful mockery: it is to give a stone to those
who plead for bread.

The second, and considerably longer, part of the
work is devoted to an inquiry into the divine right

be advised by the pastors and governors of the Church, yet he
commands what is to be done in the Church by his own authority
—not that of the Church officers.   pp. 45–6.

of various forms of ecclesiastical government; to his conclusions upon which we have already referred. Here he shows the liberalism of Chillingworth and Hales, especially quoting largely from the latter's tract on Schism; but as his arguments are mainly directed towards the establishment of the Church on comprehensive lines rather than towards the toleration of those who dissent from it, we are not directly concerned with them. The latitudinarianism of this part of the work seems generally to have drawn away attention from the wide openings left for intolerance in his theory of the civil power and its relation to the Church. Stillingfleet would have welcomed a settlement of the Church in accordance with liberal principles but he "lacked vitality of liberal conviction[1]," and, like many other men of his time, impressed by the disturbances which had been rife since his early boyhood[2] with the paramount need of a central controlling power, showed no proper appreciation of the rights of the individual conscience against authority.

Character of the Restoration. The Restoration was the result of an alliance between Presbyterians and Episcopalians in common fear of anarchy. It was far more than a restoration of the House of Stuart: it was a restoration of the old order,—of a freely elected House of Commons and of the House of Lords, as well as of the monarchy; and the natural corollary was the restoration of Episcopacy. This last fact put the *Position of the Presbyterians.* Presbyterians in an ambiguous position. They had not calculated that their escape from the visionary

[1] Tulloch, I. 411.   [2] He was born in 1635.

Fifth Monarchy Men would lead them into the hands of the oppressed and not unnaturally vindictive Episcopalians. They had supposed that they had a large party in the country; and they woke up to find themselves leaders with but a scanty following. They had allowed themselves to be deceived by the mild professions of the Church-and-King party[1]; and it soon became plain how great a divergence between profession and practice may be the result of a change from adversity to prosperity. Presbyterianism, in spite of its theoretical establishment, had never really taken root in England, and even in the Convention Parliament the supporters of Episcopacy were stronger than either Presbyterians or Independents[2]. Failure and disillusionment begat in the Presbyterians a new-found moderation. Not that they were converts to the toleration which they had so lustily denounced. On the contrary, they desired an ecclesiastical establishment supported by persecution of those outside it, with the important proviso that room should be found for themselves within. Their aim, in a word, was comprehension for themselves, and no toleration for the

[1] See the "Declaration of the nobility, gentry, and clergy that adhered to the late King in and about the City of London." "We do sincerely profess that we do reflect upon our past sufferings as from the hand of God, and therefore do not cherish any violent thoughts or inclinations to those who have been in any way instrumental in them. And if the indiscretion of any spirited persons transports them to any expressions contrary to this our sense, we utterly disclaim them." Kennett's Register, p. 121, quoted by Perry, *Student's English Church History*, 484.

[2] See *English Historical Review*, xxii. 51, Jan. 1907, Louise F. Brown, *Religious Factors in the Convention Parliament*.

sects[1]. The months immediately succeeding the
Restoration were an anxious time for them, as
they saw their supposed influence ebbing away and
leaving them more and more at the mercy of the
flood of royalism and High Churchmanship which
the Restoration had let loose[2].

Corbet:
"The In-
terest of
England,"
1660,

It was in this troublous time that John Corbet,
the Presbyterian rector of Bramshot in Hampshire,
published his book entitled "The Interest of England
in the Matter of Religion." His object was to show
how the Presbyterians and the Episcopalians might
come to an "accommodation," as indeed they ought
to do to check sectarianism and Popery (61). This
was to be preferred to toleration, for the latter
"being the daughter not of Amity but of Enmity
(at least) in some degree, supposeth the party
tolerated to be a burden" (74). In the second part
of his pamphlet, however, he proceeds to arguments
which may be applied to toleration as well as comprehension. There have been, he points out, and
always will be "doubtful disputations"; to enforce
external uniformity in such matters is to exercise a
tyranny over men's judgments, and the consequent
servility in religion leads to a dissoluteness in conversation which cannot be countervailed by all
imaginable uniformity (Part II. 61-2). Love and
peace are not incompatible with difference of judgment (Part II. 65). "Divers men are carried divers

[1] Gwatkin in *Cambridge Modern History*, v. 329.
[2] It should be noticed that the outburst of enthusiasm followed
rather than preceded the return of Charles. This was, of course,
natural.

ways as they are led by natural temper, custom,
education, or studious inquiries....There is no con-
straining of minds to one persuasion without im-
basing their judgments to perfect slavery" (Part II. 76).

Nor does he fail to urge the political inexpediency
of intolerance. "Where there are many sufferers upon
a religious account, whether in truth or pretence,
there will be a kind of glory in suffering, and sooner
or later it may turn to the Ruler's detriment." The
imposition of conformity in things unnecessary and
subscription to all particulars of doctrine, worship
and discipline, is " the sure way of endless dissension
among a people that are not bottomed on this principle of believing as the Church believes " (Part II.
83–4, 87–8). The Presbyterian party, he asserts,
will not change or disappear, because it rests on
principles of firm and fixed nature. Even were it
extirpated, it would appear again, provided Protestantism were still preached and the Bible permitted to the common people (Part I. 29, 34). Corbet
was no exponent of the principle of toleration, which
he did not propose to extend to the Romanists and
sectaries. His object was the purely practical one
of securing that under the coming settlement his
party should be inside and not outside the Church,
or if outside it, at least not persecuted. Toleration
was with him a mere *pis aller*.

This book evoked from Roger L'Estrange, a *answered*
doughty champion of Church and King, a reply *by L'E-*
with the conciliatory title, "Interest Mistaken, or *strange:*
The Holy Cheat; proving, From the undeniable *"Interest*
Mis-
taken."
Practices and Positions of the Presbyterians, that *1661.*

the Design of the Party is to enslave both King and People under the Masque of Religion." The title is a pretty clear indication of the character of the work. L'Estrange had taken service under Prince Rupert; but, betrayed into the hands of Parliament, he had spent three years in Newgate under sentence of death in "a distressing condition of expectancy." Small wonder if his pamphlet is full of bitterness, and repeatedly accuses Presbyterianism of being anti-monarchical and responsible for sectarianism; while to Corbet's warning of the risks attendant on the persecution under which many suffer, he makes the ominous reply, that "there will not be many sufferers where there are not many offenders, and there will not be many offenders where an early severity is used " (148).

Thorndike: "The Due Way of Composing the Differences." 1660.

Of a somewhat different tone was Herbert Thorndike's "The Due Way of Composing the Differences on foot, Preserving the Church." Thorndike, a man of pronouncedly High Church views, had been deprived in the Civil War of his living and his fellowship at Trinity College, Cambridge, but at the Restoration he was reinstated in both, and shortly afterwards made a Prebendary of Westminster. On the question of comprehension, he rules out the idea of any arrangement which could possibly prove an obstacle to future re-union with Rome. As to toleration, he thinks that perhaps it is justifiable for the state to allow the private exercise of religion under such moderate penalties as the disobeying of the laws of a man's country might require. He sees that the whole Reformation condemns such extreme measures as persecution to death and banishment. But such moderation must be extended also to the Roman Catholic recusants. Those Roman Catholics who think themselves bound by the bull of Pius V, excommunicating and deposing Elizabeth and absolving her subjects from their allegiance, or by similar bulls, deserve the utmost penalties as enemies to their country; but all the Roman Catholics are not of that opinion, and it is more easy to secure the state of the allegiance of Roman Catholics against a papal dispensation from it, than to secure it of the allegiance of the sectaries against a dispensation "which the pretence of God's Spirit may import when they please" (234).

The High Churchmen were blind—it was not un- *The High Church point of view.* natural if they chose to be blind—to the distinctions between the various types of Nonconformists. The Presbyterians were in their eyes responsible for the beginning of "the late troubles," and all that ensued was laid at their door. The differences between them and the Independents, who put the royal martyr to death, and the sects of religious maniacs to which Independency gave birth, were too unimportant to trouble the High Churchmen in the hour of their triumph. They alone had remained loyal to the monarch through fair fortune and foul, and the gulf between them and the various sects of rebels was so wide that the divisions of the rebels amongst themselves faded into insignificance. Besides, if a breach were once made in the Church's bulwarks to admit some of the less guilty, who could set a limit to the horde of pestilential hypocrites who would come flooding in, insidiously corrupting the faithful with their pernicious doctrines concerning resistance to the Lord's Anointed? No! let the Church present an undaunted front and abate no jot of her demands.

If comprehension was to be denied the Presbyterians they could only fall back on shadowy hopes of toleration. And these were shadowy indeed. Charles, it is true, had declared in favour of liberty of conscience, but from the first there was little likelihood that he would be allowed to fulfil the hopes which he had raised. The Presbyterians themselves were no more favourable to toleration than were the Episcopalians, and since the Restoration had been carried out by the alliance of these two parties practically no serious thought of it had been entertained. Hence the Presbyterians, if they failed to obtain comprehension, were likely to share the fate of those for whom there had never *Baptist* been any prospect of it—the Independents, Baptists, *Tracts.* Quakers and other sects. Persecution, indeed, had *"An* *Humble* begun even before Charles entered London[1]. In *Petition."* 1660 was published a pamphlet entitled "An Humble *1660.* Petition and representation of the Anabaptists[2]." It was a petition to Charles II from certain Kentish Anabaptists confined in Maidstone gaol. We have already seen that the Baptists were probably the first Christian body to declare that the magistrate has no right to interfere in religion[3]: this doctrine

---

[1] Frank Bate, *Declaration of Indulgence 1672*, 8.
[2] Printed in *Tracts on Liberty of Conscience and Persecution, 1614–1661*, pp. 297–308.   [3] p. 59.

again appears in the tract under consideration. The magistrate, as such, the prisoners urge, has no power to impose anything by force in the worship of God or on men's consciences, for, in the first place, it would follow that all magistrates in all nations must have the same power, in Turkey power to compel men to be Mohammedans, in Spain power to compel men to be Papists; in the second, the apostles refused to obey commands which were contrary to the word of God; and in the third, it is obvious that the Scriptures of the New Testament enjoining obedience to the civil power cannot have referred to religious matters, for the civil power in New Testament times was pagan. Moreover, persecution is contrary to the practice and teaching of Christ and the apostles, and a direct breach of the command to do to others what we would that they should do to us.

In the following year, one John Sturgion, "a member of the Baptized People," published "A Plea for Toleration of Opinions and Persuasions in Matters of Religion, differing from the Church of England[1]." Sturgion had been a private in Cromwell's life-guards, but had been discharged and imprisoned as the author of a pamphlet attacking Cromwell. Subsequently he, amongst others, had signed a memorial to the exiled Charles denouncing the Protector as "that loathsome hypocrite," and begging Charles to return and establish liberty of conscience. Charles had now complied with the first request, but not with the second; and Sturgion took up his parable once more. Restraint, and im-

Sturgion: "A Plea for Toleration." 1661.

---

[1] *Tracts on Liberty of Conscience etc.*, pp. 323–41.

position of articles of faith and rules of worship by the magistrate are, he says, contrary to the nature of the Gospel, which prevailed by its own piety and wisdom.   He also quotes the " golden rule " and the example of the primitive church.   He further condemns persecution on rational grounds : it is unreasonable and impious to deny men the use of their reason in the choice of their religion and to use force, for " there is nothing, under God, hath power over the understanding of a man," and we are bound to worship God according to our lights.   He hazards, moreover, the untrue, but popular, statement that persecution is always unsuccessful.

This tract was rapidly followed by another, bearing the date May 8th, 1661, the day of the meeting of the Cavalier Parliament.   It was entitled " Sion's Groans for her Distressed, or Sober Endeavours to Prevent Innocent Blood[1]," and was the work of seven Baptist ministers, two of whom had already appeared among the authors of the "Humble Petition." All that is substantial in that tract is reproduced in " Sion's Groans," which contains, however, a good deal more than its predecessor, including the following peculiar argument.   If the magistrate has power from God to command in spiritual matters, Christians must obey for conscience' sake.   Then, since it is only in cases of disobedience to the magistrate that persecution arises, anyone might be a disciple of Christ without being persecuted, and anyone persecuted would be *ipso facto* condemned. But the saints' endurance of persecutions and suffer-

"*Sion's Groans*," 1661,

[1] *Tracts on Liberty of Conscience etc.*, pp. 349–82.

ings in preference to obeying, is abundantly foretold, rewarded, and justified. It follows, therefore, that no magistrate has power from God to compel in spiritual causes. The seven ministers proceed to point out that it is unsafe for magistrates to persecute, because of their fallibility, for they all believe whatever they impose to be in accordance with the mind of God: but every man should judge for himself in matters spiritual. The magistrates should confine themselves, like Gallio, to the punishment of civil injuries and wrongs—a self-restraint which would free their governments from many inconveniences. They quote the parable of the tares and the wheat, dear to the hearts of tolerationists, and finally appeal to experience, which, they assert, has proved in France, the United Provinces, and several countries of Germany, that toleration is not inconsistent with the safety and well-being of a nation.

To " Sion's Groans " an anonymous reply was made by Henry Savage, one of the King's chaplains. His answer bears upon the title-page the name " Toleration with its objections fully confuted," but the pages are headed with the words " The Dew of Hermon which fell upon the Hill of Sion." After some abuse of the Nonconformists and defence of the Church system, he declares that religion is the foundation of all government, and the magistrate stands to his subjects in the same relation as a father to his children; hence he must look after their religion (33–5). To the argument that the justification of persecution would make men Moham-

answered by [Savage]: " Toleration with its objections fully confuted." 1663.

medans in Turkey and Papists in Spain, he replies
that all magistrates have power in religion, but not
all have the same rule to govern by: "unconverted
magistrates" have the "book of Nature": some have
the Old Testament; some the New Testament.
Hence in any case the Turk has no power to impose
the "Alcoran[1]," for the "book of Nature" does not
prescribe it: similarly the King of Spain, having
both Testaments, abuses his power in permitting
idolatry (35-6). This condemnation of the Koran
on the ground that it is not prescribed by the book
of Nature is interesting as foreshadowing the later
development of naturalism[2] to the point of rivalry
with the Biblical revelation.

The strange argument from the prophecy of
persecution is met by the reply that the magistrate
may command something contrary to the Word and
Will of God, and so abuse his power: in such cases
there is scope for persecution, for only passive—not
active—obedience is to be yielded (39). Nor will
the parable of the tares serve the tolerationists' turn,
for it "seems not to note the duty of the civil magistrate but the event of God's providence," and does
not imply that the magistrate should leave the
Nonconformists alone, any more than that he should
have spared a traitor or a murderer who escapes by
the providence of God. And in any case the magistrate cannot discover and convict, and even so ought

[1] The Koran is always, I think, so named in the literature of
the period.
[2] Later, that is, as a common subject of controversy. Herbert
was a forerunner a great distance ahead.

THE TOLERATION ACT · 103

not to kill, all wicked doers ; so that the activities of
the magistrate will not prevent the parable from
still being applicable to the state of affairs prevalent
in the world (51–2). And the fallibility of magistrates "serves only and that very well too, as a
motive to care and conscience in the exercise of
power": the magistrate has "as much security as a
judge that condemns a prisoner at the bar" (55–7).
Punishment for sins of omission or commission alone
is persecution in the scriptural sense, and this is not
persecution but justice. Hence there is no argument from the "golden rule" (57–8). In cases of
toleration alleged from foreign countries "they
tolerate not blasphemy or heathenish idolatry," and
in France and Germany there are tolerated "but two
religions, not all, as these men would have done here"
(67). All through his pamphlet, Savage is attacking
the writers of "Sion's Groans" as demanding toleration for "horrid opinions," idolatry, sedition, and
blasphemy: towards the end he gives a good specimen of the more pitiful type of argument to which
the anti-tolerationists had recourse. "He who is a
friend to unbounded liberty of opinions (such as
these men contend for) is a friend to drunkenness
too, inasmuch as he that hath liberty to think what
he pleases in anything (for hither these men would
extend liberty) will judge it lawful to take a cup too
much at some times" (80).

In 1662 was reprinted another Baptist tract,
originally published in 1615, with the title "Persecution for Religion judged and condemned[1]." The

"Persecution for Religion judged and condemned." 1662.

[1] *Tracts on Liberty of Conscience etc.*, pp. 95–183.

author, Mr. Underhill conjectures, was probably a member of Helwisse's church in London[1]. He asserts the inability of persecution to beget either faith or moral reformation: it can only produce conformity; but worship not offered up with the spirit is not acceptable to God, but most abominable. Moreover, to compel a man to conformity is not to secure his allegiance, but rather to harden his heart to work villainy. The tone of the pamphlet is not conciliatory. The burden of it is that Rome is the beast in the Revelation and the spiritual power in England is his image, and to the tyranny of either it is perilous for the conscience to submit. "The sum of all which is, that whosoever openly professeth obedience and subjection to that spiritual cruel power of Rome, the beast, or to that spiritual cruel power of England, his image (wheresoever they or either of them are exalted) such a one and such persons shall drink of the wine of God's wrath, and be tormented in fire and brimstone, and shall not rest day nor night for evermore[2]." We cannot be surprised if such language helped to raise against the Baptists a prejudice which proved a serious obstacle to toleration[3].

Relations of Episcopalians   The hopeful prospect at the Restoration that an understanding might be arrived at between the

[1] See p. 59.

[2] *Tracts on Liberty of Conscience etc.*, p. 147.

[3] Together with *Persecution for Religion Judged and Condemned* was reprinted *An Humble Supplication to the King's Majesty* (*Tracts on Liberty of Conscience etc.*, pp. 189–231), conjectured to have been written by the same author, and first published in 1620. It contains little of independent value.

Episcopalians and the Presbyterians soon disap- *and Pres-*
peared.   The exceptional opportunity of union at *byterians.*
a time when they were drawn together by common
fears and hopes was let slip, and it was definitely
decided that the Church should not be sufficiently
comprehensive to give expression to the religious life
of the nation approximately[1] as a whole. The government of the Church had been more definitely and
aggressively than before associated with the High
Church party by Laud.   In the conflict with Puritanism that party eventually triumphed at the
Restoration, and celebrated its triumph by the expulsion of its adversaries.   The schism, it is true,
might be asserted to have taken place already when
the mass of the English clergy submitted to the
abolition of Episcopacy: but this it must be remembered was regarded not as an abandonment of the
Church, but as a further reformation of it[2], involving
the ejection of the more stubborn Episcopalians.   At
the Restoration the wheel of fortune brought the
Episcopalians once more into power, and they seized
the opportunity to eject in their turn the more
stubborn Puritans.   If the step was inevitable, it *Cause of*
was so, not because of the questions at issue, but *failure to*
                                                    effect a
because of the weaknesses of human nature.   Doc- *settlement.*

[1] There would, of course, in any case have been a certain
proportion of irreconcilables—Roman Catholics, Independents,
Baptists, etc.
[2] "Now once again, by all concurrence of signs and by the
general instinct of holy and devout men, as they daily and
solemnly express their thoughts, God is decreeing to begin some
new and great period in his Church, even to the reforming of
Reformation itself."   Milton, *Areopagitica, Works* (8 vols. London,
1851), IV. 437.

trinally, there was little difference between the parties; constitutionally, the so-called Presbyterians[1] were prepared to acquiesce in " modified episcopacy," so that the apostolic succession and the episcopal order were not at stake; it was not to the order itself but to the supposed exorbitant powers vested in the order that exception was taken. The great battle-ground was the question of ceremonies: less prominent, but of deeper importance was that of episcopal ordination. But the real underlying cause of the failure to reach an arrangement satisfactory to both parties was the ineradicable effect of prolonged partisan animosity, or, as Charles had expressed it in the Declaration of Breda, " the passion and uncharitableness of the times "—and uncharitableness covers (from the eyes of the sinner) a multitude of sins. Alternating periods of oppression had almost entirely destroyed that mutual sympathy and confidence, some measure of which is an indispensable ingredient in any stable reconciliation. The Savoy Conference failed, because it was intended to fail unless the Presbyterians would surrender (as they certainly would not) upon the Episcopalians' terms. The Presbyterians were captious, the Episcopalians, with power on their side, domineering. Appointed as a consultation for peace, the conference

[1] The term is little more at the Restoration than a name for the party representing the old Puritan Churchmen. Some of them no doubt really preferred a Presbyterian Church-government, but the theory of the divine right of presbyteries was never popular in England, and the mass of them were quite prepared to allow "Episcopum Praesidem non Principem." See Corbet, *Interest of England*, part I., pp. 19, 20.

resolved itself into a judicial trial in which the
Presbyterians were plaintiffs while the Episcopalians
united the parts of defendant and judge.

This being the case, the result was inevitable, *Character*
and the Act of Uniformity completed the schism. *of the*
That, indeed, would seem to have been the object at *formity.*
which the act was deliberately aimed. "Mr George
Firmin relates, that a certain lady assured him that,
on her expressing to a member of parliament her
dislike of the Act of Uniformity when it was about
to pass, saying to him, 'I see you are laying a snare
in the gate,' he replied, 'Aye, if we can find any way
to catch the rogues we will have them[1].'" As for
Sheldon, who became Archbishop of Canterbury
in 1663, "it is related that when Manchester complained to Charles that the act was so rigid that
few would conform, Sheldon replied, 'I am afraid
they will.' Equally significant was the retort which
the same bishop is reported to have made to Dr Allen,
when he lamented that the door was made so strait.
'It is no pity,' said Sheldon, 'if we had thought so
many of them would have conformed, we would have
made it straiter[2].'" The act marked the triumph of
one party in the Church of England at the expense
of another which had existed in the Church since
the Reformation, to her considerable benefit. There
can hardly be any question that "many of the great
Puritan divines whose piety and talents have
adorned the National Church" would, if alive, have

[1] Edmund Calamy, *The Nonconformist's Memorial*, ed. Samuel
Palmer, Editor's Preface, iii n., 2nd ed., 3 vols., 1802.
[2] Frank Bate, *The Declaration of Indulgence, 1672*, 25.

been ejected with Baxter, Howe, and Calamy[1]. The difference between the Latitudinarian Churchmen— who unfortunately exerted only too little influence at this great crisis[2]—and the moderate Nonconformists was very slight; the line of cleavage in some cases separated men between whom was no difference whatever save in the interpretation put upon the declarations required[3]. But, were the difference great or small, incumbents were compelled at short notice to make the declarations or be driven out of their benefices with indecent haste a month before the great tithes became due[4]. And their expulsion was merely the preliminary to bitter persecution of those who felt bound by their office to continue preaching the word of life to their fellow men.

and of the subsequent persecution. This persecution had no solid basis in grounds of self-protection. Laud had been intolerant not only because of the conviction that his system was divinely ordained, but for reasons of political exigency—he was the leader of a governing minority[5]; but this was not the case with the Anglican leaders at the Restoration: for the first time in their history the squirearchy and the mass of the nation behind them

---

[1] Abbey and Overton, *English Church in the Eighteenth Century*, I. 384.

[2] Tulloch, II. 213.

[3] Abbey and Overton, I. 386–7 ; Hunt, II. 272.

[4] O. Airy, *English Restoration and Louis XIV.* 98. The number of those thus ejected is estimated by Mr. Frank Bate at 1800, in addition to 450 ejected between May 1660 and S. Bartholomew's Day 1662. These figures are exclusive of schoolmasters and of clergy who were merely silenced. *The Declaration of Indulgence, 1672*, Appendix II.

[5] Henson, *English Religion in the Seventeenth Century*, 213–4.

were High Churchmen. The Nonconformists (save a few extremists) were by no means in irreconcilable opposition, and the Church was practically beyond the reach of attack. It was now the case of a majority inflicting upon a minority a persecution largely inspired by a spirit, actually, if not consciously, vindictive, of which the persecutors would in the long run become ashamed[1].

"It is true that that minority was especially formidable, partly from its activity and energy, but still more from the fact that it numbered in its ranks the dissolved Puritan army. As long as those soldiers were alive it would be difficult to persuade ordinary citizens that it was safe to allow to the Dissenters an ecclesiastical organization which might easily be converted into a military organization. Such a danger would, however, of necessity grow less every year. The risk was diminished as each of Cromwell's soldiers passed intô the grave. In twenty or thirty years the Dissenters would only be known as a small minority of the population, of whom a few old men had once borne arms in a now unpopular cause. All that would then stand in the way of the grant of the liberty of sectarian association apart from the national church would be the feeling of dislike which their ideas and principles aroused. Now, however, they would not be without allies within the national church itself. The men who measured Christianity by its reasonableness rather than by its traditionary authority were not without considerable influence there, and though

[1] Gwatkin in *Camb. Mod. Hist.* v. 330.

these men would have preferred that dissent should not exist, they were not likely to oppose much resistance to the recognition of its claims[1]."

The case for the High Churchmen.

Deeply then as we may deplore the conduct of Sheldon and his associates, there is a good deal to be said in their defence. The great argument against toleration between the Restoration and the Revolution was the political argument, which appears again and again with wearisome iteration,—the Nonconformists only wanted opportunity to rebel and to overthrow Church and State as they had once already done. The memory of the Puritan domination (and to the loyalist Churchman, as we have pointed out, all Puritans were alike) had graven itself upon the national consciousness; and, in ignorance of the real causes at work in the Great Rebellion and the change in circumstances since the days of Charles I, men lived in a perpetual fear, none the less real because it was groundless, of a repetition of the days of 1641 and 1642. The failure of the republican governments in England and the attendant disorders, not

(1) Need of authority.

only produced a longing and reverence for authority (expressed in philosophical form by Hobbes), but also confirmed men's belief in the divinity of Kingship, since its overthrow was followed by such disastrous consequences. The union of Hobbes' theory of sovereignty with the theory of the divine right of kings furnished a promising and plausible basis for persecution for which the circumstances of the time won sincere and widespread acceptance.

[1] Gardiner and Mullinger, *Introduction to English History,* 156–7.

Again, it was not realized that Dissent had become (2) *Per-manence of* a permanent factor in English life. The grim words *Dissent* of Roger L'Estrange that "there would not be *unreal-ized.* many sufferers where there were not many offenders, and not many offenders where an early severity was used[1]," no doubt expressed views widely held, and probably present to the mind of Sheldon when he hounded on his myrmidons to their repulsive task[2]. It is not surprising if this was so. In the previous century the clergy had shown remarkable facility in adapting themselves to the contradictory commands of four successive Tudors; and the behaviour of the Puritan clergy in 1662 is the measure of a century's growth in religious sincerity. It must be also remembered that it (3) *In-fluence of* was but twelve years before the Restoration that *Religious* the Peace of Westphalia had closed the period of *Wars.* religious wars in Europe. Since the Reformation the opposing forces in European politics had been mainly defined by the lines of religious cleavage, and, though the religious wars survived such religious inspiration as they had, it could not be expected that men should realize as yet that religion need not be the main divisive force in politics. Indeed, in spite of the gradual rise of commercial rivalry as the successor of religious diversity in this function, there yet survived a considerable element of religious bigotry in the wars of Louis XIV. In these circumstances it is not surprising that the Church party tended to exaggerate the political antagonism involved in religious dissent, and to look upon the

[1] p. 96.   [2] See pp. 172, 218.

Great Rebellion as solely the outcome of Puritanical views, and, moreover, the normal outcome of such views, which might be expected to recur if Puritanism were allowed to gather head. Fear is merciless, and we must give fear its due allowance (however groundless it may have been) in estimating from a moral point of view the persecution of the Dissenters.

(4) Belief in necessity of religious unity. And, beyond the mere security from rebellion, the necessity of religious unity was impressed upon men's minds with a vividness which we, accustomed as we are to religious diversity, and the divorce between the ecclesiastical and political aspects of society, may find difficult to appreciate. The important lessons that order can exist apart from uniformity, that uniformity spells torpor, and that truth is to be found not in the agreement, but in the clash of minds, had not as yet been learned. Gilbert Sheldon was a man of stern purpose who made up his mind to do much which was (however he conceived of it) evil, in order to gain what he conceived of as a greater good. His tragedy lies in this, that while the greater good was not achieved, the evil that he did lives after him—a bitter heritage of religious rancour which has done much to poison the spiritual life of England from his day to our own. *(5) Habit of persecution.* And, as the belief in the necessity of religious unity was old, so was the policy to which it logically led—that of persecution. To tolerate was to innovate —this alone was for most men enough to condemn it; to persecute was to follow in the track of countless generations—this alone was for most men enough to commend it. We must not forget the force of habit,

and habit was on the side of persecution, which had
been more than usually active during the last hundred and thirty years.   "The views of all sections of
Protestant Englishmen...had been perverted by the
habit of persecuting the Catholics....The English
Puritans had helped to sharpen the weapons which
later were directed against themselves[1]."   Lastly, (6) *Asso-ciation of toleration with mili- tarism.*
while the practical extirpation of dissent in the days
of Elizabeth seemed to bear testimony to the efficacy
of persecution as a cure for the present evil,
Cromwell's attempt at toleration had not only been
a strictly partial and unsuccessful experiment, but
had discredited the policy by associating it with a
militarism which the nation abhorred[2].

As an illustration of the official attitude towards *The House of Com- mons on toleration. 1663.*
the question of toleration we may take the reasons
alleged by the House of Commons in 1663 against
the King's proposal that a law should be passed
enabling him "to exercise with more universal satisfaction that power of dispensing which we conceive
to be inherent in us" in the interest of the Dissenters[3].
Their first objection is that "it will establish schism
by a law."   That the state should countenance more
than one form of religious worship was a thing un-
precedented, and this fact was quite enough to set
against toleration an enormous deadweight of un-

[1] Frank Bate, *The Declaration of Indulgence 1672.*   Introduction by C. H. Firth, pp. x, xi.

[2] *Ibid.* p. x.

[3] The reasons given may be found in an appendix to a pamphlet
(attributed to Richard Baxter) published in 1663, entitled *Fair
Warning: or XXV Reasons against Toleration and Indulgence
of Popery.*

thinking conservative prejudice and conventionalism. That the state should divest itself of its ecclesiastical character, and stand as an impartial arbitrator between the adherents of various creeds was a conception monstrous and almost unthinkable. Comprehension indeed was a familiar idea in the Church of England; the Elizabethan settlement itself consisted in an attempt to comprehend, if possible, the whole nation in spite of its divisions: but toleration required a liberal grasp of mind which was not generally forthcoming as yet[1]. The education of prejudice by experience is slow, and we need not be surprised that toleration was long in coming: but for the exceptional state of affairs momentarily brought about by James II's blindly beneficent stupidity it might well have been much longer. In the second place the Commons urged that "it will make the government of the church precarious and contemptible." The fact that the state had never yet allowed a rival to the established Church gave rise to the not unnatural misconception of the Church's political connection as the foundation on which she rested, and an essential, if not of her being, at any rate of her well-being. In the third place they regarded it as absurd to weaken the Act of Uniformity in the next session after passing it. Fourthly, grants of indulgence would expose His Majesty to the restless importunity of dissenters, and would cause

[1] The general attitude is illustrated by a sentence in a contemporary pamphlet, *Animadversions upon a late pamphlet entitled The Naked Truth*, published in 1676: "He is blaming us for being so hard-hearted, and preaching to us *not only comprehension but toleration*," p. 45. See pp. 188–90.

an increase of the sects, leading perhaps to general toleration and even to Popery. The fear of Popery was never far from men's minds and liable to manifest itself in season and out of season, with or without provocation. The accusation of connection with the Papists, or even of concealed Popery was a frequent and extremely damaging charge against the Dissenters. Lastly, indulgence would cause disturbance.

It is worth noticing that the religious, theological, and doctrinal motives for persecution do not appear. Parliament, as appears from the preamble to the Licensing Act of 1662[1], still regarded itself as incidentally a vindicator of the divine honour, and in the Act of Uniformity of the same year had lamented among many other things that "many people have been led into factions and schisms...to the hazard of many souls," and had passed the act "for the prevention thereof in time to come." But now in 1663 it is the ecclesiastical motive which is dominant. This soon yielded the first place to the politico-social motive. The spirit of the Restoration was essentially a mundane spirit, retarded in its manifestation by the strong Puritan reaction against the ceremonialism of Laud[2], and therefore more marked when manifested at length. The political view of the question of persecution taken by the Parliament may be illustrated from the preambles to the persecuting statutes. Thus the Conventicle Act of 1664[3] was passed, *Political view of the question taken by Parliament.*

[1] 14 Cha. II, c. 33. See Appendix III.
[2] Gardiner, *Cromwell's Place in History*, 69–70, 108–9.
[3] 16 Cha. II, c. 4. See Appendix III.

ostensibly at any rate " for providing of further and
more speedy remedies against the growing and
dangerous practices of seditious sectaries and other
disloyal persons who under pretence of tender consciences do at their meetings contrive insurrections,
as late experience hath showed." These words are
repeated almost verbatim in the preamble to the
Second Conventicle Act of 1670[1], and both acts are
entitled "An Act to prevent and suppress Seditious
Conventicles." Similarly the Five Mile Act[2] penalized the Nonconformist ministers on the ground
that they " have settled themselves in divers corporations in England, sometimes three or more of
them in a place, thereby taking opportunity to distil
the poisonous principles of schism and rebellion into
the hearts of His Majesty's subjects, to the great
danger of the Church and Kingdom." The Church
was mentioned, but no doubt what weighed most
with men (except sheer prejudice) was the supposed
political danger. Fear for the Church was itself
largely political, for what was dangerous to the
Church was to most men of necessity dangerous to
the kingdom also[3].

The official attitude was, of course, that of the
Cavaliers, whose views were voiced in no uncertain
tones outside Parliament in the pamphlets of Roger
L'Estrange, whom we have already met. In 1663
his sufferings in the royalist cause were partially

[1] 22 Cha. II, c. 1. See Appendix III.

[2] 17 Cha. II, c. 2. See Appendix III.

[3] No doubt the Church was popular on religious grounds, but
its popularity was also largely due to political reasons.

compensated for by his appointment as "Surveyor of the Imprimery"—a post which provided an outlet for his energy in midnight raids on printing offices. In the same year he published "Toleration Discussed," in the form of a dialogue between Conformity, Zeal (representing the Presbyterians), and Scruple (representing the Independents). Its substance was recast and issued in another form under the same title in 1670. Its extreme tone, common to all L'Estrange's controversial writings, might be guessed very soon from a saying of "Conformity" in the earlier edition, "Without fooling, I look upon conventicling but as a graver kind of catterwawling" (2: ed. 1663), and the motto on the title-page of the latter, " *Vae vobis, hypocritae*[1]." He does, however, deal in serious argument. The Act of Uniformity limits actions, but not thoughts; therefore it does not restrain liberty of conscience, to refuse which is barbarous and ridiculous; but liberty of practice is "not only unreasonable, but utterly inconsistent both with Christianity itself and the public peace." "To ask that ye may govern yourselves by your own consciences is the same thing with asking to be no longer governed by the King's laws" (5, 6: ed. 1663, 3: ed. 1670). "Toleration of all opinions is a toleration of all wickedness, and therefore unlawful"; but if it

L'Estrange. "Toleration Discussed." 1663 and 1670.

[1] In fairness to L'Estrange it should be remembered that the accusation of hypocrisy against the Nonconformists had a good deal of excuse, hypocrites having largely swelled the ranks of Puritanism in the days of its power. These now, no doubt, conformed, and left the sincere to face the storm which their time-serving hypocrisy had done much to raise. See W. W. Wilkins, *Political Ballads* (2 vols., 1860), I. 167, "*A Turn-coat of the Times*" (1661).

is limited it will fall to the magistrate to decide to
whom it is to be limited, and those excluded would
have just the same plea of conscience as had previously been urged by those to whom toleration was
granted.   The King may if he likes, tolerate certain
opinions, but the people cannot claim toleration as
their due, and it is unsafe for a King to " submit his
regality to the claims of the people " (10–13: ed. 1663).
If the Nonconformists are honest they will be quiet
without a toleration ; if they are dishonest they will
be dangerous with it.   The inevitable war is brought
up against them, the execution of Charles I, and
their constitutional principles (15, 24–7: ed. 1663).
The Nonconformists in conjunction are in a direct
conspiracy.   Liberty of Conscience (for L'Estrange
does not remain true to his identification of it with
liberty of thought) will produce another war unless
there is a standing army (a name of abhorrence
since Cromwell's day) to prevent it, " for in this
town, a toleration of religion is cousin-german to a
licence for rebellion " (127, 134–5, 146: ed. 1670; 101:
ed. 1663).   " Liberty of Conscience turns naturally
to liberty of government and therefore is not to be
endured, especially in a monarchy " (102: ed. 1663).
The three great judges of mankind in descending
order of authority are God, magistrates, and conscience (89: ed. 1663).   In spite of violent partisan-
ship L'Estrange is not without an intelligent appreciation of some aspects of the question; as when he
asserts that there can be " no end of controversy
without a final unaccomptable judge, from whose
sentence there shall be no appeal " (226 : ed. 1670),

and for all his intolerance the seed of modern toleration is apparent in the sentence "The stress of the
question, in order to a toleration, does not bear so
much upon this point, whether your opinions be
true or false; as whether safe or dangerous" (102:
ed. 1663). With him at least the politico-social
motive is supreme, and this motive, as we have
seen, admits of being proved inadequate for the
persecution of religion as such.

In another of his pamphlets, "The Free-born *"The Free-born Subject."*
Subject; or the Englishman's Birthright," published
in 1679, the principles of liberty of conscience and *1679.*
divine right of kings are unblushingly exposed in
naked antagonism. "It is a tyranny to press a man
to a false worship; a tyranny to punish him for
adhering to a true one; a tyranny to hinder any
man from worshipping God as he ought: *but there is
no remedy*[1], for the people are not well aware that,
first, in obeying of magistrates, in all warrantable
cases they obey God also, in that civil obedience.
Secondly, supposing the command of the Supreme
Magistrate to be directly opposite to the express
will of God: I will not obey him in that case, but I
am not yet discharged of my duty to him in other
cases: for he is nevertheless a lawful magistrate;
(even for not being a Christian) and I will not resist
him in any" (8, 9). A strong feeling of the necessity
of orderly government led to the investing of the
civil power with all available sanctions, of which the
religious sanction was the most authoritative, and
the widest in its appeal. L'Estrange is prepared

[1] The italics are mine.

to condone a "bare and simple Dissent," but "when that Dissent comes to be practical" then "it is no longer a plea of conscience but a direct conspiracy against the government." "As the Act of Uniformity hath the full and solemn complement of a binding law; why may they not as well demand a dispensation for rebellion, as for schism?" (11, 12). This inability to look behind the law, which is regarded almost as something which carries with it its own sanction is a noticeable feature in the intolerant literature of the period, and is the natural accompaniment of the theory of government expounded in "*Citt and* another pamphlet by L'Estrange entitled "Citt and *Bump-* Bumpkin, in a dialogue over a pot of Ale, concerning *kin.*" matters of Religion and Government," published in *1680.* the following year. He begins with divine right: power is from God, not from the people; the idea of the sovereignty of the people is most ridiculous. But then he flounders, not very consistently, into Hobbism. "Government," he says, "is the will and power of a multitude, united in some one person or more, for the good and safety of the whole." The king is the united power and will of the people. He is presumed to be vested with all powers necessary for the protection of the community, he is obliged in duty to exert those powers for the common good, and entrusted with the judgment of all *Hobbism* exigencies of state (38–9). Hobbism was a *and* *Royalism.* doctrine with great possibilities from a royalist point of view, but it needed to be tinkered at a little before it could be regarded as really serviceable. It smacked too much of an original sovereignty of the people, and it made no attempt to show that as a matter of fact in the English constitution the sovereignty was vested in the Crown. Both these defects were remedied by a fusion with the theory of the divine right of kings, but in L'Estrange's hands the fusion was not artistically carried out. His views are worth examination, as being no doubt typical of the more uncompromising section of intolerant opinion in his day, based on certain sound but misapplied doctrines of political science as to the secular functions of the state as the guardian of order, coupled with a grievous lack both of human sympathy and of appreciation of the meaning and proper scope of conscience.

But among those who were less ecclesiastically or less politically minded, there was a growing appreciation of the moral aspect of religion as compared with the dogmatic and ritual aspects. In 1663 appeared " Religio Stoici " by Sir George Mackenzie, afterwards Lord Advocate of Scotland. In a preface described as " a friendly address to the phanaticks of all sects and sorts " he asserts that there is no divine warrant for persecution; we justify the persecution of ourselves by persecuting others. But he goes on to say that " as every private Christian should be tolerated by his fellow-subjects to worship God inwardly according to his conscience; so all should conspire in that exterior uniformity of worship which the laws of his country enjoin." He adds, however, " Since discretion opened my eyes I have always judged it necessary for the Christian to look oftener to his practice of piety than to confession of faith." It is to be regretted that his

Mackenzie: " Religio Stoici." 1663.

principles were not sufficiently effective to prevent him from earning the title of " bloody Mackenzie " by his treatment of the Covenanters after the battle of Bothwell Bridge.

Glanvill :

In the same direction—that of the recognition of the importance of morality—tended the influence of the Cambridge school. Joseph Glanvill was an Oxford man, but, revolting from the Aristotelian scholasticism of his day, he became a follower of the Cambridge Platonists and especially of Henry More.

" Scepsis Scientifica."
1665.

For the Cambridge men religion was preeminently a matter of life rather than of dogma, and the anti-dogmatic reaction found strong expression in Glanvill's " Vanity of Dogmatizing " which he published at the age of twenty-five in 1661. Four years later a revised edition appeared with the title of " Scepsis Scientifica." In this work the inroads of scepticism upon dogmatism are very noticeable ; Glanvill shows a vivid realization of the fallibility of the human mind. Without much originality or depth of thought[1] he yet puts forward the rationalist point of view with healthy vigour. " What a stir there is for mint, anise, and cummin controversies, while the great practical fundamentals are unstudied, unobserved ? What eagerness in the prosecution of disciplinarian uncertainties, when the love of God and our neighbour, those evangelical unquestionables are neglected ?...How fond are men of a bundle of opinions which are no better than a bag of cherry-stones ? How do they scramble

---

[1] I here follow Tulloch (II. 444 f.) against Hallam and Lecky, whose admiration for the book seems to me undeserved.

for their nuts, and apples, and how zealous for their petty victories?...To be confident in opinions is ill manners and immodesty....This is that spirit of immorality, that saith unto dissenters, 'Stand off, I am more orthodox than thou art': a vanity more capital than error[1]."

Like all his school, Glanvill stood for morality and reason in religion, as opposed to mere orthodoxy and credulous faith. "The sum is," he said, in his sermon Λόγου Θρησκεία, "Religion primarily is Duty[2]" (6); and he proceeded to declare that reason is infallible, and, in a sense, the word of God (23–4)— a noticeable instance of the affinity between the Cambridge school and Lord Herbert of Cherbury. Glanvill even disowned the spirit of the propagandist. "I am not concerned to impose my sentiments upon others, nor do I care to endeavour the change of their minds, though I judge them mistaken, as long as virtue, the interests of religion, the peace of the world and their own, are not prejudiced by their errors[3]." This statement is of interest in that while it seems to show a spirit essentially tolerant it could be agreed to by the most violent persecutors. The doctrinal, the ecclesiastical, the politico-social, and perhaps even the theological motives to persecution are acknowledged, at least by implication, as legitimate;

[1] pp. 199, 200, Owen's edition.

[2] Cf. Whichcote "Morals...are nineteen parts in twenty of all Religion." *Aphorisms*, 586, quoted by Tulloch, II. 107.

[3] Quoted by Owen: Preface to *Scepsis Scientifica*, xxxii, xxxiii. I have not been able to discover from which of Glanvill's writings it is taken. Similarly (as we saw, p. 69) Cudworth held that the object of religion was not to propagate opinions.

and, in the eyes of most men of Glanvill's day, the acknowledgment would have been regarded as to all intents and purposes nullifying the tolerant rule with which the sentence opens: and unfortunately *His actual* Glanvill, for all his disclaimers, did not shake himself *intoler-* free from the prejudices of his time. He seems to *ance.* have been capable of maintaining a remarkable separation between theory and practice, for in the very year after the publication of his "Vanity of Dogmatizing"—the year of the eviction of the nonconforming clergy—we find him denouncing in the abstract in one sentence, what he defends in the concrete in the next. In his preface to "Lux Orientalis" published in 1662, he writes "To tie all others up to our opinions and to impose difficult and disputable matters under the notion of confessions of faith and fundamentals of religion, is a most unchristian piece of tyranny, the foundation of persecution, and every root of anti-christianism. So that I have often wondered that those that heretofore would have forced all men to a compliance with their darling notions, and would have made a prey of them that could not bow down before the Idol of their new framed orthodoxy; should yet have the face to object persecution and unchristian tyranny to our Church appointments:...let any equal man be judge which is the greater superstition, either to idolize and place religion in things of dispute and mere opinions; or conscientiously to observe the sanctions of that authority we are bound to obey." This passage might, perhaps, be explained away as a merely relative commendation of the Church of

England as compared with the Dissenters, but
unfortunately in " The Zealous and Impartial Pro- *"The*
testant[1]" he definitely repudiates the idea of toleration *Zealous*
in the approved style of the hack pamphleteer. *and Im-*
Toleration is not the way to union : " to strive for *partial*
toleration is to contend against all government "; to *Protest-*
allow the plea of conscience is to put an end to all *ant."*
laws (26-7).   When Dissenters are chastised for *1681.*
their prejudice they will be more inclined to consider the reasons of Churchmen impartially (34).   As
for atheism, our apostle of scepticism and toleration
would have it made capital (45).   It is strange that
such a pamphlet could have been written by the
author of " Scepsis Scientifica[2]."   It is to be hoped
that the work of Glanvill, the philosopher, promoted
the cause of toleration more than that of Glanvill,
the pamphleteer, obstructed it : for the scepticism of
which he was so vigorous an exponent, and the
exaltation of reason and morality in which he joined
with the Cambridge men, must, as we have seen, be
given prominent places among the tolerant tendencies
of the age.

While the influence of the Platonists made for
toleration on *a priori* grounds, the Nonconformists
were not backward in putting before the public their
view of the practical side of the question.   Amongst
their most active writers was John Owen, an *John*
Independent, who, in the days of the interregnum *Owen.*

[1] Written 1678 : published (posthumously) in 1681. Greenslet,
Joseph Glanvill, 85.

[2] For the similar failure of Sir Thomas More to apply his
tolerant principles, see Creighton, *Persecution and Tolerance*, 104.

had been closely associated with Cromwell, and
become Dean of Christ Church and Vice-Chancellor
of the University of Oxford, in which capacity he
connived at the use of the proscribed Anglican liturgy.
After the Restoration he refused to conform in spite
of offers of high preferment from Clarendon; but he
had powerful friends at court, and was allowed to
preach.   In or about the year 1665 he published
various pamphlets, one of which, "The Grounds
and Reasons on which Protestant Dissenters desire
their liberty[1]" was mainly devoted to showing that
the Dissenters were irreconcilably opposed to Popery.

Accusation of Popery against Dissenters. Seeing that their objections to the Church of England
were largely on the grounds that she had not reformed
herself sufficiently from Popery, it might be expected
that Popish sympathies were the last charge that
could have been levelled against the Dissenters; but
as a matter of fact this served as one of the most
telling indictments against them, and there is a
certain sense in which it was not entirely without
foundation.   It is not easy to realize how prominent
was the doctrine of non-resistance at this time in the
Church of England—a doctrine which distinguished
her at once and on the same grounds from Papist
and Nonconformist.   It was the crowning heresy of
the Church of Rome that she claimed political
supremacy over kings, and of this the theocratic
tendencies of Presbyterianism were reminiscent.   The
quarrel between the Crown and the Pope, and the
sharp opposition between their respective claims, of
which a lively memory was perpetuated by the oaths of

[1] Works, vol. xxi. pp. 467–71 (21 vols., ed. Russell, 1826).

allegiance and supremacy, caused Roman Catholicism to be looked upon as preëminently anti-monarchical; and was it not notorious that the Dissenters held that there were circumstances in which it was lawful to take up arms against the King? Then was not this flat Popery? "Popery having apparently *Hickes on* corrupted the Gospel in the doctrines of obedience *the Dis-* and submission, and the divine authority of the *senters.* supreme power, especially of Kings; they cannot be sound and orthodox Protestants, who hold the very same destructive principles to regal government, by which the Papists have corrupted the Gospel in these points. No, they are not sound and orthodox Protestants, but Protestants popularly affected, Papists under a Protestant dress, wolves in sheep's clothing, rebellious and Satanical spirits transformed into angels of light[1]."

The same standpoint is emphasized in a political *"Geneva* ballad of the day entitled "Geneva and Rome; or, *and* the Zeal of both boiling over," from which the *Rome."* following verses are taken:

"Jack Presbyter and the sons of the Pope
    Had a late dispute of the right of the Rope
    Who'd merit hanging without any trope;
        Which nobody can deny.

First Jack held forth, and bid him remember
    The horrible plot on the *Fifth of November*,
    The very month preceding December;
        Which nobody, &c.

---

[1] Dean Hickes. Sermon on Jan. 30, 1681–2, quoted by Figgis, *Divine Right of Kings*, 182, to which I am indebted for much of the substance of this paragraph.

The thirtieth of January, th' other reply'd,
We heard of 't at Rome, which can't be deny'd,
Had Jack been loyal, then Charles had not dy'd ;
    Which nobody, &c.

* * *

A truce ! a truce ! quoth Presbyter Jack,
We both love treason as Loyalists sack,
And if either prevails the King goes to wrack ;
    Which nobody, &c.

The Bishops tell Charles we both have long nails,
And Charles shall find it if either prevails,
For, like Sampson's foxes, we're ty'd by the tails ;
    Which nobody, &c.[1] "

It is important to realize this point of view if
we are to understand the strength of the prejudice
which Churchmen felt against the Nonconformists ;
for prejudice did more than anything else to delay
toleration.

Owen also protested against the methods of
executing the penal laws, and especially against the
loathsome tribe of informers which they called into
existence[2].

*Owen :
" Indulg-
ence and
Toleration
consider-
ed." 1667.*
In 1667 appeared his " Indulgence and Toleration
considered in a letter unto a Person of Honour[3]."
He points out the very material difference between
the position of the Churchmen and that of the
Dissenters, in that the former imposed, without
feeling obliged in conscience to do so, things in which

[1] W. W. Wilkins, *Political Ballads*, I. 224 f.

[2] Works, vol. XXI., *A Word of Advice to the Citizens of London,*
pp. 445–56. *The Present Distresses on Nonconformists examined,*
pp. 473–80.

[3] Works, vol. XXI. pp. 373–402.

the latter could not acquiesce without violating
their consciences. He concludes from the common
practice of all mankind that it is a law of nature to
admit divergences from uniformity. "We are some
of the first who ever anywhere in the world, from the
foundation of it, thought of ruining and destroying
persons of the same religion with ourselves, merely
upon the choice of some peculiar ways of worship
in that religion." Even in the Roman Church
"particular ways of worship" are allowed[1]. It
should be noticed that Protestantism and Roman
Catholicism are conceived of as two different religions, and the gulf between them as incomparably
greater than any division between Protestants. The
solidarity of Protestantism was frequently insisted
on as a reason for toleration or comprehension by
the Nonconformists who were entirely out of
sympathy with the reverence for Catholic tradition
and the aspirations to Catholic reunion of such men
as Thorndike[2].

Owen protests against the idea that the conscience
can be considered as free apart from freedom to act,
and against the attempt to force an assent which can
only be given upon conviction and evidence of the
truth of a thing. Impositions upon men's consciences
amount to an endeavour to force them "to reject all
respects to the future judgments of God....Atheism
will be the end of such an endeavour[3]." He has discovered the important truth that it is a mistake in
policy to regard Church and State as co-extensive

---

[1] *Ibid.* p. 384.   [2] See pp. 96, 191.
[3] Works, vol. xxi. pp. 385–8.

and mutually dependent, but he bases it upon reasons which would not find much favour at the present day, and illustrates from a fresh quarter the widespread craving for political stability. The laws, he says, on which the Church order is founded may be changed by Parliament from time to time, "whereas the constitution of the civil government is founded upon no such alterable and changeable laws, but hath quite another foundation, obnoxious to nothing, but to the all-overruling providence of the Most High." This imposing and immutable structure is weakened by comparison with the Church. True to his Independent principles, Owen asserts that while every Englishman is born into the nation, he must himself choose his religion, or else he has none. Even could a general outward conformity be attained it would not increase the peace or security of the Church, but this is not in the least probable, for persecution has never yet succeeded anywhere[1]. Persecution is against the interest of the King, for it impoverishes the country. The imprisonment of Nonconformists causes disturbance in industry and commerce in which they are largely engaged; and to the discouragement of trade must be added the stimulus which it gives to emigration: moreover the natural sense of Englishmen is against it[2]. The inclination to persecute those who differ from us is no proof of holding the truth, but rather the inseparable companion of error and superstition[3]. To say that toleration is impracticable is a mere

---

[1] Works, vol. xxi. pp. 390–4.   [2] Ibid. p. 395.
[3] Ibid. p. 400.

pretence: the Nonconformists merely desire the same liberty as the Huguenots have in France and the French and Dutch churches have in England. He also gives various instances of toleration practised on the Continent, and finally urges it as giving greater security and esteem to the established order and making for tranquillity, trade, wealth and peace[1].

In the same year appeared "A Proposition for the Safety and Happiness of the King and Kingdom" by David Jenkins. There were only two ways, he asserted, of dealing with the religious question; either an "accommodation" must be granted, or else the Nonconformists must be got rid of by ruthless extirpation like the Christians in Japan (17–8). In this he was certainly right if we may allow a little for exaggeration. What was not realized by the governors of the Church or of the state was that Dissent was a permanent element in the religious life of the nation, with its roots embedded in a past more distant than the Restoration or the Long Parliament, and that ultimately the only alternative to a frank recognition of the right of this element to a peaceful continuation of its existence was a determined application of methods morally intolerable. The cleavage in English life was not sufficiently great, and the moral sense of Englishmen was too strong, for the etablishment of an Inquisition or an anticipation of the *dragonnades*

[Jenkins]: "A Proposition for the Safety and Happiness of the King and Kingdom." 1667.

---

[1] *Ibid.* pp. 401–2. The instances given are those of the United Provinces and Poland, of Lutherans in Brandenburg and Hesse, of Calvinists in many free cities of the Empire, and in some places in Denmark, and of both Lutherans and Calvinists in sundry German principalities with Romish magistrates, p. 401.

of Louis XIV. Owing to this pernicious but most natural misunderstanding of Dissent, methods were adopted, too oppressive to be otherwise than exasperating, but too vacillating to be otherwise than futile.

Jenkins next proceeds to deal with the question of oaths. It is to the oaths and declarations, he said, that the Nonconformists object, not to the doctrine, discipline or ceremonies of the Church[1]: and the oaths are useless, for a man does not change his principles though he takes the oath, and if he has "loosened the reins of his conscience" to take it, it embitters him. Oaths "make such debauchery work amongst honest minds that we shall rue the time that ever they were born into the world" (18–24). Gamaliel's argument, too, in favour of the apostles does duty in the cause of the Dissenters (35). Also the obvious fact is brought forward that persecution unites all the factions against prelacy, followed by the interesting assertion that there is a considerable public opinion against persecution (38, 41–2). Jenkins lays solemn emphasis upon the sin of doing violence to men's consciences, and declares that while the severity of the laws can only result in hypocrisy, indulgence will put an end for ever to sedition and rebellion. On political grounds, however, the Roman Catholics are not to be included (72–5, 71, 91, 61–3).

[*Tomkins*]: " *Inconveniencies of Toleration.*" 1667.   The essay of David Jenkins immediately provoked a reply from Thomas Tomkins, chaplain to Archbishop Sheldon, entitled " The Inconveniencies

[1] This, of course, was not true of the Nonconformists as a whole, but no doubt was true of some, perhaps of great numbers.

of Toleration[1]." Tomkins follows L'Estrange in pointing out that while universal toleration "layeth us open to all the folly and phrenzy imaginable," limited toleration is a confession that conscience is not so sacred but that restraints may be put upon it, and that consciences may be such that men ought not to act upon them (1). If Jenkins' arguments are valid for the Dissenters they are valid for conscientious Papists and Turks too (21); and if the severity of the laws does not remove the error it may prevent it from spreading (24). Tomkins does not miss the opportunity of calling up the extravagances of the interregnum, saddling them upon the Dissenters in a body, and concluding that, as the safety of the government depends upon its being stronger than each single person, associations must not be allowed to grow up and gather strength (28–32). Two instances may be given of the spirit that animates this pamphlet and too much of the ephemeral literature of the time. "There is no such dangerous way of libelling as that which is vulgarly called a good gift in prayer" (4). Also the Five Mile Act is referred to as "so direct, so reasonable, and withal so merciful a law": confiscation of goods, perpetual imprisonment or banishment would be reasonable penalties for a refusal of the prescribed oath (10)—an oath, be it noted, completely inconsistent with constitutional progress and liberty, involving an undertaking, the full observance of

[1] Tomkins was also a fellow of All Souls College, Oxford, rector of a London church, and assistant licenser of books. In this last capacity he nearly refused to license *Paradise Lost*, because of the comet in Book i., which " with fear of change Perplexes monarchs."

which would have made participation in the Revolution of 1688 impossible.

The fall of Clarendon in 1667 and the passing of the second Conventicle Act in 1670 mark the limits of a period of intermittent and precarious toleration for the Nonconformists, during which the stream of pamphlets on the question seems to have been much more voluminous than before. In addition to those already noticed, John Corbet[1], ejected from the Rectory of Bramshot by the Act of Uniformity, published in 1667 his "Discourse of the Religion of England. Asserting that Reformed Christianity Settled in its Due Latitude is the Stability and Advancement of this Kingdom." Adversity had had a chastening and liberalizing effect upon his views. He now had the breadth of mind and the courage to put in a plea for the Roman Catholics. In spite of the fact that Popery disposes subjects to rebellion and persecutes all other religions within its reach, he pleaded that they might have their faith to themselves without molestation, and the state always providing to "obviate" their "principles and practices of disloyalty," and the diffusing of the leaven of their superstition : but they must not be "admitted to a capacity of civil and dangerous influence upon the affairs of the kingdom, or of interrupting and perplexing the course of things that concern the public" (16). With regard to the Dissenters the Discourse is, like his "Interest of England," mainly a plea for comprehension. "A momentous part" of the Dissenters might be "incompassed in an

[Corbet]: "Discourse of the Religion of England." 1667.

---

[1] See p. 94.

establishment of such a latitude as may happily
settle this Church": others "of sound belief and
good life" should be tolerated, but their liberty
should be "measured and limited by the safety of
true religion in general; and of the public established
order" (38). A third class of persons might be
allowed "a connivance" (28), but Corbet does not
descend to particulars.

His book was soon answered by Dr Richard [*Perrin-
Perrinchief[1], who had been ejected by the parlia- *chief*]:
mentary commissioners from his fellowship at Mag- *"A Dis-
dalene College, Cambridge, but had received a *course of
London rectory at the Restoration, and in 1664 *Tolera-
been appointed a prebendary of Westminster. In *tion."
"A Discourse of Toleration" he perversely identifies *1667. ?–8.*
a plea for dissenters with a plea for dissensions in
religion, and then sets himself the easy but ineffectual task of showing the evil origins and results
of the latter. He makes his task more easy and
more ineffectual still by absurdly assuming that the
Dissenters are analogous to the less satisfactory types
of heretic in the early Church. His theory of persecution is that it "may take off all encouragements
to error, and so make men more diligent in the
search of Truth, when it will not be safe to deceive
or be deceived." Moreover, he naïvely adds that,
as dissensions arise from lusts (he has already proved
this easily in his own fashion), we cannot hope that
carnal desires will grow modest by being tolerated

---

[1] Also by an anonymous pamphlet entitled *Dolus an Virtus?*
—a bitter attack which describes Corbet's book as "a seditious
discourse," and contains nothing relevant to our subject.

(16, 18). This pamphlet shows a deplorable lack of discernment and sympathy; it is perhaps the least intelligent in the whole controversy (which is to say a great deal), and is only noteworthy as showing to what an extremity it was possible for blind prejudice to drive a man.

It was not left unanswered: Corbet wrote "A Second Discourse of the Religion of England," and Owen "A Peace-Offering in an Apology and Humble Plea for Indulgence and Liberty of Conscience[1]." The latter is a plea that the Dissenters should be judged by the actual principles which they profess, which will free them from the charge of responsibility for "the late troubles." Owen emphasizes the agreement of the Dissenters with the Church in doctrine and in acknowledgment of the royal supremacy in' ecclesiastical affairs[2]. To justify toleration in the abstract, he appeals to the law of nature. In things within the power of men, he argues, the law of nature commands that the individual should make concessions for the good of the community: but some things, uniformity of stature and visage, for example, are not within the power of men, and it is a principle of the law of nature that unavoidable differences should be allowed. He holds that the "diversity of men's apprehensions of things spiritual and supernatural" is to be reckoned among unavoidable differences[3]. He attacks persecution on the grounds of its ineffectiveness and its contrariety to the spirit of Christianity[4]. The arguments of unlawfulness,

Owen:
"A Peace-Offering."
1667. ? -8.

---

[1] *Works*, vol. XXI. pp. 403–44.   [2] *Ibid.* pp. 411, 415–8.
[3] *Ibid.* pp. 421–2.   [4] *Ibid.* p. 424.

sedition, confusion, error and uncleanness against
Dissenters are, he points out, the same as have
always been used by persecutors. They will serve
any party in power, and have oftener been managed
in the hands of error, superstition and heresy than
in those of truth and sobriety[1]. Persecution for
opinions was originally invented for the service of
error (he means by the Roman Catholic Church),
and cannot be justified where infallibility is disclaimed. Unanimity as to the worship of God has
never existed and cannot be effected by punishments, being itself impossible, and the means not
being suited to the procurement of it[2]. To assert
that all sorts of evils will result from toleration is
to imply either that truth and order have lost the
power of preserving themselves, or that such evils
have actually followed whenever toleration has been
granted; but the latter is notoriously untrue, and,
for the former, the Gospel has never so prevailed as
when there was full liberty to dissent from it[3]. But
for all his liberal principles, Owen is careful to confine their application to Protestants[4]. He appeals,
too, to the commercial motive, as usually in his
pamphlets, pointing out how largely the trade and
wealth of the nation depend on the Dissenters[5].

Corbet's "Second Discourse of the Religion of
England" is a less solid contribution to the question.
As in his previous treatises—"The Interest of Eng-
land" and the "Discourse of Religion"—his main aim
[Corbet].
"Second
Dis-
course."
1668.

[1] *Works*, vol. xxi. pp. 434–5.   [2] *Ibid.* p. 435.
[3] *Ibid.* p. 436.   [4] *Ibid.* p. 437.
[5] *Ibid.* pp. 439–40.

is the advocacy of a comprehensive latitudinarian
church. He is largely in agreement with the Anglican
writers, except that he thinks that room for his party
should be found in the Church: and he justifies his
contention by saying that the points of difference
between Dissenters and the Church are of less
weight than points on which Churchmen differ
among themselves and yet keep the peace (9, 35).
He, too, is profoundly impressed with the importance
of civil order and the ease with which it may be
disturbed by religious differences. Both the comprehended and the tolerated, he says, should prefer
the common interest of religion and the settling of
the nation before their own particular persuasions.
Considerate Nonconformists will never promote their
own liberty by such ways and means as would bring
in a toleration of Popery (which now, in spite of
the plea in his former Discourse, he definitely dis-
countenances); and a fixed state ecclesiastical is
necessary as a precaution against infidelity; otherwise Christianity would be much endangered. He
urges, too, that episcopacy will gain more by moderation than by severity (42–5).

[Perrin-
chief]:
" Indulg-
ence not
Justified."
1668.

Owen's and Corbet's treatises summoned the redoubtable Perrinchief once more into the arena; his
" Indulgence not Justified" being intended as an
answer to them both. He disposes of comprehension
and toleration successively in a single sentence. "The
measure of a people's mutual confidence," he says,
"and so consequently of their quiet among themselves, will be according to the degrees of purity and
unity which are observed in that religion professed

by the State " (1). Owen's assertions that "men's
apprehensions of things spiritual and supernatural...
are not absolutely in their own power," and that
therefore "these apprehensions and the exercise of
conscience towards God upon them cannot be the
subjects of the laws of civil societies," Perrinchief
disposes of easily, *more suo*, by a flat denial (6–7).
He cites Christ, the apostles, the primitive Christians,
the first Christian emperors and modern princes as
supporters of persecution : comprehension and toleration are the projects of enemies to the establishment,
save possibly in some few cases where men are mistaken "in the simplicity of their hearts" (9–30).
Necessity only can justify a toleration, and a standing
army is necessary to make it safe (49).

Another reply to Corbet's "Discourse" came from
the pen of Thomas Tomkins, whose acquaintance
we have already made. In "The Modern Pleas for
Comprehension, Toleration, and the taking away of
the Obligation to the Renouncing of the Covenant,
Considered and Discussed[1]" he propounded the question, What if the King feels bound in conscience to
suppress doctrines which I feel bound in conscience
to preach ? If it is urged that the King's conscience
should give way because he is not concerned with
religion, it may be replied that in the first place
religion has great influence on civil government and
therefore does fall within his care (99–102). Soul

*[Tomkins]:
"Modern
Pleas etc."
1675.*

[1] This was also an answer to Wolseley's "Liberty of Conscience, upon its true and proper grounds asserted and vindicated,"
(see p. 141) ; and was not published till 1675, in which year Tomkins died at the age of 37.

and body are so closely related that what affects one
affects the other, at least to the point of making
a man consider. Experience shows that the corporal
penalties in religious matters have great effect upon
the mind, and, indeed, otherwise correction must be
superseded in civil affairs as well as religious (121).
Secondly, the subject is as likely to be wrong as the
sovereign (99–102). This latter seems to us an extraordinarily weak argument; but it is an instructive
one. Nowadays we give the benefit of the doubt
to liberty of conscience; Tomkins with the spirit of
his age gave the benefit of the doubt to authority
in the interests of order. Fear of the disturbance
of order seems almost to have been a perpetual
nightmare to the party which he represents. Thirdly,
magistrates are obliged in conscience to use to the
honour of God the authority which God has given
(99–102). Tomkins admitted that "to act against
our conscience is always a sin; but," he continued,
"I shall add this further, That it is very frequently
a grievous sin to act according to it....Conscience is
not a safe rule for any man to act by in his private
capacity" (150–1). How it is a safe rule for the
magistrate to act by, he did not make clear. The
private consciences of men, he said, are not trusted
in their ordinary dealings; if all were wise and
honest we could do without coercion, not only in
religious matters, but in civil matters also (168 f.).
As it was, toleration meant chaos in religion, and
danger to the civil government, for a sect might
easily become a party and perhaps gain supremacy.
"Gathered churches," he said, with significant refer-

ence to the Puritan army, "are most excellent
materials to raise new troops out of" (153–67).

It must be remembered that Cromwell's terrible
soldiers were dispersed about the land, many of
them no doubt still capable of bearing arms[1]; and
Tomkins was only voicing a widespread apprehension
when he hinted that the Presbyterians, if allowed to
gather head, would be prepared to repeat the measures
of 1642 (144).

In the same year as the "Second Discourse of
Religion," 1668, were published two anonymous
pamphlets written by Sir Charles Wolseley. The
son of a sequestrated Royalist, Wolseley had nevertheless been a strong supporter of the Protectorate.
He had been a leader of the Cromwellian minority in
the Barebone's Parliament, one of Oliver's Lords, and
a member of the councils of both Cromwells, father
and son. At the Restoration he had been pardoned,
and thenceforward lived in retirement, gardening
and writing pamphlets. Of the two with which we
are now concerned the first is entitled "Liberty of
Conscience upon its true and proper grounds asserted
and vindicated," and the second "Liberty of Conscience the Magistrate's interest." In the former
Wolseley defines conscience as the knowledge men
have of themselves in reference to God, and draws the
conclusion that the "simple actings" of conscience
cannot be forced (6, 11). He then proceeds to deal

*[Wolse-
ley]:
"Liberty
of Con-
science...
asserted
and vin-
dicated."
1668.*

[1] A soldier under twenty-five at the Restoration would still be
under forty when Tomkins wrote. Even as late as the time of
the Rye House Plot (1683) "little groups of the Cromwellian army
signified their readiness to bear arms." Gooch, *English Democratic Ideas in the Seventeenth Century*, 339.

with the magistracy, of which he finds the basis in the light of nature and the historical origin in the family : the magistrate's power exists for the total suppression of all moral evil and the encouragement of all moral good : he is to see all the laws of Christ put into execution, and to take care that all things in the church be duly administered (12, 14, 25). It might seem that this comprehensive view of the duties of the magistrate would lead up to a justification of persecution, but Wolseley does not see clearly whither his principles would lead him.   The magistrate, he explains, is to have the care and oversight of the Gospel, but is not to use the temporal power in it : " he is to see that done...which he is by no means to force the doing of " : the civil and ecclesiastical powers are distinct and ought to be kept so (26–7).   No prince or state ought by force to compel men to any part of the doctrine, worship or discipline of the Gospel, and against such use of force eight reasons are alleged.   It is against the light of nature ; it has not been appointed by Christ and is therefore unlawful ; it cannot change a man's views ; God accepts only a willing service ; it is contrary to the practice of Christ and the Apostles ; it supposes infallibility in the power applying it ; it is obligatory upon a man to follow his private judgment (on this considerable emphasis is laid) ; and, finally, it meets with ill-success (28–45).   Men may indeed be enjoined to hear the Gospel preached, without being forced to give their assent to it ; but " the plainest truths of the Gospel ought not to be enforced upon men, much less those more doubtful

and obscure, concerning discipline and order"; and
it is unreasonable and unnatural to force men "about
things wholly supernatural and purely spiritual; and
so are all the matters of the Gospel which lie seated
in men's belief and persuasion, in reference to their
own eternal condition" (48, 51–2). Toleration, however, is not to be universal: nothing is to be tolerated against the "common light" and the common
interest and natural good of mankind (52). It will
be remembered that Stillingfleet, in his "Irenicum[1],"
appealed to the law of nature, but with an instructive difference. For Stillingfleet the law of
nature merely determined certain exceptions from
the general rule of the magistrate's control; for
Wolseley the "common light" determined certain
exceptions from the general rule of toleration.

This pamphlet, as has already been seen, is not
a very practical one. It is all very well to assert
that the magistrate is to promote the Gospel, but
if he is not armed with the ultimate appeal to force,
how is he, as magistrate, to promote it? Wolseley
can give no clear definition of the means to be
employed, and indulges in an obscure comparison
of the church, as he would have it regulated, with
the College of Physicians, who, as he sagely points
out, are not forced to give physic (27).

This weakness is commented upon, and a remedy *"A Peace-*
for it suggested in "A Peaceable Dissertation" pub- *able Dis-*
lished in the following year[2]. The anonymous author *sertation."*
justly observes that to say that the magistrate may *1669.*
not use the temporal sword in religion is to say that, as

---

[1] See pp. 86–92.   [2] See p. 167.

magistrate, he has nothing to do with religion. But as a matter of fact he may punish the clergy for neglect of duty and the people for not coming to church (24). He must see that the people worship God according to their consciences; otherwise he is not executing the will of God. He may justifiably (if he is acting according to his conscience) restrain men from doing what they conscientiously are impelled to do, but may not constrain them to do what they conscientiously cannot do; for though it is God's will that men should never act against their consciences, it is also His will that men should not act according to them when they are erroneous (26–9). What, then, is to happen to the man who cannot conscientiously come to church? But this obvious question is apparently beyond the limit of our author's vision.

[*Wolse-ley*]: "*Liberty of Con-science the Magis-trate's interest*." 1668. Wolseley's treatment of the subject from a more purely political aspect in the second pamphlet, "Liberty of Conscience the Magistrate's interest," is far more satisfactory—indeed this short paper of less than two dozen pages is one of the most capable contributions to the controversy from the tolerant side, full of acute insight and pithy statement. Liberty of Conscience is the magistrate's interest because if he allies himself with one party and supports it by persecution, all the other parties are engaged against him (3). And here follows the exposure of a fallacy which lay at the very root of the current theory of persecution: "'Tis not the having several parties in religion under a state, that is in itself dangerous, but 'tis the persecuting of

them that makes them so" (3). Could but this
truth have been realized in the most influential
circles and acted upon, one of the least pleasant
chapters of English history need never have been
written. Wolseley goes on to show that the magistrate will find his safety rather in a prudent balance
of divided parties than in supporting a single united
party; he should make himself a common father
to the whole Protestant religion (3–4). In these
calculations of the magistrate's interest there is a
noticeably secular tone, which is a striking illustration of the wane of theological rancour, and in itself
a strong force in the tolerant direction; for, where
public opinion is a power, purely political motives
are not likely to be strong enough or venerable
enough long to support the odium which persecution
for religion excites[1]. There are also several shrewd
observations which are in striking contrast to the
often crude and generally conventional views of the
pamphleteers. "By how much the principles of any
party are less taking and plausible, the less dangerous
still is that party." Supposing that it is true that
those who demand liberty of conscience are factious;
grant them what they ask, and they will either be won
over to obedience or will lose their excuse and fall into
general contempt and become inconsiderable. "'Tis
marvellous prudence to separate between conscience
and faction, which can never be, but by a liberty for
the one, so that they may distinctly punish the

---

[1] In the case of the English Roman Catholics the motive was
from time to time renewed by real or supposed plots at home and
actual or rumoured attack from without. See pp. 30–1.

other." "Foolish and absurd opinions are only put
to nurse by persecution " (4–5). The effect of denying
liberty of religion in a Protestant state has always
been mischievous; nor is enforced uniformity consistent with Protestant principles. Moreover it dis-
obliges the best sort of men in every party and
dissatisfies the generality of the nation (6–7). In
this statement we may see a testimony to the change
in the feelings of the nation: the Cavalier Parliament, elected in the full excitement of the royalist
reaction accompanying the Restoration, " more
zealous for royalty than the King, more zealous
for episcopacy than the bishops," might still pass the
second Conventicle Act two years later than the date
of this pamphlet, but the tide of feeling in the country was already setting slowly and uncertainly in the
direction of toleration. It is knowledge, Wolseley
continues, which causes differences in religion, and
knowledge is a thing which princes should encourage:
religious imposition on the other hand makes men
heartless in their calling, and either ignorant or dis-
satisfied (7–8). The interests of trade, too, must be
considered: it is the trading part of the nation upon
which the persecution mainly falls, and liberty of
conscience would be a more serious blow to Holland[1]
than all the victories yet gained (9–10). The interests of religion demand the same thing: liberty
of conscience is the best way of securing the Protestant faith, both as being a breach with the Romish
principle of persecution, and as diffusing a know-

[1] See p. 148.

ledge of divine things: the Roman Catholics cannot
be included in toleration because of their refusal to
give assurance of their fidelity and because their
principles prevent them from being good subjects in
a Protestant state (11, 12, 14). The arguments now
used against the Nonconformists, the Papists also
use against the Protestants, and in the early days of
Christianity the heathens used against the Christians.
" He that would have the magistrate force all men to
his religion, will himself be burnt by his own principles
when he comes into a country where the state religion
differs from him. To say that he is in the right,
and the state that does it in the wrong, is a miserable begging the question. If one magistrate be to
do it, all are to do it, and there can be no other
rule of truth and error in that case but what they
think so" (16, 19). Wolseley had also grasped
Chillingworth's doctrine that religious liberty is
of the essence of Protestantism. "Liberty of conscience," he said, "lies as naturally necessary to a
Protestant state, as imposition to a Popish state"
(21).

One of the most interesting things in this in- *Growth of popular feeling in favour of toleration.*
teresting tract is the witness which it bears to the
growth of popular feeling in favour of toleration.
Already, four years ago, while the Conventicle Act
was still new, Pepys' pity had been aroused at seeing
some Nonconformists, one August Sunday, led by in
custody for worshipping God in their own way. " I
saw several poor creatures," he writes, "carried by,
by constables, for being at a conventicle. They go
like lambs without any resistance. I would to God

they would either conform, or be more wise, and not
be catched[1]!" And many persons, who set more
store by the feelings of common humanity than the
subtleties of ecclesiastical and political argument,
must have seen and felt with Pepys. Jenkins, too,
in his "Proposition for the Safety and Happiness of
the King and Kingdom," which we have already
noticed[2], asserted that there was a considerable
public opinion against persecution[3], and suggested
that a plebiscite should be taken in a county selected
at random, confidently expecting a verdict in favour
of liberty of conscience (41–2). Probably this was
an unjustifiably sanguine estimate; but it was not
for nothing that men saw Nonconformists dragged
through the streets to waste their lives in noisome
gaols, herded together with the offscourings of the
nation, for no fault save that of following the harmless
dictates of their consciences.

Commercial considerations.   Dissent, in accordance with an extremely interesting tendency, flourished chiefly among the
trading classes; and the consideration that it was
upon these classes that the persecution mainly fell,
and that thus English commercial expansion was
checked at a time when the bases of our power were
being laid in India and America and we were
engaged in a convulsive struggle with the Dutch
for commercial supremacy, is one which appears
frequently in contemporary literature. We have

---

[1] *Diary*, Aug. 7, 1664. The Conventicle Act was passed in
the previous May.

[2] p. 131.

[3] The same fact is attested by Owen. See p. 130.

already seen it exemplified in the writings of John
Owen[1], and emphasized by Sir Charles Wolseley[2].
It also formed the substance of a document written
by a more influential person than these. About this
time, Anthony Ashley Cooper, now Lord Ashley, but *Ashley.*
better known by his subsequent title, the Earl of
Shaftesbury, addressed a memorial to Charles II on
the subject of toleration[3]. In the days of the Protectorate a member of the Barebone's Parliament,
Ashley was one of the so-called Presbyterian minority
in the Cavalier Parliament, who, after the Act of
Uniformity became the nucleus of a party in favour
of toleration. He was now one of the group of
ministers known as the Cabal who took the place of
the fallen Clarendon, and favoured a tolerant policy.
In his memorial to Charles II, he proposed that *His me-*
office should still be confined to members of the *morial to*
Charles II.
Church of England, but that with the exception of *? 1668-9.*
Roman Catholics and Fifth Monarchy men, liberty
of conscience should be allowed. He urged that this
would check emigration from England and attract
population from abroad: the result would be that
the value of land would rise and industry and commerce be stimulated. It is interesting to notice
that a committee of the House of Lords appointed
in 1669 to consider the fall of rents and the decay of
trade reported " that ease and relaxation in ecclesi-

[1] See pp. 130, 137.
[2] See p. 146.
[3] Printed in full in Christie's *Life of the first Earl of Shaftesbury*, vol. II., Appendix I. Christie gives the date as between
October 1668 and November 1669.

astical matters will be the means of improving the
trade of this kingdom[1]."

At a time of acute commercial rivalry with the
Dutch it was natural that men should attempt to
examine the foundations of Dutch prosperity, with a
view to learning lessons which might be applied at
Petty: home.   Sir William Petty in his "Political Arith-
"Political metic[2]," which was apparently written between 1671
Arith-
metic." and 1677 (though it was not published till 1690[3],
1690. two years after the author's death), considers the
example set by Holland in the matter of toleration,
and its effects.   The Dutch granted liberty of conscience, he supposes, because "they themselves broke
with Spain to avoid the imposition of the clergy";
because the dissenters are usually sober and industrious; because no man can believe what he
pleases, "and to force men to say they believe what
they do not, is vain, absurd, and without honour to
God"; because they were conscious of fallibility;
because where most endeavours have been made to
preserve uniformity, heterodoxy has most abounded;
because, it being natural for men to differ, there
must be some heterodox; and because of the external
similarity between the positions of the dissenters and
of the primitive Christians.   He makes the further
observation that the trade of all countries is chiefly
managed by the heterodox; "from whence it follows
that for the advancement of trade, if that be a

[1] Christie's *Life of the first Earl of Shaftesbury*, vol. II.,
Appendix I., p. v, n.
[2] Recently reprinted in Aitken's *Later Stuart Tracts*, pp. 1–67.
[3] A spurious edition appeared in 1683.   Aitken.

sufficient reason, indulgence must be granted in matters of opinion: though licentious actings, as even in Holland, be restrained by force[1]."

The example of Holland was also held up in "A Letter from Holland touching Liberty of Conscience" written in 1688. Toleration is advocated, without reference to contemporary English politics, as having been beneficial to "this Commonwealth," because by providing a refuge for the persecuted it attracts population, and the persons thus attracted are generally the most sober and industrious. A pointed example is given in the contributions made to the growth of Amsterdam by the persecutions conducted by Mary and by Laud (2). Religious liberty also, the author continues, encourages people to be more industrious and "more freely to venture their stocks [capital] in trade," and takes away all colour for faction or rebellion (3). The question is dealt with mainly from the point of view of trade and industry in England and Holland; and it is hinted that France (though France is not mentioned by name) will suffer commercially from the establishment of toleration in England. The tone is purely worldly, and quite in keeping with that general change of feeling which in the latter half of the seventeenth century was making commerce, instead of religion, the matter of primary importance in politics and the cause of wars[2].

"A Letter from Holland." 1688.

---

[1] Aitken, 20–2.

[2] The author of this pamphlet pays a hardly deserved tribute to the much-abused British climate as "a Climate where they shall never need Stoves in the Winter nor Grotta's (*sic*) in the Summer" (4).

*Temple:
"Observations on
the United
Provinces."
1672.*

Sir William Temple, for some time English ambassador at the Hague, put in a plea for toleration in his " Observations on the United Provinces of the Netherlands[1]," published in 1672. The ends of religion, he said, were two—our happiness hereafter, and our happiness here. " Now our way to future happiness has been perpetually disputed throughout the world, and must be left at last to the impressions made upon every man's belief and conscience....For belief is no more in a man's power than his stature, or his features." Those who say that their opponents must inform themselves mean that they must go on doing it till they agree with them. He could not understand why such great stress was laid by religious men upon "points of belief which men never have agreed in, and so little upon those of virtue and morality in which they have hardly ever disagreed. Nor, why a state should venture the subversion of their peace and order, which are certain goods, and so universally esteemed, for their propagation of uncertain or contested opinions."

*Seculariz-
ation of
persecu-
tion.*

Concern for another world was being withdrawn from practical politics. Political order and commercial prosperity were at least recognizable and within the scope of civil government; men began more and more to doubt whether the same was true

---

[1] Chapters 5 and 6 quoted in *A Collection of Testimonies in favour of Religious Liberty*, 1790, pp. 62–4. Temple had been for two years a pupil of Cudworth at Emmanuel College, Cambridge. His election as M.P. for the University in 1679 was unsuccessfully opposed by Peter Gunning, Bishop of Ely, because of this expression of his views in favour of toleration. *Dictionary of National Biography*.

of other men's relations with their Maker. And though this secular attitude was bound to make for toleration, it was not confined to writers on the tolerant side alone. Whilst they advocated toleration as a means of turning disorder into quiet, their opponents argued for persecution as the only means by which disorder could be kept in check.

Indeed the case of the Dissenters had never given much scope for the action of the religious and theological motives, the latter of which is practically absent from the controversy. The New Testament indeed was wrested into giving persecution the sanction of a divine command, but none save extremists could consider that the very small actual differences which divided the mass of Dissenters from the Church involved either disparagement to the Creator or serious danger to the soul. In the case of persons denying Christianity or the doctrine of the Trinity, the religious motive at any rate survived a good deal longer ; but, as concerned the Dissenters, the other-worldly motives, if they may be so described, were largely excluded owing to the material agreement of the parties on all save the questions of church-government and ritual.

Moreover, since these questions are not directly decided by Scripture, Protestants, who disclaimed infallibility, could not without inconsistency plead the certainty of the truth of their doctrine upon them as a justification for persecution; and though men are by no means always consistent, the inconsistency in this case, eagerly pointed out by those interested and by impartial witnesses, was too glaring

not to be seen at length. Persecutors were more
and more compelled to rely on mere worldly considerations, and persecution which had claimed to
stand for the honour of the Almighty, the salvation
of men's souls, and the purity of the Church, was
degenerating into a mere matter of police.

Relations of church and state.   It was not merely among laymen that it was so
regarded. The Church had made herself the willing
handmaid of the state, and, in return for the oppression of the Dissenters, constituted herself the
champion of the existing order. Each trespassed
in the other's sphere : the state refused to grant
religious liberty ; the Church inculcated, as part of
Christianity, doctrines inconsistent with the continuance of civil liberty. The state undertook to
maintain the ecclesiastical order ; the Church undertook police-duties. Thus we find the secular aspect
of the question clearly exemplified in the ablest
statement of the theory of persecution made in the
Parker : "Dis-course of Ecclesias-tical Polity." 1669?–70[1].   period. This was "A Discourse of Ecclesiastical
Polity," by Samuel Parker, the successor of Thomas
Tomkins as chaplain to Archbishop Sheldon[2]. He
begins with "A general account of the necessity of
sovereignty over conscience." Conscience, he asserts,
Necessity of sove-reignty over con-science.   is what has most troubled governments, and rivalled
princes in their supremacy. Everything any man

[1] The title-page bears the date 1670, but Owen's reply *Truth and Innocence vindicated* (see p. 168) is dated 1669.

[2] Parker as a young man at Oxford had held pronounced
Puritan views ; but these underwent considerable modification
after the Restoration, and he took orders in 1664. In 1670 he
was appointed Archdeacon of Canterbury, perhaps as a reward for
his *Discourse.*

has a mind to is his conscience, and for men to claim
supremacy for conscience is to defy the princes'
authority and to acknowledge no governor but
themselves (4, 6, 7).   This being so, the supreme
magistrate must be vested with a power to govern
the consciences of his subjects with regard to religion; and his power over conscience in matters
of divine worship is identical with that over conscience in matters of morality and all other affairs
of religion.   The prime end of government is the
peace of the commonwealth, and this can never
be effectively secured unless religion be subject
to the authority of the supreme power (10, 11).
Carried away by the memory of the obstinacy
shown, and the disorders caused, by the sectaries,
Parker declares that it is an incomparably harder
task to restrain extravagances of zeal than those
of lewdness and debauchery; and proceeds to
draw the not very obvious conclusion that there
is as much need to suppress zeal as to suppress
immorality.   Indeed, he continues, remiss government of conscience is the most fatal miscarriage
in all commonwealths, and impunity of offenders
against ecclesiastical laws the worst sort of toleration.   "It were better to grant an uncontrolled
liberty by declaring for it, than, after having
declared against it, to grant it by silence and impunity" (18–20)—presumably a reference to the
intermittently tolerant policy of Charles and the
Cabal.   Religious affairs, Parker continues, must be
submitted to the supreme civil power and not to
another: otherwise subjects would be "obliged to"

contradictory commands. All supreme power, both in civil and in ecclesiastical affairs, issues from the same original, and is based on the necessity of a supreme power to decide the quarrels and controversies resulting from the passions, appetites, and follies of men (25–8). Here is something like Hobbes' doctrine of the social contract by which a sovereign was created to save men from the horrors of the state of nature. But Parker steers clear of any view which would derive sovereignty, however remotely, from the people[1], and finds the origin of monarchy in paternal authority, which is the source of all government both civil and ecclesiastical[2] (31). By some ingenious rather than capable reasoning, he easily finds that Scripture supports his intolerant views; and secure of the divine sanction he returns to the political question, and proposes a dilemma for the tolerationists. Upon their principles a prince must be either a tyrant or impotent—a tyrant if he exerts a power over conscience to which he has, *ex hypothesi*, no right, impotent if he allows his subjects to follow the dictates of their consciences. So strongly does Parker feel the importance of religion as a political bond that he implies that ecclesiastical authority is more valuable to a ruler than the power of the militia or the prerogative of ratifying civil laws (63)[3].

[1] Compare L'Estrange, p. 120.

[2] Elsewhere, however, he speaks of government as instituted only in order to the common good : see p. 164.

[3] Cf. Charles I's statement that episcopacy would sooner bring back to him the control of the militia, than the control of the

In his second chapter, a "More Particular account of the Nature and Necessity of a Sovereign Power in Matters of Religion," Parker further develops the analogy between worship and morals which he has already put forward. Stress upon the importance of morality, which we have seen as one of the forces making for toleration, does duty in his hands on the other side. The duties of morality, he says, are "as great and material parts of religion, as pleasing to God, and as indispensably necessary to salvation as any way of worship in the world"; all religion indeed, must be resolved into enthusiasm or morality. It follows (since the magistrate's right to control matters of morality is admitted), that every man's conscience is and must be subject to the commands of lawful superiors in the most important matters of religion; it is strange therefore that men should wish to exempt its means and subordinate instruments from the same authority. As the magistrate may enjoin anything in morality that contradicts not the ends of morality, so may he in religious worship, if he does not oppose its design. He may command anything in the worship of God that does not tend to debauch men's practices, or their conceptions of the Deity: all the subordinate duties both of morality and of religious worship are equally subject to the determinations of human authority (67 f.).

Analogy between worship and morality.

This specious analogy is, of course, faulty and misleading. The state enjoins obedience to certain

(The analogy examined.)

militia episcopacy. Hallam, *Constitutional History*, II. 186, ch. 10, part I., 3 vols., Murray, 1897.

moral laws, not because they are moral laws, but
as part of its duty to maintain the public peace
and order, to protect the civil rights of individual
citizens, and to promote their material welfare.   It
punishes a man, for instance, for obtaining money
under false pretences, because he thus inflicts material
damage upon a fellow-citizen, but it does not punish
a man merely for telling a lie.   This principle is not
undeviatingly followed, but, speaking generally, the
state is not a guardian of morality as such, but
interferes in moral questions as a rule only as protector or reformer of the social structure.   If then
we are to press the analogy between morality and
worship, it may interfere in the latter, too, in this
capacity only; that is, not at all with worship as
such, but only when worship involves actions which
are otherwise punishable as undermining the structure of society in general or of the state.

It is true that there is a stage in social evolution
in which community of religion is extremely important to a state.   But what men like Parker, not
unnaturally, failed to see was that even so it is
not mere religious diversity which is inimical to
solidarity, but the disintegrating force of the passion
thereby provoked in intolerant spirits.   But if the
intolerance of the public mind becomes, from one
cause or another, less actively violent, solidarity
becomes proportionately less dependent on religious
unity, and therefore persecution gradually ceases to
be politically advantageous.   Thus the state, con-
tinuing to persecute while the persecuting spirit
is on the wane, may actually come to be the

disturber, in this particular respect, of the public peace which it is the object of its existence to preserve. It appears that this position had already been reached in England at this time, so that Parker's analogy, even if correctly conceived, could only be applicable to a stage of evolution already passed.

Dealing in his third chapter with "the Inward *Identifica-*
Actions of the Mind, and Matters of Mere Con- *tion of conscience*
science," Parker, as might have been expected, *and judg-ment.*
makes the usual vicious identification of liberty of
conscience with liberty of intellect. Of conscience
he says "the commands of lawful authority are so
far from invading its proper liberty, that they cannot
reach it"; "mankind therefore have the same natural
right to liberty of conscience in matters of religious
worship as in affairs of justice and honesty, that is,
a liberty of judgment, but not of practice"; and
practice includes "venting" such wild opinions
as tend to the disturbance of the public peace
(91-2).

Thus far Parker has, in the main, reproduced *Attack on*
the views of Hobbes, and the natural climax of his *Hobbes' views on*
system would seem to be Hobbism pure and simple. *morality,*
It was not without justice that he was afterwards
described as "the young Leviathan that followed
Hobs[1]." But though he has assumed that the
magistrate has power over his subjects' consciences,
Parker is not prepared to assign to him the source
of morality, the principle of which he undertakes
to vindicate "against Mr Hobs, with a full con-

[1] John Humfrey, *Free Thoughts* (1710), 56. See p. 300.

futation of his whole hypothesis of government[1]."
"No circumstances," he declares roundly, "can alter
the principles of prime and essential rectitude," and
every man has "a natural right to be virtuous,...not
so much because subjects are in anything free from
the claims of the supreme power on earth, as because
they are subject to a Superior in heaven" (113).
Hobbes did, indeed, recognize, in theory, immutable
and eternal laws of morality; but in practice his
moral sanction was derived from the command of
the sovereign, and therefore ultimately from the
compact into which men entered with one another
to obey the sovereign. The weakness of this theory
as a source of moral obligation is seized upon by
Parker. To remove obligations antecedent to human
laws, he points out, is to remove the only obligation
to submit to those laws (114). "If private interest
be the only reason and enforcement of the laws of
nature, men will have no other reason to obey their
constitutions than what will as strongly oblige to
break them." "If justice and fidelity be not supposed to be the law and duty of our natures, no
covenants are of power enough to bring us under
any obligation to them" (130, 132). Apparently
Parker did not see that in refuting Hobbes he was
undermining his own system. But, clearly, the more
he insisted on the priority of morality to law, the
less tenable he made his theory as to the extravagant claims of the ruler. But in the elaboration
of political philosophy one of the greatest difficulties
encountered was that of fixing the relations of

[1] Heading of ch. 4.

politics to religion and morality; and Parker, not seeing clearly the issues involved, attempted to retain Hobbes's superstructure while repudiating his foundations.

However, having despatched the Leviathan to his own satisfaction, Parker proceeds to "A Confutation of the Consequences that some men draw from Mr. Hobs's Principles in behalf of Liberty of Conscience[1]." He complains that "a belief of the indifferency, or rather imposture, of all religion is *and the* now made the most effectual (not to say most *indiffer-* fashionable) argument for liberty of conscience": for *religions.* if no obligations at all lie upon men except the will of the sovereign, then religions are in reality nothing but cheats and impostures—tales publicly allowed and encouraged, to awe the common people to obedience; and it is immaterial which imposture princes single out for their people to befool themselves with, nor is it policy for them to side with one party more than another and so exasperate some of their subjects (137–9). In reality, he says, it is very important what religion is taught in a state; and he adds the characteristic reason that some are peculiarly advantageous to the ends of government and others tend to its disturbance (144). What follows is clearly an unjustifiable generalization from the Great Rebellion and the Interregnum, which the royalist churchmen either could not or would not realize to have been produced by an exceptional combination of circumstances and not merely by religious causes. Parker lays it down

[1] Heading of ch. 5.

*Govern-
ment and
religious
sects.*

that sedition always goes with fanaticism. "To
permit different sects of religion in a commonwealth
is only to keep up so many pretences and occasions
for public disturbance": if opposing religious sects
are tolerated, "whenever the grandees fall out, 'tis
but heading one of these, and there is an army."
Unless a standing army is kept up, "indulgence to
dissenting zealots does but expose the State to the
perpetual squabble and wars of religion." Toleration, indeed, might be possible if it were used
modestly, but human nature renders this impossible: similarly, men might be left to be a law
unto themselves if they were as wise and honest
as Socrates (154–62).

Turning to consider "the power of the civil
magistrate in things undetermined by the Word of
God[1]," Parker asserts that the main objection to
the magistrate's power in religion, viz. that he may
use it to command something sinful, lies equally
strongly against his power in civil affairs and all
government whatever. It is true that ecclesiastical
jurisdiction may be abused, but even so it is less
mischievous than liberty of conscience. It often
happens that it is necessary to punish men who
have innocently adopted error; but they must suffer
for the public good (210–20).

This admission we may regard as a hopeful sign.
When the theory of persecution has reached the
point of punishing innocent persons for purely
political ends, we are not far from toleration; for it
will not be long before it dawns upon men that the

[1] Heading of ch. 6.

protection of the innocent is one of the ends of the state.

In his eighth chapter, Parker returns to the *Conscience and the law.* opposition between the respective claims of conscience and of the law. If, he says, tenderness of conscience be a sufficient excuse for disobedience, it is a destruction of the force of laws, giving every man liberty to exempt himself (269). This, of course, is perfectly true. As Professor Ritchie says: " The assertion of a ' Universal Right of Conscience ' in any absolute and indefeasible sense would oblige a government to take the word of every individual for his own sincerity in saying what his conscience ordained. If we refuse to allow the individual to judge in his own case (as every well-regulated society must in a great many instances refuse to do), we give up any absolute right of individual conscience, and fall back upon the authority of the legislature and the law courts[1]." But what the legislature is unable to concede in principle, it should concede as far as possible in fact, by reducing to a minimum the possibility of friction between statutory obligations and the moral sense of any members of the community; that is, by eliminating such possibility altogether save in cases where it inevitably arises from the faithful discharge of the state's legitimate secular functions. It is the recognition of this fact which is responsible for the change in the attitude of the state between Parker's day and our own. The spirit of reverence for authority which the reaction from innovations of the " late troubles "

[1] *Natural Rights*, 158-9.

produced, showed itself in an exaggerated respect
for the law. "Doubts and scruples," Parker declares,
"are outweighed by the obligations of the law:...
unless I am absolutely certain that the law is evil,
I am sure disobedience to it is." Obedience to
authority he held forth as one of the greatest and
most indispensable duties of mankind (286 f.). "In
cases and disputes of a public concern, private men
...are not to be directed by their own judgments...
but by the commands and determinations of the
public conscience." The imposer of the command
is responsible: the subject's duty is to obey. In
all such matters the commands of public authority
are the supreme rules of conscience (368–9). How
this pronouncement is compatible with due regard
to the "principles of prime and essential rectitude";
and where the point lies at which those principles
assert themselves at the expense of the obligation
to obey the public authority; and by what means
the position of that point is to be ascertained—to
all these obvious, awkward, and pertinent questions
Parker has no real answer. Men should submit
themselves, he says, except in matters of indispensable duty (which unfortunately he does not specify),
to the public judgment, because of their obligation to
advance the welfare of mankind and particularly of
the society they live in—an obligation antecedent
to those of government, which is instituted only in
order to the common good. Though we are not to
submit our understandings to any human power,
yet we are to submit them to the fundamental laws
of charity (314–6). Parker in effect assumes that

the will of his sovereign in some way reflects the
general will (else it is a mere mockery to describe
him as the "public conscience" and the "public
judgment"), and that government is not only instituted in order to the common good, but consistently
exercised in such a way that obedience is always
more conducive to that end than resistance: and
both these assumptions are certainly untrue.

Parker's Ecclesiastical Polity brings out clearly *Conse-*
how damaging was the legacy of the Great Rebellion *quences
to the Dis-*
to the Dissenters. This may be seen in two distinct *senters of
the Great*
respects. In the first place it caused an almost *Rebellion.*
indissoluble union in the minds of men between *(1) Identification of*
the ideas of Dissent and of sedition. The religious *Dissent*
differences which had played so large a part in *with
sedition.*
bringing about the Civil War seem to have entirely
eclipsed in the general imagination the other causes
that were at work, and to have been held responsible
for all that followed[1]. Hence it was concluded that
sedition was of the essence of Dissent; laws were
made against the Dissenters as being seditious,
and were held to be justified by their non-sub-
mission; for was not this proof of their sedition, and

[1] Sir Frederick Pollock well points out that when men are
discontented with the government they live under, and the church
is part of this, their discontent is directed against the church.
Hence arise sectarianism and infidelity. "It is both natural and
convenient for Churchmen to invert the real order of cause and
effect, and assign the origin of every general disorder to the heresy
and infidelity which is in truth only a symptom of it." *The
Theory of Persecution* in *Essays in Jurisprudence and Ethics,*
171. This, however, is only partially applicable to the present
case, for Puritanism was by no means "only a symptom" of
disorder.

even sedition itself? And this brings us to the second point in which the memory of "the late troubles" was a ruinous heritage for the Dissenters.

(2) *Exaggerated reverence for the law.* The failure of an illegal revolution which had not spared the head of the state, in flagrant defiance of the principles of law and justice, and the aversion with which the government subsequently set up was regarded, stimulated to intensity the reverence felt for the law, as such. Bitter experience of the results of breaking with the law, made men shy of tampering with it, and unwilling to look behind it[1]. In some quarters obedience to the law came to be looked upon almost as one of the rudimentary virtues: it was as though the nation existed for the law and not the law for the nation. In the face of this attitude it was not relevant to urge that the Dissenters as a body were perfectly loyal and that their principles were subversive neither of monarchy nor of order; or to point out how circumstances had changed since 1641, and that the Presbyterians at any rate had had nothing to do either with the sectaries or with the execution of Charles I; or to show that during the brief periods of toleration accorded no evil results had ensued, and that it was persecution and not toleration that caused disturbance. The appeals to reason and to experience alike were stifled. On the side of this reverence for the law was thrown the great influence

[1] It made prominent and general a current of thought which it did not originate, and which may be seen earlier in the legalism of Coke, and in the demand, made by both the Levellers and Harrington, that the government should be by laws and not by men.

of Hobbes; and while abusive denunciations were
cast upon the philosopher, immense contributions
were levied from his philosophy.

Parker's elaborate exposition of the theory of
persecution was naturally not allowed to go unchallenged. In an anonymous pamphlet entitled
"A Case of Conscience...together with Animad- *"Animad-*
versions on a new book entitled Ecclesiastical Polity; *versions*
...as also A Peaceable Dissertation," the first part *on a new book."*
is an answer to Patrick's "Friendly Debate[1]," which *1669.*
does not concern us; the third is the comment upon
Wolseley's "Liberty of Conscience," which we have
already considered[2]; and the second is an answer
to Parker. How, it is asked, shall a man be subject
to the magistrate for conscience' sake, if the command of conscience has not in it a superior and
more prevalent power than his? (9). To Parker's
analogy between moral and religious matters, it is
replied that the magistrate has indeed some power
in religion as in morals, but he has power over
conscience in neither: the subject must not obey
in either case if the command is contrary to his
conscience, the dictates of which he must follow in
his outward as well as his inward acts (9–10).
Parker's refutation of Hobbes, it is also pointed
out, recoils upon himself, for if nothing intrinsically
evil may be commanded, what becomes of the magistrate's power over conscience? (11).

A more weighty indictment came from the in-

---

[1] An unsympathetic and strongly anti-Nonconformist work,
published in 1669, not strictly relevant to our subject.

[2] See pp. 141–4.

[*Owen*]:
"*Truth
and Inno-
cence Vin-
dicated.*"
1669.
defatigable John Owen, in his "Truth and Innocence Vindicated." In his survey of Parker's first chapter he concedes that the magistrate has all the power necessary to preserve the public peace; but what, he asks, is the extent of that power? Does it, for instance, include the power of determining whether there is a God or no? whether any religion is needful in and useful to the world? and, if so, then to determine what all subjects shall believe and practice from first to last in the whole of it? His answer is that the nature of government itself "hath nothing belonging unto it but what inseparably accompanieth mankind as sociable"; and that there is a determination of what is true and what is false in religion, which gives obligations or liberty to men's consciences antecedent to the imposition of the magistrate (92–4, 100–1). He too falls upon the inconsistency of Parker in allowing that it is the subject's duty to disobey the magistrate in the cause of the moral virtues (102). Parker, he goes on to assert, ascribes more authority to the magistrate than to Christ. "The power and authority here ascribed unto princes is none other but that which is claimed by the Pope of Rome (with some few enlargements) and appropriated unto him by his canonists and courtiers" (103–7, 116). Thus Popery became an accusation mutually exchanged between the upholders and the impugners of the doctrine of divine right[1].

Owen proceeds with the pertinent question, why should not the sense of duty, which is to make men conform contrary to their consciences in the interest

[1] See p. 126.

of the public peace, prevent them, if given liberty
of conscience, from disturbing the public peace?
(121). On Parker's principles, he points out, a
Christian probably may conform in Turkey, and
certainly a Protestant may in Roman Catholic
countries (127). The public peace is much better
founded on openness, plainness of heart, sincerity
and honesty, and a respect for God in all things,
than on principles such as these (129).

On Parker's comparison between religion and
morals, he denies that the right to control morals
implies the right to control worship. The two
things are different in kind: on the first all are
agreed, on the second there is no agreement: the
magistrate cannot mistake about morals, but all
differ about worship. And even so the power of the
magistrate over moral virtues is not such as to make
virtue what was not virtue before; mankind is
obliged to observe all moral virtues antecedently
to the command of the magistrate, nor can the
magistrate give men dispensation from the performance of them (232–48).

As to the severance made by Parker between
judgment and practice, Owen declares that this
leads to "atheism and thereby the subversion of
all religion and government in the world." Liberty
of acting according to conscience should be granted
to all whose principles are not inconsistent with
public tranquillity or opposite to the principal truths
and main duties of religion, on grounds of "natural
right, justice and equity, religion, conscience, God
Himself in all, and His voice in the hearts of all
unprejudiced persons" (256–8). The admission that

men are subject to a power in heaven superior to the magistrate should be extended to all things in which men should have regard to that power; and then all the preceding chapters fall to the ground (283).

Owen sums up as follows:—" The principal design of the treatise thus far surveyed, is to persuade or seduce sovereign princes or supreme magistrates unto two evils that are indeed inseparable, and equally pernicious to themselves and others. The one of these is to invade or usurp the throne of God; and the other, to behave themselves therein unlike him. And where one leads the way the other will assuredly follow" (383).

Improved position of the Dissenters after the fall of Clarendon.

Since the fall of Clarendon, as has been already mentioned, the position of the Dissenters had been somewhat improved. No new persecuting acts had been passed, the administration of the existing acts was from time to time practically suspended (the Conventicle Act indeed had expired in 1668[1]), and there were among the King's advisers open advocates of toleration, of which Charles had more than once declared himself in favour. A scheme, usually

Wilkins' scheme.

associated with the name of Dr Wilkins[2], who became Bishop of Chester in 1668, including both comprehension and toleration, had been drawn up. But when Charles spoke in favour of toleration, the

1667.

Commons petitioned for the enforcement of the penal laws; and when Wilkins' scheme was drafted, the

Intolerance of Parliament, 1668.

Commons decided that no bill having comprehension for its object should be received. At the opening of

[1] Pepys' *Diary*, Aug. 11, 1668.

[2] " He married Cromwell's sister; but made no other use of that alliance but to do good offices." Burnet, *History of My Own Time*, I. 321 (? 322).

Parliament in 1670, Charles tacitly dropped his idea of toleration, and Parliament promptly set to work to provide a successor to the defunct Conventicle Act.

In these circumstances John Owen returned once more to the charge with a tract entitled "The State of the Kingdom, with respect to the present Bill against Conventicles[1]." He appealed at once to the motives most likely to have influence. The kingdom, he urged, was in peace and quietness; the bill if passed would produce disorder in trade by the ruin of many merchants, clothiers and other traders, and by the failure of mutual trust, that is, the shaking of credit. There was no reason to fear sedition if it should not be passed, and the uniformity which it aimed at would be no compensation for the trouble caused; by persecution neither religion nor conformity is promoted. "Many wise and judicious magistrates," he added, "have openly declined what lieth in them, all engagements in these persecutions[2]." This statement is borne out by the fact that a clause was inserted in the act to the effect that justices of the peace and chief magistrates not performing their duty should be fined £100[3]. The parliamentary zeal for persecution was outrunning the popular feeling

Second Conventicle Act, 1670, protested against by Owen: "The State of the Kingdom," 1670,

---

[1] *Works*, vol. xxi. pp. 457–71.   [2] *Ibid.* 459-64.

[3] Second Conventicle Act: see Appendix III. Similar clauses contemplating neglect of duty by sheriffs, officers, and gaolers appeared in the first Conventicle Act 1664, 16 Cha. II, c. 4. According to Neal, on the passing of the second Conventicle Act, "many honest men who would not be the instruments of such severities quitted the Bench." *History of the Puritans*, iv. 393–4 (5 vols. London, 1822).

which alone could keep it alive under a free government. Unfortunately it was by no means outrunning *but en-* the feeling of the leaders of the Church. Archbishop *dorsed by* Sheldon sent a circular letter to all the bishops of *Sheldon's* *circular* his province strongly recommending the diligent *letter.* execution of this merciless law as being " to the glory of God, the welfare of the Church, the praise of His Majesty and Government, and the happiness of the whole kingdom[1]." He was still able to allege the religious and ecclesiastical reasons for an act passed by Parliament as a matter of political expediency. In any case the persecution was very bitter. According to one account the act "was so severely executed that there was hardly a conventicle to be heard of all over England[2]." This, however, would seem either to be an exaggeration, or to describe a purely temporary state of affairs: the act was by no means everywhere persistently enforced[3].

[Penn]: Within a year of the passing of the Second *" The* *Great Case* Conventicle Act appeared the completest exposition *of Liberty* of the theory of toleration in our present period. *of Con-* *science."* " The Great Case of Liberty of Conscience Once more *1671.* Briefly Debated and Defended," was written by the Quaker, William Penn, and was dated, in a manner most fitting a plea for liberty, from Newgate, where the author was a prisoner.

(Attitude The advocacy of toleration on the part of the *of the* *Quakers* Quakers sprang, it should be noticed, not from the *on tolera-* fact that they were persecuted, but directly from *tion.)* their religious views. To a believer in the inner

---

[1] Neal, *History of the Puritans,* iv. 396.   [2] *Ibid.* 394.

[3] Frank Bate, *The Declaration of Indulgence 1672,* 70.

light, the prescription of any particular form of religion
by authority must constitute a violation of an indefeasible right of man, and thus the Quaker held on
a priori grounds a belief in toleration to which other
parties were slowly and reluctantly approximating
under the force of circumstances[1].   Penn set himself
in methodical manner to demonstrate certain propositions, of which the first was that imposition,
restraint, and persecution for matters relating to the
conscience directly invade the Divine Prerogative ;
in proof of which he asserted that government over
conscience is the incommunicable right of God, that
it constitutes a claim to infallibility, and that the
operation of God's spirit alone can beget faith
(12–14).   His second proposition was that the use
of force in matters of faith and worship involves
the overthrow of the Christian religion ; for Christ's
kingdom is spiritual, not carnal, and restraint and
persecution are unchristian, obstruct the promoting of the Christian religion by preventing
the "further informing and reforming" of those
who use them[2], and prevent many from receiving
eternal rewards, for the recompense of slavish religion
is condemnation (14–16).   Thirdly, he declared imposition, restraint, and persecution repugnant to the
plain testimonies and precepts of the Scriptures (16).
Fourthly, that they are destructive both of "the
great privilege of nature" and of the principle of

[1] G. M. Trevelyan, *England under the Stuarts*, 436 n.

[2] Penn put this point—the obstruction offered to truth by
persecution—better in his *Address to Protestants* (see p. 178).
"God did never ask men leave to introduce truth, or make further
discoveries of his mind to the world," p. 200.

reason—of "the great privilege of nature" because
they invade the natural right to liberty of one's
fellow-creatures, rob mankind of the use and benefit
of their natural intuition of God, and destroy
all natural affection:—of the principle of reason,
because they are unreasonable in view of confessed
fallibility, and because we cannot judge, will, and
believe against our understanding: indeed a man
cannot be said to have any religion that takes it
by another man's choice; and if he that acts doubt-
fully is damned, how much more he that conforms
against his judgment? The principle of reason is
further violated in that all hopes of recompense in
the next world are frustrated, because men's acts,
if compelled by fear of penalties, are unavoidable,
and therefore without merit. All true religion is
subverted, "for where men believe, not because it is
true, but because they are required to do so, there
they will unbelieve, not because 'tis false, but so
commanded by their superiors." Persecution, too,
unmans men by taking away their understanding,
reason, judgment, and faith: "shall men suffer for
not doing what they cannot do? Must they be
persecuted here if they do not go against their
conscience, and punished hereafter if they do?"
Lastly, there is no adequation of means, viz. fines
and imprisonments, to the end, viz. the conformity
of judgments and understandings (19–23).

Penn's fifth proposition was that force in matters
relating to conscience carries a plain contradiction
to government in the nature, execution, and end
of it. These last he dealt with separately. The

nature of government, he said, is justice, and persecution contradicts it, because justice demands of one to do as one would be done by; because the Nonconformists were overcharged for the necessities of government, but not protected; and because corporal penalties are disproportionate to a purely intellectual fault (23–4). The execution of government is prudence, and persecution contradicts it, because the persecuting laws are temporary and alterable and therefore must not be regarded as immutable[1]; because a time of connivance has brought "no ill success to public affairs"; and because persecution causes resentment. Moreover the prudential considerations alleged in favour of persecution would equally justify it in France and Constantinople, and would have prevented the Reformation. Persecutors cannot be sure of the friendship of those who are brought to a hypocritical conformity; and persecution not only damages the revenue and power of a country, but is ineffective. "Force never yet made either a good Christian or a good subject" (24–8). Lastly, the end of government is felicity, and persecution contradicts it because by causing disturbances peace is broken, plenty is converted into poverty, and unity is destroyed (28–9).

Summing up the case against persecution as inimical to government, Penn wrote "The single

[1] This, as Penn puts it, is not strictly logical. It was meant as a protest against the exaggerated reverence for the law, as such, which we have seen in Parker's *Ecclesiastical Polity* (see pp. 164, 166) and elsewhere, which led men to give the mere fact of the existence of the persecuting laws as an ultimate reason for persecution. Cf. p. 188 and n.

question to be resolved in the case, briefly will be this. Whether any visible authority (being founded in its primitive institution upon those fundamental laws that inviolably preserve the people in all their just rights and privileges) may invalidate all or any of the said laws, without an implicit shaking of its own foundation, and a clear overthrow of its own constitution and government, and so reduce them to their *Statu* (sic) *quo prius*, or first principles : the resolution is every man's at his own pleasure " (30).

He proceeded to point out that the Dissenters were in the same position as that which the Protestants had occupied at the Reformation; both must be justified or both condemned : moreover, wars and revolutions were caused, not by toleration, but by intolerance (32, 34). Ancient and modern instances were given of the advantages of toleration, and various authorities were quoted in its favour, including Hammond and Taylor (39–43). Penn ended with a solemn disclaimer of seditious principles, and an assertion that in spite of persecution the Quakers must meet (48–9). In a postscript he maintained that the terms of the persecuting acts applied only to those who formed conspiracies under pretence of religion, and not to those who assembled really to worship, and on behalf of the Quakers disclaimed the terms used *seriatim*. To declare the Quakers' meetings, as such, seditious was, he justly claimed, simply a misuse of words; while to decide that Quakers' assemblies were not really for the worship of God was to assume more than papal power (51–4).

After this brief but comprehensive statement of

his views upon the question of toleration, Penn had little to do in later publications but to develop at greater length thoughts which he had already expressed. Four years after "The Great Case of Liberty of Conscience," appeared "England's Present *"England's* Interest Discovered," in which he laid further stress *Present* on the political and commercial reasons for toleration *Interest* which were more likely than theories of *a priori* *Discovered."* 1675. right to meet with favourable consideration. He urged the damage which persecution caused to trade, and the check which it offered to immigration : by increasing the number of beggars it would raise the poor-rate (42–4)[1]. Moreover, if a foreign country were to offer the Dissenters liberty of conscience, a million people might emigrate; it was by such methods that Holland had risen to greatness (44–5). Penn also enlarged upon the fact that the persecuting measures supposed to be the only defence against anarchy were really a source of insecurity to the government. The point at issue was, of course, whether or no the persecution was capable of bringing the whole nation into the Church. If it was, another bond of national unity would be formed, however variously the value of that bond might be estimated : but if it was not, it must be regarded not merely as a failure, but as positively destructive of the unity which it was designed to

[1] The special force of this objection lay in the fact that at this time the poor-rate was almost intolerably high: towards the end of the century Gregory King calculated that of a population of $5\frac{1}{2}$ millions about a quarter was more or less dependent on parochial relief. Cunningham, *Growth of English Industry and Commerce*, II. 572 (ed. 1903).

s.   12

promote, and a danger to that order which it was
designed to secure. Penn saw that the latter was
the truer view. "The interest of our English
Governors," he wrote, "is like to stand longer upon
the legs of the English people, than of the English
Church" (59). Severity was an inducement to
conspiracy, and united all other interests in opposition to the Church, while toleration would unite all
interests in support of the established order and
therefore would not make for Presbytery or Popery
(46–51). As a Quaker, Penn naturally opposed the
idea of comprehension of the Presbyterians, on the
ground that its aim was the suppression of the other
dissenting persuasions; he therefore tried to magnify
the differences between the Presbyterians and the
Church (50–2).

The Quakers were frequently confounded with
the Roman Catholics, and the sufferings inflicted on
the society by the anti-Romanist fanaticism of the
"Address
to Pro-
testants."
1679.
Popish Plot scare called forth from Penn his "Address
to Protestants on the Present Conjuncture,"—a survey
of all the evils under which the nation was suffering,—
in which he laid especial stress upon the necessity of
distinguishing between the provinces of church and
state—the things of Caesar and the things of God
(194–5), and repeated several arguments from his
previous pamphlets. Virtue, Truth, and Sincerity,
he found to be the only firm bond of human society
and more necessary to government than Opinion
(195).

It is possible that King Charles's motive in
dropping his advocacy of toleration at the opening

of Parliament in 1670[1], and in assenting to the
second Conventicle Act was not entirely a desire for
the money of which he was always more or less (and
at that particular juncture especially) in need. It is
quite in keeping with the zig-zag course of his
diplomatic chicanery that he should assent to a
bitter persecution in order to win the Dissenters
to the support of his long-cherished scheme of toleration in which the Roman Catholics should be included.
Be that as it may, in 1672 he issued his Declaration
of Indulgence suspending the execution of the penal
laws and granting rights of public worship in specially
licensed places to Protestant Nonconformists, and of
private worship to Roman Catholics[2]. The reasons
alleged are worth consideration. "It being evident
by the sad experience of twelve years, that there is
very little fruit of all these forcible courses, we think
ourselves obliged to make use of that supreme power
in ecclesiastical matters, which is not only inherent
in us but hath been declared and recognised to be
so by several statutes and acts of Parliament. And
therefore we do now accordingly issue out this our
royal declaration, as well for the quieting the minds
of our good subjects in these points, for inviting
strangers in this conjuncture to come and live under
us, and for the better encouragement of all to a
cheerful following of their trades and callings, from
whence we hope, by the blessing of God, to have many
good and happy advantages to our government; as
also for preventing for the future the danger that

*Declara-
tion of In-
dulgence.
1672.*

[1] See p. 171.
[2] The Declaration will be found in full in Grant Robertson,
Select Statutes, Cases and Documents, p. 42.

might otherwise arise from private meetings and
seditious conventicles."

The confession of the ineffectiveness of the persecution made clear an important point which was
as yet insufficiently realized. The recognition of
the permanence of Dissent is only one step short of
the recognition of its right to exist. For the rest
the Declaration is typical of the purely practical
considerations—political and commercial—by which,
rather than by the recognition of principles, the cause
of toleration was being advanced. We may perhaps
see in it the hand of Ashley, whose memorial to
Charles upon the subject of toleration has already
come under our notice[1], and whose support of the
Declaration won him the Earldom of Shaftesbury.

Charles compelled to withdraw it, owing to   But Parliament, which had itself but lately refused to grant toleration[2], was in no mood to coun-
tenance a grant of it by an unwarrantable stretch
of the royal prerogative; and on meeting in 1673 it
promptly compelled the withdrawal of the Declaration, in spite of Charles's expression in his opening
speech of determination to maintain it[3].

the fear of Popery, which found ex- pression in   The fear of Nonconformity had given way to
the fear of Popery. "The unnatural alliance with
France to destroy the Protestant State of Holland,
the presence of a standing army under officers whose
religion was suspect, the ill-concealed Romanism of

[1] See p. 149.
[2] See p. 170. It was, of course, the same Parliament which
had passed the Clarendon Code.
[3] On February 4th Charles said "And I will deal plainly with
you, I am resolved to stick to my Declaration": on March 8th he
cancelled it.

the Duke of York, who commanded our fleets, and
of Clifford who controlled our counsels, the abeyance
of the penal laws throughout the country, and the
'flaunting of Papists' at Court, all combined to
create a panic which for a few weeks overcame the
desire of pensioners to earn their reward, of Dissenters to enjoy the Declaration of Indulgence, and
of Anglicans to persecute Dissent[1]." These indications were indeed far short of the truth that Charles
had agreed with Louis XIV to establish Roman
Catholicism in England by French arms, but they
were enough to lead to the overthrow of that design.
The reply of Parliament to the Declaration of In- *the*
dulgence was the Test Act[2], which excluded all *Test Act.*
Roman Catholics from office, and the coercion of *1678.*
Charles into peace with Holland by the refusal of
supplies for an army which was regarded as a possible
menace to Protestantism and English liberty. Thus
the effect of the Declaration of Indulgence was
wholly disastrous to the Roman Catholics whom it
was intended to serve. The private worship which it
openly permitted had previously been connived at[3];
and for this merely temporary recognition a heavy
price was paid in the imposition of the test.
Churchman and Dissenter were temporarily at one
in face of the common enemy; on the one hand the
Dissenters supported the Test Act, on the other a
bill for the "Ease of Protestant Dissenters" (so great
a change had come over affairs since the second
Conventicle Act of 1670) was carried in the House

---

[1] G. M. Trevelyan, *England under the Stuarts*, 377.

[2] 25 Cha. II, cap. 2: see Appendix III.

[3] Frank Bate, *Declaration of Indulgence 1672*, 84.

of Commons.   But while the former passed into law,
the latter failed in the Upper House owing to the uncompromising hostility of the bishops.   Shaftesbury,
however, having discovered Charles's real designs,
had already made a sudden change of policy.   He
had pressed for the withdrawal of the Declaration
of Indulgence; he had vehemently supported the
Test Act; and now he set himself to organize
an anti-Romanist party in alliance with the Dissenters,—a party standing for toleration (now
confined to the Dissenters alone) and parliamentary
supremacy.

Charles turned to the Church of England;   Charles's Romanizing policy had failed, and
he abandoned his hopes of establishing Roman
Catholicism in England; but his hopes of exalting
his own power he did not abandon.   The Roman
Catholics being no longer available for the purpose,
he turned to the Church of England and gave his confidence to Danby, who, in opposition to Shaftesbury,
built up a party standing for intolerance and the
royal prerogative.

Thus the Declaration of Indulgence had proved
to be the signal for a complete change of the politico-
religious kaleidoscope.   Previously the Dissenters,
oppressed by an intolerant Parliament, had received
intermittent relief from Charles who hoped to make
them instruments in carrying out his Romanizing
plans: now they had the favour of a considerable
party in Parliament, but Charles, his Romanizing
plans having proved abortive, had no further use for
them, and gave his countenance to the Church
in the work of persecution.   And as the fear of
Popery subsided, zeal for the "ease of Protestant

Dissenters" subsided also, and the work of persecution proceeded apace.

But the effects of the Declaration of Indulgence could not be wholly undone. Charles had liberated a force which he could not recapture. A very large number of licenses had been issued for Nonconformist places of worship, and these were not finally recalled till 1675. Thus many congregations had a two or three years' breathing-space, and an opportunity was given the various Nonconformist bodies to organize themselves. Ordinations among the Presbyterians, which had not been held since the Restoration, were resumed. There seems to have been a considerable drift from the Church to the Dissenters, who were henceforth too strong for repressive measures to put them down[1]. *but the effects of the Declaration were permanent.*

And time was on the side of toleration. As the ineffectiveness of persecution became more and more apparent, and the vivid memory of the Cromwellian oppression grew fainter, and the palpable fact that the periods of toleration had not fulfilled the forebodings of the intolerant party became gradually more recognized (together with the natural corollary that the assumptions by which the persecution was justified were false), and, finally, as the century-old fear of Popery resumed the place in men's minds from which the fear of Nonconformity had only temporarily ousted it, the party for toleration could *Drift of opinion towards toleration.*

[1] Frank Bate, *Declaration of Indulgence 1672*, 140–2, and Introduction, ix, x. In Appendix VII. Mr Bate gives a list of about 2500 licenses. According to Evelyn, the Declaration acted "to the extreme weakening of the Church of England and its Episcopal government, as it was projected." *Diary*, Mar. 12, 1672.

not but grow in numbers and influence. Nonconformity was slowly winning its way to recognition as no passing craze which could be stamped out by prompt and active measures, or dangerous form of fanaticism inimical to the very structure of society, but as a permanent element in English religious life, the natural expression of the religious feeling of a considerable section of the English people.

[*Croft*]: "*The Naked Truth.*" 1675.

This movement of thought shows itself very clearly in the pamphlet entitled "The Naked Truth, or the True State of the Primitive Church," published in 1675. The author concealed his identity under the title of "An Humble Moderator," but was in reality no less a person than Herbert Croft, the Bishop of Hereford, who could now look back over a troubled life of more than seventy years. His father, a friend of Lord Herbert, had become a Roman Catholic late in life, and the son followed his example while still a boy. But after some years he returned to the English Church, and held various preferments. Of these he was deprived by the Rebellion, but the Restoration elevated him to the episcopate. Now in his old age he came forward as a peacemaker. In a preface addressed to the Lords and Commons assembled in Parliament, he urged that though unity was to be desired the laws had not produced the desired effect: meanwhile the divisions between English Protestants made for the growth of Popery, which in itself constituted a strong reason for peace. In a second preface addressed to the reader he laboured to free the Nonconformists from the charge of perverseness. Men, he said, might be divided upon religion to the extent of laying down their lives for different opinions, when their differences were due merely to education " having in their youth so imprinted their own opinions in their mind, as you may sooner separate their body than their opinion from their soul." " Those that have been educated," he continued, " in that way as to sit at Communion, and baptize their children without the Cross, had rather omit these sacraments than use kneeling or the Cross ; and those that have been educated in kneeling and crossing, though they acknowledge they are mere ceremonies indifferent, yet had rather omit the sacraments than omit the ceremonies, just as if a man had rather starve than eat bread baked in a pan, because he hath used bread baked in an oven. So that religion in many is merely their humour, fancy passeth for reason, and custom is more prevalent than any argument."

With regard to articles of faith, Croft pointed out that the Apostles' Creed was enough for the primitive church : what need was there of more now ? Even less sufficed Philip for the eunuch. The imposition " by zealous men " of " that which they conceived truth" on the Dissenters had caused furious wars, and such an act is " to promote the truth of the Gospel contrary to the laws of the Gospel, to break an evident commandment to establish a doubtful truth." " Men's understandings are as various as their speech or their countenance " : hence it is that there are understanding, moderate, and conscientious men alike among Papists[1], Lutherans, and Calvinists

[1] This admission is no doubt the result of Croft's knowledge of

(1, 2). As for the mysteries of Christianity, they are unintelligible to human reason and must not be elaborated by it: it is unsafe to speak of divine matters but in the very words of Scripture (4–5). And Croft pointed out that the Church was not actually, as was professed, suppressing seditious practices, but enforcing a confession of faith (8). He also put forward a dangerous Calvinistic argument: " 'Tis evident that upon preaching of the Gospel as many as were ordained by God to Eternal Life, believe: and surely those who are not ordained by God to Eternal Life can never be brought thither by the ordinance or power of man " (9).

" As to ceremonies," Croft said, " I wonder men of any tolerable discretion should be so eager either for or against them ": but he continued that all subjects are bound to conform to the ceremonies of that church whereof they are members, unless there be anything flatly against the Word of God; otherwise they break an evident commandment (for to disobey our superiors is directly against the Word of God) to satisfy themselves in a doubtful thing. At the same time parents ought not to provoke their children to disobedience by imposing unnecessary things and very offensive (15–16). To refuse to abandon one ceremony or one line of the Prayer Book to gain thousands of Nonconformists is the utmost of sectarianism and fanaticism (24). Finally, however, he advised the Nonconformists to submit,

the Roman Catholic Church from the inside. It did not, however, prevent him from taking energetic measures against Popery in his episcopal capacity.

because there is no scriptural authority for con-
demning any ceremony of the Church of England,
because it is safer to err by way of humility than by
way of pride, and because the separation was bringing
great mischief on the Church by contributing to the
advance of Popery (64–6).

The appeal to the common-sense aspect of the
question caused a considerable stir[1], and provoked a
storm of criticism. In 1676 appeared "Lex Talionis: *"Lex
or the Author of Naked Truth stript naked," an Talionis."
anonymous pamphlet variously ascribed to Peter 1676.*
Gunning, who had taken a prominent part in the
Savoy Conference and had just been appointed
Bishop of Ely; to William Lloyd, afterwards successively Bishop of S. Asaph (in which office he became
one of the famous seven Bishops), Lichfield and
Coventry, and Worcester; and to one Philip Fell, a
fellow of Eton College[2]. The point of view of the
author was that conformity was a duty which the
Nonconformists deliberately ignored. "The thing
complained of," he wrote, "is that men turn away
their faces, shut their eyes, and will not lay their
heads to consider what is set before them: and if
the immorality of error be once cured, there will be
a speedy account of its misadventures in speculation
and theory....The will of man has a higher pretence
to freedom than the intellect; tyranny can make me

[1] "The appearance of this book at such a time was like a
comet." Anthony Wood, quoted in *Dictionary of National Biography*, art. on Herbert Croft.

[2] Hunt, II. 13 n. ascribes it (? by confusion with Philip Fell) to
John Fell, Bishop of Oxford, 1676–86, and hero of the famous
rhyme "I do not like thee, Dr. Fell."

suffer, but cannot oblige me to approve, much less to
choose: and yet it is not impertinent or irrational
to require men to will, and what is more than that,
actually to perform their duty " (5).

The main point of " Naked Truth " had evidently
been quite wasted upon this writer, who was impervious to the lesson (which, after all, has not been
very widely learnt even yet) that there are many
important questions upon which men who differ will
never be brought to an agreement by mere consideration, and that there are fundamental differences
of temperament and mental outlook which argument
cannot reach. The pamphlet is largely devoted to
attacking Croft's reading of Church History and
displays on the whole a rather unintelligent conservatism. On the question of ceremonies, however,
a sensible and practical point is made, viz. that
concessions to Nonconformists would cause offence
to Conformists, and "surely the scandalizing those
who do their duty, by our breaking the laws, is a
greater mischief than to displease those who violate
their duty by our keeping the law " (20)[1].

[*Turner*]: A more formidable attack was " Animadversions
"*Animad-* upon a late Pamphlet entitled The Naked Truth,"
versions by Francis Turner, Master of St John's College, Cam-
upon a late bridge, afterwards Bishop of Ely, and, like Lloyd, one
Pamph- of the famous seven. He too charged the Noncon-
let." 1676. formists with wilful blindness. " God," he said, " is

---

[1] The use of the words "breaking" and "keeping" instead of
"altering" and "maintaining" characteristically illustrates the
prevalent tendency to regard the law as something ultimate and
immutable. Cf. p. 175 and n.

wanting to no man in necessaries: and the reasons
which help every man to see these truths, at least
when they are showed and pointed out to him, is a
vulgar, a popular thing....He that shuts his eyes yet
pretends to see clearly, is an hypocrite already: and
we that would oblige him to open his eyes, whether
he will or no, do not go the way to make him an
hypocrite, but a true convert from his sinful hypocrisy." Belief in the inability of a man to discern
fundamental truths when they are laid before his
eyes leads us "into the very dregs of Mr Hobbs's
divinity; that is fatality." For "he that believes not
shall be damned," therefore to assume that a man
cannot believe, is to assume that he cannot be saved
(12, 13). Consistently with this view the Dissenters
are to be forced into the Churches "that they may
hear our defences of an honest cause" (14). If,
Turner continued, a Christian magistrate might, as
Croft admitted, punish those that troubled the
Church of Christ with doctrines, contrary to the
clear text of Scripture and such as are destructive to
Christianity, who, on the hypothesis advanced in
"Naked Truth," should be judge of what is clear
and what is thus destructive? the party accused or
the civil magistrate? (13). This was an awkward
question. Croft had only looked at the present and
aimed at some formula calculated to secure the Dissenters from punishment; and for this purpose his
proposal was probably adequate, for none but a
bigoted minority could describe the differences of
the Dissenters from the Church as contrary to the
clear text or as destructive of Christianity; but as a

theory of toleration in general it was, as Turner's
question showed, seriously faulty in that there was
no guarantee of any general agreement as to the
exact limits set by this formula to the jurisdiction of
the civil power. The only remedy lay in the removal from that jurisdiction of all purely religious
questions[1].

On Croft's assertion that "our case is not in
repressing seditious practice, but enforcing a confession of faith, quite of another nature," Turner's
comment was "I say only this; the very act against
them calls them seditious conventicles: and openly
to break so many laws of the land after so many
reinforcements, is not this to be turbulent?" (15)—a
more than usually frank advocacy of the proverb,
"Give a dog a bad name and hang him."

The pamphlet largely deals with comprehension,
which is discounted on the grounds of introducing
confusion into the Church of England, and laying
her open to accusation by the Roman Catholics of
breaking with primitive tradition (46, 65)[2].

*Exclusive
state sup-
port sup-
posed to be
necessary
to the
Church.*
The intolerance of this pamphlet, as indeed the
general intolerance of the age, was largely due to
the fact that the recognition of a second form of

[1] Even so, of course, the difficulty is not completely overcome,
for it still rests with the civil power to decide what questions are
purely religious. It alone can fix in practice the limits of its own
jurisdiction. But the advantage of this arrangement is that the
room for difference of opinion on the question, though not
abolished, is reduced to a minimum.

*A Modest Survey of the most considerable things in a Discourse
Lately Published, entitled Naked Truth* by Gilbert Burnet, afterwards Bishop of Salisbury, contains some sensible reflections on
comprehension on similar lines.

worship by law was a thing hitherto unknown[1], and not only was considerable imaginative power necessary to conceive such a state of affairs at all, and considerable breadth of mind to conceive of it as good, but also a considerable amount of insight was required to see that it did not involve the fall of the established Church. For that was what seemed its natural implication to many who only knew of the English Church as bolstered up by persecuting laws, neither allowed nor attempting to stand by her own strength. And, as a matter of fact, the nearest approach to toleration yet seen in England had resulted in the parish churches being "filled with sectaries of all sorts, blasphemous and ignorant mechanics usurping the pulpits everywhere[2]," and preaching "feculent stuff[3]" to the horror and disgust of those who clung to the memory of "the Church of England in her greatest splendour, all things decent[4]." Hence the strength of the ecclesiastical reason for persecution, in urging which many of our divines speak as though the intolerance of the state was the rock upon which not merely the Church of England, but Christianity itself, was built. A very remarkable feature of the literature of the toleration controversy is the comparative rarity of confidence in the power of truth to win its way without being fostered by the state[5].

This attitude of mind found clear expression in Thorndike's "Discourse of the Forbearance or the

---

[1] See pp. 113–4, and n.   [2] Evelyn's *Diary*, Aug. 3, 1656.
[3] *Ibid*. Dec. 4, 1653.   [4] *Ibid*. July 2, 1637.
[5] Corbet's *The Kingdom of God among Men* (1679, p. 119 f.) affords a noticeable exception.

*Thorn-
dike:
" Dis-
course of
the For-
bearance
etc."
1670.*

Penalties which a due Reformation Requires," which
was published in 1670, and had anticipated many of
the arguments put forward in the last two pamphlets mentioned.   How could the Reformation stand,
he asked, unless the Clergy were bound to "reduce"
recusants to the Church, and enabled to convince
them that they ought to embrace it[1]?   And the
rule of reforming the Church requires "that it be so
reformed as to continue a member of the one Catholic
Church, as it was unreformed; saving the unity,
which cannot be held, without the consent of those
that will not be reformed."   Otherwise there would
be no plea to justify the bringing of recusants to
church (7–10).   Like the authors of the two pamphlets against "Naked Truth" just noticed, Thorndike
would not allow the credit of honest search to the
Dissenters.   "It is a horrible reproach to Christianity,"
he said, "to say that any doubting conscience is not
under a light sufficient to resolve it," for the same
principle might be applied when the question was
one of turning Christian or not.   To escape this
conclusion he propounded the remarkable view that
"faith provides a resolution that they who have
scruples in conscience are bound in conscience to
lay them aside" (59–60).   Moreover "the plea of
weak consciences cannot be allowed those that
engage in conventicles," for they have renounced
the faith rather than continue in the Church (63).
"Running into conventicles" is "worshipping an idol
of their own setting up," that is, "by worshipping

[1] Apparently "it" is the Reformation as exemplified by the
Church of England.

God according to an imagination of their own erecting"; hence both kinds of recusants—Roman Catholics and Nonconformists alike—are punishable on the same grounds, those of idolatry (154).

Thorndike's book was largely a plea for the revival of ecclesiastical discipline, and from this standpoint he found a new reason for persecution. If conventicles were not penalized, he urged, those excommunicated from the Church could take refuge there, and excommunication would be no longer a weapon against those who did not carry out the Christianity which they professed. And how should the Church and religion subsist when no man need do so ? (161–2)[1].

This same note of disbelief that religion could be trusted to stand alone, and to win its way by its own merits, is struck by a sermon preached in the year 1680 by Stillingfleet, now Dean of S. Paul's, upon the "Mischief of Separation." He professed to regard the Nonconformists as scrupulous and conscientious men (15), but the ecclesiastical liberalism of the youthful rector[2] appears considerably modified in the middle-aged dean; and the unsympathetic

Stillingfleet: "The Mischief of Separation." 1680.

---

[1] So practical a view did Thorndike take of ecclesiastical discipline, that he even proposed that the law should "make it a disgrace and a degree of infamy to stand excommunicate, whether by themselves or by the Church" by forbidding Christian burial to all who had not received the Holy Communion within the year (pp. 164, 169). This, be it remembered, would have included, and was intended to include, all the Nonconformists except such as might escape by occasional conformity. But in Thorndike's view Christianity seems to have been confined to the Catholic Church as conceived of by himself.

[2] For Stillingfleet's *Irenicum*, see p. 86 f.

tone of the sermon hardly bears out the professions of the preacher. The constitution of the
Church, he said, which cannot be perfect, must
involve inconveniences to some (47–8). This was
cold comfort, but what followed was little short of
brutality. It was not the way to peace for the
Dissenters to complain of persecution ; the laws had
been so gently executed that others had complained
of the indulgence shown to them (54). As for toleration, " an universal toleration is that Trojan Horse
which brings in our enemies without being seen, and
which after a long siege they hope to bring in at
last under the pretence of setting our gates wide
enough open to let in all our friends " (58)—words
almost prophetic of the policy of James II. " If all
men were wise and sober in religion," Stillingfleet
continued, " there would need no toleration ; if they
are not, we must suppose, if they had what they
wished, they would do as might be expected from
men wanting wisdom and sobriety, that is, all the
several parties would be strong and contending with
each other which should be uppermost." The result
would be that religion would be brought into contempt, or submission would be made to the tyranny
of the Pope, as a means to unity (58–9). Stillingfleet urged that whatever reasons the Nonconformist
ministers might have for their secession owing to
the oaths and declarations required, the people had
no such excuse : but, save for this, his sermon shows
little insight, and is quite unworthy of a man of so
great a reputation with allies and opponents alike.

Whatever might be the merits of " The Mischief

of Separation," it certainly raised a storm of controversy. In 1675 had been published a pamphlet by two Nonconformists, John Humfrey and Stephen Lob, entitled "A Peaceable Design." A second edition of this was now issued as "An Answer to Dr Stillingfleet's Sermon, by some Nonconformists, being the Peaceable Design Renewed." This treatise advocated comprehension for the Presbyterians and toleration for the Independents. Renunciations of the Covenant, oaths, and subscriptions, the authors pointed out, only served to keep the forbidden views and doctrines in men's minds; and men cannot swear away their thoughts and beliefs. "Whatsoever it is we think or believe, we do think it, we do believe it, we must believe it, notwithstanding any of these outward impositions. The honest man, indeed, will refuse an injunction against his conscience, the knave will swallow it, but each retain their principles, which the last will be likeliest to put to any villainous practice" (26–8). They even dared to put in a word for the Roman Catholics. The Papists, they said, must not have public worship, for they were idolatrous; or public office, for the supremacy of the Pope was inconsistent with the authority of the King; but as to private religion, they stood upon the same ground as others who refused to come to Common Prayer (32).

Another reply to the sermon came from the pen of John Howe, domestic chaplain to both rulers of the House of Cromwell, who had been ejected from his Devonshire living in 1662 because he could not reconcile himself to reordination. His tract bore the

[Humfrey and Lob]: "The Peaceable Design Renewed." 1680.

[Howe]: "A Letter written out of the Country." 1680.

title "A Letter written out of the Country to a Person of Quality in the City." It bears upon the theory of toleration only indirectly as a vigorous justification of the Nonconformists' position, broadly based on the obligations of conscience and the divine law. Howe contends that they cannot receive the sacraments in church because of their conscientious objections to the ceremonies used ; therefore they must hold meetings of their own and administer the sacraments. "When," he says, "we are satisfied that we cannot enjoy the means of salvation in his [Stillingfleet's] way without sin ; and he tells us, we cannot without sin enjoy them in our own: We...cannot think the merciful and holy God hath so stated our case as to reduce us to a necessity of sinning to get out of a state of damnation" (14). Indeed, the course taken by the Nonconformists is not only lawful, but a duty, for divine precept lays upon them the necessity of availing themselves of the means necessary to salvation (17). Their meetings also are a duty, in spite of human laws, in places such as London, where the church accommodation is wholly inadequate. "We acknowledge," says Howe, "order and unity are very lovely and desirable things, but we think it is of greater importance that the ministers with whom such fault is found conduct men, though not in so accurate order (which they cannot help) to Heaven, than let them go in the best order, yea (and as the case is) without any at all, to hell[1]" (36). It is a case of setting the saving of souls against the preservation of "certain human institutions and

---

[1] The same justification was pleaded by John Wesley.

rules, confessed by the devisers of them not to
be necessary to the being of the Church, which
common reason sees unnecessary to its well being...
and which experience shows to be destructive " (39).

In answer to the many attacks[1] which his sermon *Stilling-*
had called down upon him, Stillingfleet wrote a *fleet:*
"The Un-
lengthy book entitled "The Unreasonableness of *reason-*
ableness of
Separation," which displays the same hard, cold, *Separa-*
undiscerning spirit as the sermon which it was *tion."*
1680 ?–1.
written to defend. Answering the "Letter from the
Country," he wrote, "The dispute lies in a narrow
compass, and men may see light if they will. But
what if they will not? Then we are to consider
how far a wilful mistake or error of conscience will
justify men? I say it doth not, cannot justify them
in doing evil; and that I am sure breaking the
peace of the Church for the sake of such scruples,
is" (372–3). Stillingfleet was clearly incapable of
understanding the Nonconformists, and imagining
himself in their position; but even so he need not
have offered them the gratuitous insult of describing
them as "an enraged, *but unprovoked,* company of
men" (Preface xxxix).

On the question of toleration he developed two
lines of defence. The first was the destructive
nature of the thing itself. A general toleration was
the means by which the Roman Catholics had aimed
for many years from the Restoration onwards to
break in pieces the constitution of the Church of

[1] Most of them dealt with the ecclesiastical questions at issue
between the Nonconformists and the Church, and therefore do not
concern us here. Hunt, II. 16 f. gives accounts of several.

England.   If indulgence were given to the Nonconformists alone, it could not logically be kept
there : the same reasons must cause its extension to
the Roman Catholics ; and it is impossible to root
out Popery where toleration is allowed (Preface xxii,
lxxix).   In the second place Stillingfleet urged the
obligation of submission to the authority of the
National Church.   A National Church, he asserted,
has power to appoint rules of order and decency not
repugnant to the word of God, which on that account
others are bound to submit to ; and if any disturb
the peace of this Church, the civil magistrate may
justly inflict civil penalties upon them for it (305).
" I am of opinion," he said, "if the people once thought
themselves bound to do what they may lawfully do,
towards communion with us, many of the ministers
who seem now most forward to defend the separation, would think of putting a fairer construction
upon many things than now they do " (Preface lv).
Stillingfleet's conception of the National Church
involved active support of it by the civil power ;
hence this contention was practically an appeal
to the moral obligation to obey the law of the
state, in preference to all but the most imperative
dictates of a scrupulous conscience.   And if that
obligation were fully admitted, his contention was
no doubt true ; but the question of the relative
weight of moral obligation to obey the commands of
the civil authority was one of the points on which
the disputants were in most serious opposition, and
had become more and more important as toleration
became more and more an unmixed matter of politics.

John Owen soon published anonymously " An [*Owen*]: Answer to Dr Stillingfleet's Unreasonableness of *"Answer to Un-* Separation, so far as it concerns the Peaceable *reason-* Design." He disputed, as an Independent naturally *ableness of Separa-* would, Stillingfleet's view of the sinfulness of sepa- *tion."* ration from the National Church; separation, simply *1680.* considered, was neither good nor evil (33). He agreed with the "Peaceable Design," that if the legal obligation to attend the parish churches were removed, the schism would be *ipso facto* ended; for, were the meetings of the Nonconformists legalized, they would become parts of the National Church (36, 30). This view is interesting as illustrating from an unusual standpoint the ecclesiastico-political theory of the state. The High Anglicans refused toleration on the ground that the tie of ecclesiastical unity was a necessary property of the well-ordered state, and held that the ecclesiastical unity and the political unity should be at once organically separate and actually coextensive—an end which could be gained only by persecution: the Independents aimed at securing their coextensiveness by finding the ecclesiastical unity in the political unity, that is merely in common recognition by, and common subordination to, the civil power.

"Some Additional Remarks on the Late Book of *"Some* the Reverend Dean of St Paul's by a Conformable *Additional* Clergyman" bore more directly upon the theory of *1681.* toleration. Separation upon probable reasons, which are not conclusive, but such as honest men may not be able to escape, must be endured, it was contended, in this state of weakness and imperfection, the

remedy being worse than the disease (23). As for the
accusations of wilful blindness, the author believed
that some Dissenters did consider the question impartially ; but it was a matter of difficulty for either
party to do so, and what if the Dissenters did
not ? Were they therefore insufferable ? (29). "Why
persons of some schismatical principles (provided
the main of their doctrine be sound, and consistent
with Christianity) may not have as much favour as
drunkards and other immoral men, I know not" (11).
"I do not think it lawful to separate as often as
men scruple joining in communion; yet I do believe
it lawful to tolerate some unlawful separations, yea,
and necessary too" (33); for men "will never agree
unless it be in a few plain, great, and necessary
things," and "in this diversity of men's understandings it is impossible it should be otherwise." And
"under this diversity of apprehensions there will be
some diversity of practices, too, where men fear God
and have a value for their own consciences" (30–1).
Here are views widely divergent from the current of
thought represented by Parker and L'Estrange, to
whom the "conformable clergyman" is in direct opposition as regards their view of the law as the ultimate court of appeal, declaring that "it is not in the
laws but in the equity and justice of them that the
obligation lies; and that is the question at issue " (10).

"Toleration of separation on tolerable scruples"
(whatever he meant by tolerable scruples) would
not, he said, destroy the government of the Church,
and the time for suppression by persecution was
past. "Some things may be done, and some severi-

ties may be used to crush and prevent the increase of it [separation] when budding; which may not be done to extinguish and root it out, when it's grown and increased" (34). Personal instruction and kindness, he urged, are more agreeable to the spirit of Christ, than the "military methods of converting the Dissenters" which brought no good (11). In spite of his liberalism, however, he carefully disclaimed the idea of universal toleration, and classed Socinians and Quakers among "sectarian infidels" (11). Indeed, this pamphlet is chiefly remarkable, not as being the product of a grasp of the principles of toleration—the author's grasp of principle was slight—but as exemplifying the theory of persecution *The theory* in advanced decay. For the "sectarian infidels" of *of persecution in* whom the reverend author conceivably knew little *decay.* or nothing, the old intolerant spirit survives in full vigour; but his knowledge of the Dissenters was sufficient to make him respect their scruples and understand that prejudice was not all on one side; and where respect is felt the persecuting spirit receives a serious blow. "They are persons of holy lives," he wrote, "and upright conversations, at least some of them; and I would not have a hand in persecuting and undoing them, for all the preferments this Church or this world affords" (10). The "conformable clergyman," no doubt, represents the drift of a great body of opinion, determined not by the *a priori* considerations that commended themselves to Penn, so much as by the gradual pressure of events and the recognition of obvious facts. It was this drift of opinion which eventually found expression in the Toleration Act.

[*W. Sherlock*]: "*A Discourse about Church-Unity.*" 1681.

Stillingfleet was not left to fight the battle alone. In "A Discourse about Church-Unity" Dr William Sherlock came to his aid under the pseudonym of "A Presbyter of the Church of England." Sherlock was a London rector, who became in this year a Prebendary of S. Paul's, and four years later Master of the Temple. He showed a lack of sympathy, equal to Stillingfleet's, with the addition of no small measure of uncharitableness and abuse. The main body of the work contains little relevant to our subject, but in the Preface Sherlock has something to say on toleration. The plea of conscience, he urged, if admitted, must hold good in all cases, and in answer to a plea that a distinction should be made between those that subvert Christianity and those that err in small things consistent with salvation, Sherlock replied, "Thus our governors have already distinguished[1]" (Preface vii–ix).

Difficulty of determining the limits of toleration.

It is easy to blame this narrowness of view, because we have proved by long experience that toleration is not a very formidable thing, but it must be remembered that at this time that proof was not available[2]. The principle was clearly perceived that it would be impossible to allow every man to do everything for which he chose, whether justifiably or not, to allege the plea of conscience: the question was, what limit was to be set? Many of the advocates of persecution could not discern the difference between an abandonment by the govern-

[1] The argument was carried on in further treatises on both sides with increasing violence and abuse.

[2] The proved harmlessness of temporary relaxations of the penal laws was useful as cumulative evidence, but was of course a very different thing from long experience.

ment of all meddling in religious matters and a
willingness to defer to any pleas of conscience whatever. Hence what they refused was not what the
Dissenters asked for, but a concession which all
states, by their very nature, are compelled to refuse.
They could not see any stable half-way house between absolute toleration of everything for which
conscience could be alleged, and the maintenance
of the existing law. That no toleration should be
given outside the Church of England was an obvious
principle santioned by immemorial custom; if once
that principle were infringed it would be by no
means easy to find a new and satisfactory bulwark
against the irruptions of Popery, fanaticism, and
infidelity. As a contemporary rhymester expressed
it,

> "The starry rule of Heaven is fixt,
> There's no dissension in the sky:
> And can there be a mean betwixt
> Confusion and Conformity ?
> A place divided never thrives :
> 'Tis bad where hornets dwell in hives,
> But worse where children play with knives[1]."

To many toleration must have appeared, if not as
inevitably pernicious, at any rate as a leap in the
dark : why for the scruples of a few obstinate persons
should the cause of Christianity in England be imperilled ?

A treatise of much the same tone as Sherlock's
was "Evangelical and Catholic Unity maintained in

---

[1] W. W. Wilkins, *Political Ballads*, i. 205, "*The Geneva
Ballad*" (1678).

*Saywell:
"Evan-
gelical and
Catholic
Unity
main-
tained."
1682.* the Church of England" by William Saywell, Master
of Jesus College, Cambridge.   Toleration, according
to him, spelt confusion, and was an inlet even for
atheism: in an illuminating sentence he said that
were toleration granted "it will be no thanks to the
government that there is any such thing as religion
amongst us" (129).   Moreover, it was what the
Papists were aiming at in order to damage the
Church: hence the Presbyterians were really favour-
ing Popery (131).   Commenting on a plea which
had been put forward that toleration should be
granted for seven years so that the tolerable and
the intolerable might be distinguished, Saywell
said, "When hell has been let loose so long to rage
amongst us...they shall have conjured up the people
to the humour they were of in '41."   Then would
follow the reimposition of the Covenant (133–4).
Baxter was quoted as saying in his "True and Only
Way of Concord" that only those are to be silenced
who, *consideratis considerandis,* are found to do
more harm than good.   But toleration, it was objected, involved setting up a formal schism, and the
Nonconformists, being guilty of schism, did more
harm than good[1].   Saywell advocated moderate
penalties for the Nonconformists, supplemented not
by death or torture but by sober conference and
reasons, the penalties being continued "to make
them hearken and attend to them, which generally

[1] Preface "To the Reader." In the same year Sherlock declared that separation from the Church of England was a schism,
and schism was as damning a sin as idolatry, drunkenness and
adultery. *Continuation and Vindication of the Defence of Dr
Stillingfleet's Unreasonableness of Separation,* p. 389.

Dissenters and lazy people will not do[1]"; for the claims of the Church require long arguments to be proved, "and therefore (here the Master of Jesus rises to the level of genius) many out of mere sloth, and to avoid trouble will run away from the Church." The Dissenters followed their teachers blindly and therefore should be compelled to receive instruction. If they still dissented after understanding the matter, they must still be punished to make them consider better, but not put to death or tortured (224-7)— a generous concession. Divines of this school were quite willing to recognize the power of prejudice, but by no means willing to recognize that perhaps they themselves were prejudiced[2].

Fortunately men like Stillingfleet and Sherlock and Saywell had not the sole voicing of the views of the Church of England. Stillingfleet, indeed, ranked as a latitudinarian, but others who bore that name *The Lati-* showed much greater liberality upon the question *tudin-* of toleration. The controversialists of the period *arians.* between the Restoration and the Revolution were mainly engaged upon the problems already dealt with by Hales and Chillingworth—the problems raised by the conflict of the rights of conscience with ecclesiastical dogmatism; and we have already seen[3] that it was on his inheritance of the tradition of Hales and Chillingworth that Stillingfleet's title to

---

[1] Preface " To the Reader."

[2] See especially the preface to *The Unreasonableness of Separa-tion: the Second Part*, an anonymous continuation of Stilling-fleet's book, by T. Long, published 1682.

[3] See p. 86.

latitudinarianism is based. The exalted speculations
of the Cambridge Platonists, on the other hand, had
gone on far above the heads of the pamphleteers
whose eyes were fixed upon the petty details of
ecclesiastical disputes; but as time went on the
influence of the school began to penetrate downwards
into the arena of the controversy, and showed itself
in the growing importance of a more liberal and
practical latitudinarianism than that of Stillingfleet.
But the Cambridge philosophy could not but be
coloured by the intellectual strata through which
it percolated; and thus, as its influence was com-
municated to the sphere of practical life, it gave rise
to "the more commonplace and worldly liberality of
the Revolution period, which adopted and applied
the Cambridge principles, rather than intellectually
lived in them[1]."   Its most obvious characteristics
were the elevation, in the spirit of the Cambridge
school, of morality in religion as compared with
dogma and of reason as compared with authority
or "enthusiasm."

[Fowler]:
"Prin-
ciples and
Practices
etc." 1670.
In 1670 a defence of the "latitude-men" was
published by one of their number, Edward Fowler,
afterwards Bishop of Gloucester. His father and
elder brother had been among the ejected in 1662,
and he had himself conformed only after prolonged
hesitation. His book was entitled "The Principles
and Practices of certain Moderate Divines of the
Church of England, (greatly misunderstood) Truly
Represented and Defended; Wherein (by the way)
Some Controversies of no mean Importance, are

[1] Tulloch, II. 440.

succinctly discussed: In A Free Discourse between Two Intimate Friends." Fowler first defends the character and practices of the latitudinarians (1–40): they preached, he says, the reasonableness of the Christian precepts (42 f.) and of the points of mere belief (93 f.). They are accused of preaching up only a moral righteousness, but there is no difference betwixt evangelical righteousness and that which is in the best sense moral (117, 119 f.). As to questions of doctrine they dislike none more than the monopolizers of truth to a party (296). Charity is to solve the problems of religious controversy: "let the professors of Christianity labour for the true spirit and temper of Christians; and it will be as well with the Christian world as if we were all of the same mind. I mean let us not magisterially impose upon one another, and be so charitable as to believe well of Dissenters from us that live good lives, are of modest and peaceable deportment, and hold no opinions that directly oppose the designs of the Christian religion, and of making men like to God[1]; and then we shall see, that there will be little reason to desire an infallible judge of controversies, to make us all of one opinion" (308–9). On church government and ceremonies they occupy a middle position: episcopacy is the best form of government but not indispensable (323–4); rites and forms of prayer may be imposed, but they must be indifferent and agreeable to Scripture (327–8). Their attitude had been put with greater pictur-

[1] Compare Whichcote's description of religion as "a seed of a deiform nature," p. 67.

esqueness and force by an earlier apologist than Fowler[1]. "As for rites and ceremonies of divine worship, they do highly approve that virtuous mediocrity, which our Church observes between the meretricious gaudiness of the Church of Rome and the squalid sluttery of fanatic conventicles."

After what has been said about charity and "magisterially imposing upon one another" it is surprising to find that Fowler refers with approval to the way in which the subject of the authority of the civil power in ecclesiastical affairs is handled in Parker's lately published "Discourse of Ecclesiastical Polity[2]" (326-7); but he continues that while the "latitude-men" believe that magistrates must be obeyed when they command things inconvenient if lawful, yet they "are not more for obedience to all lawful commands of authority, than desirous that mercy should be shown to those whose consciences will not permit them to comply with their governors in some things disputable" (329, 332-3). Here is the key to the diverse attitudes on the question of toleration taken up by members of the latitudinarian school. There was room for a very wide divergence of opinion according as stress was chiefly laid on the one hand upon the right of the civil power to impose, or on the other upon its duty to exercise that right sparingly and with caution.

Tillotson.   Typical of the latitudinarianism of the Revolution

---

[1] "S. P. of Cambridge," in *A Brief Account of the new Sect of Latitude Men.* See p. 70 n. The quotation is from *The Phenix*, II. 503.

[2] See pp. 154–165.

on its higher side was John Tillotson, the future Archbishop of Canterbury. Brought up a Puritan, he was ejected from his fellowship at Clare College, Cambridge, at the Restoration; but he conformed after the Act of Uniformity. A man of wide sympathies, counting among his friends the Independent John Howe, the Quaker William Penn, and the Unitarian Thomas Firmin, he naturally soared above the littleness of mind which elevated party shibboleths into indefeasible principles and confined charity within the limits of ecclesiastical communion. "I had much rather," he said, "persuade anyone to be a good man, than to be of any party and denomination of Christians whatsoever; for I doubt not but the belief of the ancient creed, provided that we entertain nothing that is destructive of it, together with a good life will certainly save a man, and without this no man can have reasonable hopes of salvation, no, not in an infallible Church, if there were any such to be found in the world[1]."

When engaged in the congenial occupation of preaching against the Church of Rome, Tillotson advocated the right of private judgment in terms which would seem to imply a thorough belief in toleration. But when it came to applying principles to practice, so strong was the tide of feeling in favour of authority that even he was swept away. Preaching at Whitehall in 1680, he declared "I cannot think (till I be better informed, which I am always ready to be) that any pretence of conscience

[1] Quoted by W. Sherlock in *A Letter to Anonymous* (1683), p. 50.

warrants any man that is not extraordinarily com-
missioned as the apostles and first publishers of
the Gospel were, and cannot justify that commission
by miracles, as they did, to affront the established
religion of a nation, though it be false, and openly
to draw off men from the profession of it in contempt of the magistrate and the law[1]." The sermon
was published by Charles's order, and called down
much criticism upon the preacher as savouring of
Hobbism[2].   Perhaps the proximity of his most
religious and gracious King had been too much for
him, for subsequently in talk with John Howe he
"fell to weeping freely" and owned his mistake.
But it is said that by " the established religion " he
meant Protestantism, and was so understood by the
Nonconformists[3].

Another prominent latitudinarian was Gilbert
Burnet, who was made Bishop of Salisbury at the

[1] Sermon xxvii , Works ii. 458-9 (10 vols., London, 1820).
Cf. Sermon xxi. also preached at Whitehall. "Neither doth this
liberty of judging exempt men from due submission and obedience
to their teachers and governors. Every man is bound to obey the
lawful commands of his governors ; and what by public consent
and authority is determined and established, ought not to be
gainsaid by private persons, but upon very clear evidence of the
falsehood or unlawfulness of it. And this is every man's duty,
for the maintaining of order, and out of regard for the peace and
unity of the church ; which is not to be violated upon every
scruple and frivolous pretence: and when men are perverse and
disobedient, authority is judge, and may restrain and punish
them." Works, ii. 266. In both sermons private judgment is
advocated as against the Roman Church : they are an instructive
illustration of the spirit of the times.

[2] Debary, *History of the Church of England, 1685–1714,* 248–9.

[3] *Dictionary of National Biography,* art. on Tillotson.

Revolution. Born in 1643 of Scottish parents, he inherited two strongly opposed ecclesiastical traditions. His father, a Scotch lawyer, was a moderate but stubborn Episcopalian, while his mother was "most violently engaged in the Presbyterian way." Almost immediately after his birth his father's objection to the Solemn League and Covenant made it advisable that he should temporarily retire, not for the first time, to the continent; and in general the early years of little Gilbert's life were troublous and rapidly changing times north of the Tweed, as well as south of it. In 1663 on a visit to England he was impressed by the preaching of Whichcote at S. Anne's, Blackfriars, and "charmed by the candour and philosophic temper of More." He also became acquainted with Tillotson, Stillingfleet, and Wilkins[1]. Thus it would seem that his parentage, early environment, and later associations coöperated to produce in him the tolerant spirit of which he was a most sincere and consistent advocate.

In a sermon[2] preached at the election of the Lord Mayor of London on September 29th, 1681, he attacked the "hot and bitter temper" of persecution. Zeal, he said, was one of the pretences by which it was supported, but "that zeal which is acceptable to God must be suitable to his nature, full of goodness, mercy, and compassion. If it makes us hate, defame or persecute our brother, we are sure this is not the zeal which will commend

"Exhortation to Peace and Unity." 1681.

[1] This paragraph is based on Clarke and Foxcroft, *Life of Gilbert Burnet, Bishop of Salisbury*, 1–12, 16, 36–9.

[2] Published under the title *An Exhortation to Peace and Unity*.

us to God....And we must never forget that we ought to be zealous for peace as well as for truth" (14). Nor was the pretence of safety to be admitted. "Perhaps no severities are very prudent except they be extreme as are the inquisitions of Spain; but we may see what the Church of Rome has gained by their cruelties in the last age. Violence alienates those further, whom we ought to gain upon, and likewise increases their party by the compassions of all good-natured people...and so the sharpness of rigour, instead of being a security often proves the ruin of those who depend upon it" (15, 16). Those who are in error "may be good men in the main, for ought we know," and "there must be a great evidence to make us conclude a man a hypocrite" (16–17). Such counsel was sorely needed, but the seed did not fall upon altogether inhospitable soil. Burnet's views, however, did not prevent him from countenancing measures against the Roman Catholics and pleading self-preservation in excuse. He urged the danger of Popery as a reason for cultivating peace at home, but at the same time desired that more charity should be shown towards the Roman Catholics. "We ought to carry it so towards them that it may appear we do not hate their persons, and do nothing against them, but as we are compelled to do it for self-preservation" (29–31).

Preface to Lactantius. 1687. His views were set forth in more detail in the preface to his translation of Lactantius' "Relation of the Death of the Primitive Persecutors," published at Amsterdam in 1687. He made an unusually wide distinction between Church and State. Actions

concerning human society, he wrote, belong to the
authority of the magistrate, but thoughts with relation to God, and actions arising therefrom, and in
which others have no interest, are God's immediate
province, and can belong to no other jurisdiction.
The violation of the laws of a society " can only
infer a forfeiture of all that one had or might have
expected by virtue of it"; hence doing what is only
contrary to our religion must not make us forfeit
our temporal estates and liberties, which we hold
not by virtue of our Christianity, but as members
of the state (17–20).   Burnet also laid stress upon
the argument from fallibility, pointing out that if
education and temper have hit together, it will
require a very extraordinary elevation to rescue a
man from their force; and one man is no more
likely to be right than another (12, 16).   The less
usual argument that truth may be trusted to prevail
is used; and the still less usual one, to which more
attention might well have been paid earlier, that
" persecution does extremely vitiate the morals of
the party that manages it" (17, 44).

The *régime* of James II seems to have somewhat
modified Burnet's attitude on the Roman Catholic
question.   In spite of the persecuting principles of
the Church of Rome and especially of the Jesuits,
he said, the mass of Roman Catholics know nothing
of these points and are not really formidable : to
requite persecution by persecution is so unchristian
and so contrary to Protestantism "that I do not
stick to say it, that I had rather see the Church of
England fall under a severe persecution from the

Church of Rome, than see it fall to persecute Papists, when it should come to its turn to be able to do it....It would be too near an approach to the cruelty of that Church, which we cannot enough detest: but how much soever we must hate their corruption, we must still remember that they are men and Christians, though perhaps of a course (*sic*) grain" (51-2).

Burnet had come to be a whole-hearted believer in toleration as far as it was practicable, on *a priori* grounds. "I have long looked," he wrote in his "History of My Own Time," "on liberty of conscience as one of the rights of human nature, antecedent to society, which no man could give up, because it was not in his own power; and our Saviour's rule, of doing as we would be done by, seemed to be a very express decision to all men, who would lay the matter home to their consciences, and judge as they would willingly be judged by others[1]."

Naturalism. Parallel and somewhat akin to the Platonist influence was the influence of naturalism, applied to the conceptions both of law and of religion. Stillingfleet in his "Irenicum[2]" had perpetually appealed to the law of nature; Wolseley[3] had fixed upon the light of nature as the canon of what was and what was not to be tolerated; long before these Lord Herbert[4] had discovered a natural religion

[1] Vol. v. p. 107, 6 vols. Oxford, 1823.   [2] See p. 86 f.

[3] See p. 143. Of course I do not imply that Stillingfleet or Wolseley had anything to do with the origin of naturalism; they are merely instanced as controversialists with whom we have already dealt.

[4] See p. 74 f.

which made revelation superfluous. In 1681 appeared an anonymous book entitled "Liberty of Conscience in its order to Universal Peace, impartially stated: and proved to be the just, right and genuine effect of true natural and Christian Religion in immunity from penal laws, church censures, and private animosities." Herbert's embarrassing conclusion as to revelation was avoided by identifying "natural religion and fundamental Christianity; one essential rule of both which is, love, peace, and mercy to all that are centred in this natural Christian Religion[1]." "The fundamental liberty of conscience is, that the laws that oblige it are implanted in it for a nature, are framed into it to be its very constitution, are so adjusted as to be its excellency and perfection; the laws that bind it are its liberty" (2). Natural Religion is the standard of human penal laws, i.e. no man is to be punished unless he violates the precepts of natural religion; men must however, as far as they possibly can, communicate with the national religion (49–50, 117). Liberty of conscience (all points of plain natural religion and morality being secured) takes away pretences for disturbance, and gives free course to the arguments for the true religion. Roman Catholicism, however, on grounds of self-preservation, must not be tolerated (15–20).

"Liberty of Conscience in its order to Universal Peace." 1681.

Similar in tone to this book was a pamphlet published in 1689[2] entitled "Liberty of Conscience

"Liberty of Conscience

---

[1] Preface "To the Reader."

[2] Apparently before the passing of the Toleration Act. Its authorship is attributed to one George Care.

Asserted and Vindicated." A careful distinction is
drawn between errors against the light of nature by
which the conscience forfeits all claim to freedom,
and errors " merely against the Gospel." The magistrate may resist moral errors and impieties by
coercion ; but he may not punish " errors and heresies
merely concerning the faith of Christ, where there
is not sufficient mixture of moral impiety "; his
resistance may only take the form of support of
orthodoxy (1, 3). Education makes error as easy to
be believed as truth, and why should a man be
punished for not believing perfectly, when he is not
punished for not living perfectly ? (10, 11). Persecution either makes sects or makes the sectaries
obstinate, while the magistrates become merely the
minister's executioners in matters which they cannot understand, and which men who study all their
lives cannot agree about. Persecution also makes
magistrates parties in the factions of their subjects, and consequently bands men together against
the government ; nor is it to the magistrate's
interest that men who might be useful to the
commonwealth should be in jail (15–16). Finally,
there is urged the necessity of union among
Protestants ; liberty should be denied to the
Papists because of their idolatry, intolerance, introduction of a foreign power, and cruelty when themselves in power, but not because of their heresy
(17, 23).

In the same year as " Liberty of Conscience in
its order to universal peace " appeared the first of
a series of four " Conformist's Pleas for the Noncon-

formists[1]" written anonymously by Edward Pearse, *the Non-*
a Welsh clergyman who held in plurality three *conform-*
ists."
Northamptonshire livings.   He pleaded in favour of 1681-3.
comprehension rather than toleration, and further
exemplified what we have already noticed in "Some
Additional Remarks[2],"—the growing respect for the
Nonconformists, which was forming a basis for
toleration.   Pearse laid considerable stress upon the
worthiness of the Nonconformists and defended them
against the perverse accusation that their meetings
were seditious.   It was undeniable, he said, that
many suffered merely for religious exercises, and
"if it be for Nonconformity...they will suffer for
religion, and for no other but the Protestant religion,
what Papists never did but for treason[3]."   Many
instances were given of the harsh treatment to
which they were subjected, and emphasis laid upon
the activity and rascality of the informers.   It was
also urged that the things required for assent were
much too big for the capacities of the young and
"unstudied," and the imposition of them amounted
to something like a claim to infallibility[4].   Moreover,
the system was futile; they might with safety preach
to five at a time, why not to five hundred?   Was not

[1] The first was entitled *The Conformist's Plea for the Nonconformists* and the others *The Conformist's Second, Third, Fourth
Plea* etc., respectively.

[2] See p. 201.   This, like *The Conformist's Plea*, was published
in 1681.   Perhaps the Popish Plot may have influenced to a considerable extent the attitude of the writers.

[3] *Second Plea*, pp. 61, 26.

[4] *Plea*, pp. 54-5.

private preaching more dangerous than public? "If they are men of pernicious principles," Pearse wrote, "they are allowed too much, if not, they are allowed too little[1]." The use of force without reason only tended to disunion; nature tells us that men must worship God according to the light and freedom of their minds and wills, and by force "you convert the schismatic into a hypocrite or atheist....And what will the Church be better for such?" Persecution rendered the Nonconformists altogether unserviceable to Church and Kingdom in time of need[2].

The first of the series also throws some sidelight upon the feeling in the country and the intentions of the persecutors. Pearse bears out Owen's statement that the justices disliked administering the persecuting acts[3], and in an interesting passage says "If some could have executed the laws, or prevailed with magistrates so to do, we should have had a militant church indeed. In the year 1669 we had several articles sent down to the clergy with private orders to some to make the conventicles as few and small as might be. The eighth and last was this, *Whether do you think they might be easily supprest by the Assistance of the Civil Magistrate?*[4]" Clearly Sheldon was still hoping in 1669 that Nonconformity was a temporary craze which might yet be stamped out, as indeed it seems almost to have been for a

---

[1] *Plea*, p. 60.

[2] *Second Plea*, pp. 42, 33; *Fourth Plea*, pp. 9, 20.

[3] *Plea*, pp. 9-10. For Owen, see p. 171.

[4] *Plea*, p. 36.

time by the Second Conventicle Act in the following year.

The " Conformist's Pleas " were issued at a time when the Nonconformists needed all the pleading for them that they could get. The anti-popery *Anti-* agitation set on foot by Shaftesbury when he went *popery* *agitation,* into opposition in 1673 received such an immense 1678-81, impulse from the lying revelations of Titus Oates and the discovery of actual Roman Catholic schemes, that from the autumn of 1678 it became a national fanaticism. But it was too wild to last. In the controversy over the Exclusion Bill Charles gave the Whigs enough rope to hang themselves with; their violence and the fear of civil war discredited them with the nation, over which there swept a tumultuous Tory reaction not unlike that of twenty *ending in* years before. The triumph of the Church and King *Tory re-* *action and* party would in any case have been fraught with *consequent* disaster for the Nonconformists; the fact that it *persecu-* *tion of the* had triumphed in circumstances resembling those *Noncon-* *formists.* of 1641, and because of the fear that similar circumstances would lead to similar results, made it doubly disastrous. The ghost of the Great Rebellion still walked, a bogey to the Tories, to the Nonconformists an avenging Fury. From 1681 the persecution was bitter, and as malignant as ever[1]. The Nonconformists were made responsible for the plots of the prostrated and malcontent Whigs with whom their cause was associated. An order for the

---

[1] For a long time John Howe had preached in houses without interference, but now it was not safe for him so much as to appear in the streets. *Dictionary of National Biography.*

suppression of Nonconformists in Devonshire, issued on October 2nd, 1683, by the quarter sessions of the county, begins, " We have been so abundantly convinced of the seditious and rebellious practices of the sectaries and fanatics," and goes on to speak of " horrid treasons," and " fury and malice "; " the Nonconformist preachers are the authors and fomenters of this pestilent faction and the implacable enemies of the established government, and to whom the late execrable treasons...are principally to be imputed[1]." And the Bishop of Exeter—Thomas Lamplugh, who became Archbishop of York in 1688 —commanded the order to be published by all his clergy in Devonshire[2].

Thus Charles II's reign which had begun with such bright hopes ended in gloom for the Dissenters, *James II's Romanizing policy.* and James II's accession brought no better prospects. On the contrary their sufferings were increased; and Monmouth's rising, which seemed at first like a new Puritan rebellion, reduced them to a yet more evil case. But suddenly an offer of relief came from an unexpected quarter. The theory of the divine right of kings acted in England as a

[1] The order is quoted at the beginning of Baxter's *The English Nonconformity as under King Charles II and King James II truly stated and argued* (2nd ed. 1690) : also at the end of an anonymous pamphlet entitled *A Plea of the Harmless Oppressed against the Cruel Oppressor*, which also quotes similar orders of Jan. 10th, 1681, and Apr. 4th, 1682, respectively forbidding poor-relief except to regular church-goers, and ordering that none should keep ale-houses but such as repair to church and produce a certificate of the reception of the sacrament ; these orders, it is stated, received the high approval and applause of the Bishop of Exeter.

[2] Baxter, *The English Nonconformity*, postscript to the order.

bulwark of defence against Rome : James attempted
to use it as an instrument to bring about the very
thing which it existed to prevent[1]. In this he
made a miscalculation. English Churchmen were
ready enough to preach the divine right of kings ;
but it was always assumed that the king was a
supporter of the English Church. A king, whose
object it was to overthrow it, was a phenomenon
which had not seriously entered into their calculations ; and, as has frequently happened in
other departments of thought, the old theory was
seriously modified by the discovery of a new fact.
Not that it was repudiated till the Revolution,
when the repudiation came in a very practical, if
not openly acknowledged, form ; but English Churchmen by no means showed that acquiescence in
James's Romanizing measures which, from their
professions of loyalty, he had expected. The Church
having refused to acquiesce in its own abasement,
James turned to the Nonconformists, and in his
Declaration of Indulgence of April, 1687[2], offered *Declara-*
them liberty of conscience as a bribe for their sup- *tion of In-*
dulgence.}
port in his schemes. The grounds alleged were 1687.
much the same as those of Charles II's declaration
of fifteen years before, but James laid claim to
higher motives and took a more comprehensive
view than did his brother: "...it is and hath long
been our constant sense and opinion (which upon
diverse occasions we have declared) that conscience
ought not to be constrained, nor people forced in

[1] Figgis, *Divine Right of Kings*, 209.
[2] For the full text see *The London Gazette*, April 4th–7th, 1687.

matters of mere religion; it has ever been directly contrary to our inclination, as we think it is to the interest of government, which it destroys by spoiling trade, depopulating countries, and discouraging strangers; and finally that it never obtained the end for which it was employed; and in this we are the more confirmed by the reflections we have made upon the conduct of the last four reigns. For after all the frequent and pressing endeavours that were used in each of them to reduce this kingdom to an exact conformity in religion, it is visible the success has not answered the design, and that the difficulty is invincible." He proceeded to abrogate religious disqualifications, and to grant freedom of public worship to Roman Catholics and Dissenters alike. To the latter the temptation to desert the cause of the constitution for that of the King must have been almost overwhelming. For more than twenty years they had suffered persecution which had not abated with time; indeed, as we have seen, the first two years of James's reign had been among the bitterest they had known. They had loyally aided the cause of Protestantism, to their own loss, in supporting the Test Act; and the only rewards they had received were the additional disqualifications which that act imposed, and the renewal of persecution as soon as the fear of Popery had somewhat abated. They might well doubt or deny the fact that the great undercurrent of popular opinion was making for toleration, and think it hopeless to look for anything but oppression from the Church. Had they, smarting as they were under recent

persecution, eagerly accepted the proffered alliance
with Rome, their political sagacity might have been
questioned, but their action would not have called
for surprise and would hardly have merited reproach.

The toleration controversy, which had flagged of *Revival*
recent years, started into new life. Supporters of *of the*
toleration
toleration for the Roman Catholics were either *contro-*
created or emboldened by the royal favour, and *versy.*
pamphlets on every side came pouring from the
press. The author of "Two Plain Words to the
Clergy" took an extreme view of the situation; "Be
wise, therefore, O ye people," he proclaimed, "and
hearken to the Voice of God by His Vice-gerent,
who calls you to liberty from bondage." On the
other hand "A Letter from a Freeholder to the rest
of the Freeholders of England" declared that "the
laws against the Papists are religious laws; they
are laws made for the high honour of God, as well
as for the common profit of the realm[1]," indeed they
were necessary to the being of the kingdom—a belated
instance of the religious motive in persecution.
Between these two extremes, various shades of
opinion were expressed upon the Roman Catholic
question: of persecuting the Dissenters there was
no further talk; that would have meant driving
them into the arms of the King. Indeed, it is from
the Declaration of Indulgence that the actual freedom of Dissent in England must be dated.

As we have seen, Churchmen were fain to recast

[1] Licensed June 28th, 1688, two days before the invitation was
sent to William of Orange. I make no attempt to observe chrono-
logical order in dealing with the pamphlets of 1687-8.

Attitude of the Church. their theories to meet the new situation. Of a sudden the Church was all tenderness and contrition; it was no longer a question of whether the Dissenters should receive toleration or not, rather the Church and the King were in excited competition as to which should have the honour of bestowing it upon them. A great stir was caused *[Halifax]:* by a pamphlet entitled "A Letter to a Dissenter," *"Letter* by T. W.—initials which concealed the identity of *to a Dis- senter."* George Savile, Marquis of Halifax[1]. He pointed *1687.* out that the declaration was unconstitutional, and that the Dissenters in accepting it as the basis of an alliance would be bartering their civil liberty for a precarious indulgence in religious matters; "the constitution of England is too valuable a thing to be ventured upon a compliment." And the interests of the Dissenters and the Church were in the end identical. The Church was convinced of its error, and "common danger...hath turned the spirit of persecution into a spirit of peace, charity and condescension" (6–8). The Church party was indeed *Ambiguous* in an ambiguous and compromising situation. It *position of* had always been understood that the same party *Church- men.* stood for Church and King, and that the two interests were identical; but now those who had acknowledged the claims of Church and King alike, without suspicion of possible embarrassment by the double allegiance, were called upon to make their choice between the two. Most chose the Church,

---

[1] It was suggested that T. W. was merely an inversion of W. T., and the author Sir William Temple. *Animadversions on a late Paper entituled A Letter to a Dissenter* by H. C. (Henry Care).

and thus turned a political somersault which brought them into opposition to the King; some few chose the King, and turned an ecclesiastical somersault involving a denial of the claims hitherto put forward on behalf of the Church. Acrobatics of some sort were inevitable for those who had held in conjunction two principles which had now become incompatible; of Church and King it was no longer possible to continue to support the one without withdrawing support from the other[1].

Among those whom political allegiance held more tightly than ecclesiastical allegiance was the redoubtable Roger L'Estrange, who among many others took upon himself to answer the "Letter to a Dissenter." He had for some time been suspected of Popish inclinations, and had in consequence been burnt in effigy by the London mob, and knighted by the King. He begins by urging the prudential and religious grounds for toleration which come strangely as a sequel to a quarter of a century's virulence on the other side. L'Estrange as a tolerationist was an object to move men, according to their disposition, to mirth or to indignation; but inconsistency on the toleration question was the natural accompaniment of the unflinching maintenance of his political views[2]. "God forbid," he said, "that any honest Englishman should envy any

Supporters of the royal prerogative.
L'Estrange: "Answer to a Letter to a Dissenter." 1687.

---

[1] Most consistent of all were those clergy (including five of the famous seven bishops) who, by resisting the Declaration of Indulgence and afterwards becoming non-jurors, withdrew their support from both successively.

[2] Apparently he still objected to toleration as a principle. See *Dictionary of National Biography.*

of his fellow-subjects the benefit of the King's mercy; because (in effect) a man can hardly do it without some sort of reflection upon his sacred wisdom and goodness" (17). In view of James's gross stupidity and more than questionable morals this is rather strong measure[1], but it was the glamour of the sacred office that dazzled L'Estrange's vision; kingship came immediately from God (49). "The law of the land is sacred and so is the law of the prerogative, which is the law of the land as well as the other, and nothing ought to be called a trespass against a human law, that is authorized by the indispensable equity of a law divine" (32).

Parker.

L'Estrange was by no means alone. It seems odd at first to find the author of the "Discourse of Ecclesiastical Polity" urging the abrogation of the Parliamentary Test; but such was the fact. Parker and L'Estrange alike had exemplified the Hobbist line of thought which made ecclesiastical questions ultimately dependent upon the civil authority. When, therefore, the civil authority proclaimed toleration, both were prepared to jettison the subsidiary arguments by which they had shown it to be *malum in se*, out of respect for the principle in accordance with which they had hitherto opposed it as also *malum quia prohibitum*. Parker had shown Roman Catholic leanings, and in 1686 had been appointed Bishop of Oxford; the King expected that he would "bring round his clergy." In 1688 he wrote and published anonymously "Reasons for Abrogating the Test, imposed upon all members

[1] Or is L'Estrange referring to God's wisdom and goodness?

of Parliament Anno 1678[1]." It is mainly a re- *"Reasons for Abrogating the Test."* 1688. futation of the charge of idolatry made against the Roman Catholics. On the question of the test (it does not deal directly with that of mere toleration) it is a feeble production, very different in tone from the vigorous "Ecclesiastical Polity," but contains the sound argument that it is absurd to demand from all members of Parliament a pronouncement upon an abstruse doctrine "that is morally impossible for them to understand" (9–11).

Besides those who applauded the Declaration of *Advocates of religious freedom.* Indulgence as an act of royal prerogative sanctioned by divine right, there were others who did not regard the matter merely from a political standpoint, but were genuinely attached to the cause of religious freedom. These therefore advocated not merely a royal suspension, but the parliamentary repeal, of the penal laws, and the definite inauguration of the reign of liberty of conscience. "An Expedient for *"An Expedient for Peace.'* 1688. Peace" urged the impossibility of agreement in religious matters. "Force and violence may make a congregation of bodies, but no unity of minds" (7). No man is a schismatic but he that departs from a good life; no man a heretic but he that teaches ill life (9). Custom, chance, prejudice, and constitution give most men their way in religion and create their conscience too (15). "All sides have been really to blame, and really criminal" (34). Agreement in

---

[1] It should be noticed that the direct object of Parker's attack was the Parliamentary Test Act of 1678 (see Appendix III), not the act of 1673. Was it with a view to clearing the way for Romanist bishops into the House of Lords?

religion being impossible, the next thing is "to make all things as innocent and easy and suitable to government as possible." This is to be done by a Great Pacific Charter compelling the contending parties to peace (40).

"*Some Free Reflections.*" 1687.

In "Some Free Reflections upon Occasion of the Public Discourse about Liberty of Conscience" it was pointed out that the test and penal laws had not given security and rest, nor hindered the spread of fanciful opinions, but had caused inclination to sedition and rebellion, and made government uneasy and insecure. Why then, it was asked, should they be alarmed at the prospect of a change which "affords more lively hopes of stable comfort"? (6–7). The test, which was a real infringement of liberty of conscience, should be abolished together with the penal laws. Natural and Christian liberty is so fundamental a law that we ought not to transgress it for any advantage (10–11). "Let us all renounce the principle of persecution and let that be the only test upon which our government be modelled." This would be "incomparably a better security for us against any particular usurper, than our several factions have been hitherto one against another" (14).

"*A Letter from a Gentleman in the City.*" 1687.

"A Letter from a Gentleman in the City to a Gentleman in the Country, about the Odiousness of Persecution" exposed the fallacy that it is lawful for true Christians to persecute erroneous Christians, showing that this is simply a license to those actually in power to persecute, and gives a right of judging truth, implying infallibility, to the civil power in

every state (20-2). Persecution is against the principles of Christianity, and happens because "the
beast gets the better of the man" (24). The penal
laws, the author says, were always laxly executed,
because the government enacting them did not intend
their rigorous execution. He also testifies to the
detestation in which informers were held and the
dislike existing in the popular mind for the enforcement of the penal laws for mere religion[1] (25-9).

"A Discourse for Taking off the Tests and Penal *"A Dis-*
Laws about Religion" emphasizes the separateness *course for*
Taking off
of ecclesiastical and temporal laws. The close as- *the Tests*
and Penal
sociation of the state with religion seemed to be *Laws."*
grounded on the maxim that "dominion is founded 1687.
in grace" (9). Tests, the author says, are contrary
to the liberty of the subject and analogous to de-
priving him of liberty and property (7-8); and moreover their effects had been bad. There was no
danger of Papist domination, for the interests of the
Papists lay in the firm establishment of liberty of
conscience (34-6).

On the side of toleration at this crisis the pro- *[Penn]:*
tagonist was William Penn. His views on liberty *"Good*
Advice to
of conscience we have already considered[2]: he now *the Church*
of Eng-
carried his arms into the enemy's country, and in *land etc."*
"Good Advice to the Church of England, Roman 1687.
Catholic, and Protestant Dissenter," attacked the
test and the very existence of a national church.
"I cannot apprehend," he said, "the necessity of
any predominant religion" (60). Compulsion on

---

[1] Cf. *Prudential Reasons for repealing the Penal Laws*, p. 4.

[2] See pp. 172-8.

the part of a state church is unreasonable, for she
cannot oblige the conscience unless the state which
established her be infallible. As for Popery, the
laws against sedition are sufficient protection against
what is dangerous in it, and there is no need of
laws against religion (12–13). Penn strongly supported the Declaration of Indulgence (15 f.): the
argument that it was unconstitutional did not appeal
to him. He went behind the English constitution
to the constitution of human nature; and for him
the right to follow reason and conscience was a
fundamental right infringed by the penal laws.
It was therefore justifiable to use the opportunity
offered by the Declaration to recover it[1].

"Some Re-
flections on
a Dis-
course
called
Good
Advice."
1687 ?–8.   Penn's "Good Advice" called forth a reply entitled "Some Reflections on a Discourse called Good
Advice to the Church of England[2]." The gist of it
was that the Church had learnt her mistake (the
responsibility for which the author tried to shift on

[1] Cf. *The Great Case of Liberty of Conscience*, p. 29. No
"temporary subsequential law" "can invalid so essential a part
of the government as an English liberty and property." At this
crisis Penn also wrote *The Reasonableness of Toleration, and the
Unreasonableness of the Laws and Tests. Wherein is proved by
Scripture, Reason and Antiquity, that Liberty of Conscience is the
Undoubted Right of every Man, and tends to the Flourishing of
Kingdoms and Commonwealths; And that Persecution for mere
Religion is Unwarrantable, Unjust, and Destructive to Human
Society* (1687), the contents of which are sufficiently indicated by
its title ; and *The Great and Popular Objection Against the Repeal
of the Penal Laws and Tests Briefly Stated and Considered. By a
Friend to Liberty for Liberty's sake* (1688) in which he said
"A National Religion by Law, where it is not so by number and
inclination is a national nuisance " (p. 23).

[2] This pamphlet will be found in *State Tracts (Charles II)*,
pp. 363–71.

to the Court) and would never persecute the Dissenters again: but Popery could not have liberty of conscience, "for though there may be some things retained in Popery, which may be called matters of religion, yet in the bulk and complex of it, it is a conjuration against all religion, and a conspiracy against the peace of societies and the rights of mankind[1]."

Fortunately the nation generally cared more for the English Constitution and the English Church than Penn did; and, when the time of trial came, James found himself practically alone.   Late in 1687 the views of William and Mary upon the *Views of William and Mary made public.* religious question had been made known through a letter written for publication by Fagel, the Grand Pensionary of Holland, declaring that their Highnesses held that no Christian ought to be persecuted for his conscience, or be ill-used because he differed from the public and established religion.   The Dissenters therefore should have entire liberty for the full exercise of their religion.   As for the Roman Catholics, they too should have full liberty of conscience, and permission to exercise their religion "provided it be managed modestly, without pomp or ostentation."   But they must be kept out of both Houses of Parliament and all public employments; their Highnesses could not consent to the repeal of the test or those other penal laws which secured the Protestant religion, being convinced that it would be dangerous to that religion and to the safety of

[1] *Ibid.* p. 366.

the nation[1]. The letter, which was translated by Burnet and widely distributed in England, was admirably calculated to conciliate public opinion, guaranteeing, as it did, liberty of conscience, and yet guarding, by the maintenance of the test, against the peril of Popery.

Flight of James.

Thus, when James paid the price of ambition and stupidity, the prospects of a religious settlement were hopeful. For the fourth time in thirty years[2] the Church had been forced into an alliance with the Dissenters by common peril, and now there was at the head of affairs a prince honestly desirous of bringing about a lasting accommodation.

The Toleration Act, 1689,

The result was the Toleration Act[3], by which freedom of worship was granted to Dissenters who should take the oaths of allegiance and supremacy[4], and make the declaration against transubstantiation and the invocation of saints prescribed by the Parliamentary Test Act of 1678[5]. The old fear of sedition appeared in the provision that the benefit of the act should not extend to any who met for religious worship with locked doors. Dissenting ministers, who, in addition to the oaths and declara-

---

[1] The letter will be found in a pamphlet entitled *Their Highnesses the Prince and Princess of Orange's Opinion about a General Liberty of Conscience,* published 1689. The letter itself is dated Nov. 4, 1687, and was printed in 1688 in Amsterdam.

[2] The previous occasions were, of course, the year of anarchy, the declaration of indulgence of 1672, and the Popish Plot.

[3] 1 Will. & Mary, cap. 18. Grant Robertson, *Select Statutes,* p. 70.

[4] New oaths had been provided by 1 Will. & Mary, cap. 1. Grant Robertson, *Select Statutes,* 55–6.

[5] 30 Cha. II, St. II. cap. 1.

tion, subscribed the thirty-nine articles, excepting
the thirty-fourth, thirty-fifth, thirty-sixth, and part
of the twentieth—those, that is, which deal with
the questions of ceremonies, the homilies, and the
consecration of bishops and ministers—were granted
freedom to officiate in dissenting congregations.
Special provisions were made on the one hand for
the toleration of Baptists and Quakers, and on the
other for the denial of "any ease, benefit, or advantage to any papist or popish recusant whatsoever,
or any person that shall deny in his preaching or
writing the doctrine of the Blessed Trinity, as it is
declared in the aforesaid articles of religion."

It should be carefully noticed that the Toleration *did not repeal, but merely*
Act did not repeal the persecuting laws; it merely *granted*
granted exemption from them to such persons as *exemptions*
should fulfil certain prescribed conditions[1]. It was *from, the penal laws,*
not a concession of the principle of religious free-
dom (which, indeed, by implication it definitely
disclaimed), but merely a recognition of the fact
that, within certain limits, religious dissent did not
imply hostility to the state or to the social order.
It was the outcome of political exigency, not of *and owed its form to*
reverence for the rights of the individual conscience. *political*
Already, as the principles implicit in the Refor- *considera-*
mation were gradually discovered, and still more *tions;*
gradually worked out in practice, belief in persecution for religious and theological reasons had lost

[1] Thus in 1787 the Methodists had to be licensed as Dissenters
to escape the penalties of the Conventicle Act. Gwatkin, in *Cambridge Modern History*, v. 336. The Toleration Act allowed no
assembly for religious worship without previous registration
(§ xix.).

its hold; and these motives had played a very small part in causing the persecution of the last two reigns, which was mainly inspired and kept alive by political considerations. "The Puritans," writes Professor Pollard, "are not hated because they refuse to subscribe the thirty-nine articles, but because they had cut off the head of a King, and had closed the theatres. Romanists are not feared because they believe in Transubstantiation but because they were thought to be in league with Louis XIV. The motive was, in fact, largely, if not mainly, political; and the party leaders use religious passions for political purposes[1]." Thus, when toleration came, it came in a form determined by political considerations and not by enthusiasm for religious liberty arising from noble motives. It had indeed been pointed out by Chillingworth that Protestantism implied more than mere toleration, and the exaltation of the dignity of man by the Cambridge Platonists made in the same direction; and among the lesser men who actually participated in the controversy after the Restoration were some like Penn and Burnet who based their pleadings upon *a priori* considerations of human nature. But, important as these considerations were in disposing public opinion, the spirit of persecution, armed with the plea of political expediency, must be met with its own weapons; and circumstances made it clear that political expediency was really on the side of at any rate partial toleration; while the treatment recently meted out to the Huguenots by Louis XIV

[1] *Factors in Modern History*, 204.

no doubt created in some quarters and intensified in others detestation and distrust of a system which logically culminated in such enormities.

" At last the time had come when English Protestants were ready to let one another worship God. All their parties were exhausted with fifty years of revolution, bloodshed and terror, culminating in the recent narrow escape of their common religion. Like dogs that have been flogged off each other, Anglican and Puritan lay down and snarled....First the Dissenters, because they were hopeless of supremacy and crushed by persecution, had allowed their powerful friends to inscribe Toleration on the party banner. And now in the year 1689 the political situation compelled the Church to follow[1]." William's publicly expressed views upon the question, the promises which the Church had made in the hour of danger, the preparations across the Channel for an invasion whereby that danger might be renewed in still more formidable guise, alike compelled to peace[1].

The act, as might be expected of a compulsory peace, was a poor fulfilment of the hopes expressed by Penn and others for a Great Charter of Liberty of Conscience[2]; it was but a mutilated edition of the programme put forward by William of Orange *it was,* in Fagel's letter[3]; but it must not be excessively *however,* depreciated. If it lacked width and exalted motive, *durable,*

[1] G. M. Trevelyan, *England under the Stuarts,* 449–50.
[2] See Penn's *Great and Popular Objection*; also *An Expedient for Peace,* and *Three Letters tending to demonstrate how the security of this Nation...lies...in the Establishment of a New Law for Universal Liberty of Conscience.*
[3] See p 231.

it was eminently practical. Its very pedestrian character was at once a safeguard against repeal and a guarantee of success within its own limited sphere. A more radical measure would have outrun the popular feeling now necessary to maintain in vigorous life a law so nearly and obviously related to men's everyday interests; indeed it may be questioned whether the nation as a whole would for some generations yet have contentedly acquiesced in a grant of more extended liberty. And though the act did not concede the principle of religious *and conceded the principle of state-recognition of religious diversity.* freedom, it did concede a principle pregnant with great results—the principle of recognition by the state of more than one form of religious worship: the state gave up the claim to decide the one particular mode, in which, to the exclusion of all others, men might acknowledge their relations to their Maker[1]. Later steps, which increased the number of alternatives between which the individual might choose, were of far less importance than the earlier one, however modest, which first gave him the right of choice.

Such as it was, then, with all its incompleteness, the Toleration Act marked a momentous advance towards that religious liberty so ably advocated in Locke's "Epistola de Tolerantia," which appeared, a few months later, in an English translation.

[1] This aspect of affairs was further emphasized by the re-establishment of Presbyterianism in Scotland, in spite of the union of the Crowns. The union of the states in 1707 consequently brought about what was (on the ecclesiastico-political theory of the state) the monstrous absurdity of the coexistence in one state not merely of two forms of religion, but of two distinct establishments.

CHAPTER IV

LOCKE ON TOLERATION

LOCKE made his first appearance as an author late in life, but the views which he then made public had long been maturing in his mind. In 1652 he entered Christ Church, Oxford, where, in spite of his dislike for the studies pursued, he was no doubt confirmed in the tolerant principles of the Independents, of which, as we have seen, John Owen, then Dean of Christ Church and Vice-Chancellor of the University, was a prominent exponent. The Independent view of the church as a voluntary association of like-minded persons for purposes of worship lies at the root of Locke's theory of toleration[1].

Long before the publication of the "Epistola de Tolerantia," that theory had been drawn up in rough outline and committed to paper in the form *"Essay concerning Toleration."* 1667.

---

[1] In or about 1682 Locke wrote *A Defence of Nonconformity* which he never published. According to Fox Bourne, it was inspired by Stillingfleet's *Mischief* and *Unreasonableness of Separation*, and contains a detailed justification of the Dissenters in grouping themselves in independent churches. Extracts from it are printed in Fox Bourne's *Life of John Locke*, vol. I. pp. 457–60.

of an "Essay concerning Toleration," written in
1667, but first published in Fox Bourne's "Life of
John Locke[1]." In this essay, which displays, as
compared with contemporary pamphlets, a noticeable grip of principle and power of expression, Locke

*Authority
of the
magistrate
simply for
the good,
preserva-
tion, and
peace of
the society.* says the authority of the magistrate is simply for
the good, preservation, and peace of the society over
which he is set. He proceeds to apply the principle
to the various activities of man. In the first place,
purely speculative opinions and divine worship (and
these alone) have an absolute and universal right to
toleration : for purely speculative opinions do not
influence my actions as a member of society, and as
I cannot control them myself I cannot give the
control of them to the magistrate; while divine
worship is purely a matter between God and myself.
These involve no guilt or sin at all, provided there
be sincerity and conscientiousness (175–8). Secondly,
"practical principles, or opinions by which men think
themselves obliged to regulate their actions with
one another" ("all these opinions being things either
of indifferency or doubt"), have a title to toleration
so far as they do not tend to disturb the state or to
cause greater inconveniences than advantages to the
community. But no such opinion has a right to
toleration merely as a matter of conscience, for the
magistrate should frame his laws with a view to the
good of all his subjects—not to the persuasions of
a part (178). In this connection Locke distinguishes
three degrees of imposition in matters of opinion;

[1] Vol. I. pp. 174–94, to which the bracketed numbers in the
text refer.

restraint upon publication or "venting," compulsion
to renounce certain opinions, and compulsion to
assent to their opposites. The last two, he says,
ought not to be practised (179–80). Thirdly, dealing
with moral virtues and vices, Locke says the magistrate has nothing to do with these, except so far as
they are subservient to the good and preservation
of mankind under government; he has nothing to
do with the good of men's souls, or their concernment in another life (181–2). Hence he draws three
conclusions: first, that the magistrate is not bound *Conclu-*
to punish all vices; secondly, that he ought not to *sions*
drawn
command the practice of any vice, for it cannot be *from this.*
subservient to the good of the people or the preservation of the government; and thirdly, that,
should he do so, the subject must disobey and submit to the penalty (183).

Locke next deals with the classes of persons *The*
whom the magistrate need not tolerate, and of these *magistrate*
need not
he discovers two classes   The first consists of those *tolerate*
who hold opinions logically destructive of the society *(1) opin-*
ions de-
in which they live; and he gives as an instance *structive*
of the
Roman Catholics who are not subjects of the Pope, *society, or*
and whose ecclesiastical allegiance to him therefore
interferes with their civil allegiance to the prince in
whose dominions they live (183). A little later he
mentions the doctrine that faith is not to be kept
with heretics as an instance of a class of opinions
and actions which are in their natural tendency
destructive of society, and therefore ought not to
be tolerated at all (186). The second case which
Locke excepts from toleration is more interesting.

(2) *a distinct party which appears dangerous.* When "men herd themselves into companies with distinctions from the public," and a "distinct party is grown or growing so numerous as to appear dangerous to the magistrate, and seem visibly to threaten the peace of the state," the magistrate should do all he can to suppress it. "For, though the separation were really in nothing but religious worship, and he should use as the last remedy force and severity against those who did nothing but worship God in their own way, yet would he not really persecute their religion or punish them for that more than in a battle the conqueror kills men for wearing white ribbons in their hats or any other badge about them, but because this was a mark they were enemies and dangerous; religion, i.e. this or that form of worship, being the cause of their union and correspondence, not of their factiousness and turbulency." Force however, he adds, is the worst way to dissolve such a party and the last to be used (184–5).

The latter exception a blemish. This odd-sounding exception from the general rule of toleration detracts seriously from the liberalism of the essay. The vague language might be made into an apology for a very high degree of religious oppression. The "distinctions from the public" immediately present to Locke's mind were perhaps the eccentricities of dress and manners affected by the Quakers; but, in any case, the analogy is, of course, grossly false. It is only the occurrence of the battle which justifies the conqueror in killing the men of the white ribbons, but Locke's magistrate would persecute the men of the distinct religion (which[1] corresponds to the white ribbons) with nothing to correspond to the battle. The ribbons are a sign of membership of the opposing force; the distinct religion may be a sign of nothing at all ulterior to itself, as Locke admits. It is a striking proof of the strength of the public fear and prejudice that even Locke had not at this time freed himself from the idea that association unauthorized by the state was in itself factious and turbulent, but shared, though in a milder form, those apprehensions of rebellion so vividly entertained by Tomkins, Parker and other champions of persecution. By the time that he wrote the "Epistola de Tolerantia," he had become, perhaps under the stimulus of political persecution, more liberal.

Applying his theories to the then state of England, Locke comes to the conclusion that in the first place the Papists must not be tolerated, for the double reason that their opinions are destructive of government and that when in power themselves they are intolerant. He enunciates as a general principle that only the tolerant are to be tolerated. The Nonconformists should be tolerated; for persecution does not convince, and only makes them, if they conform, hypocrites and secret malcontents, and enemies instead of persons merely

Application of his theory.

---

[1] I.e. the religion itself, not the signs which distinguish its members, which latter have nothing corresponding to them in the imaginary battle-scene. This is the inevitable conclusion to be drawn from the text, but it may be seriously doubted whether Locke clearly separated in his mind the ideas of the signs and the thing signified.

separated in opinions, if they stand out: moreover it forces their separate parties to unite, and uniformity cannot be gained by anything short of extirpation.

Possibility that the essay influenced Ashley.

Though the essay was not published, it is quite possible that it was not without its effect in influential circles. In the year in which it was written the fall of Clarendon made way for the Cabal, and in the same year Locke went from Oxford to London and became a member of Ashley's household. But whether Ashley ever read the essay, and if so, whether it was in some degree responsible for his attitude on the question of toleration, remain matters of conjecture. Ashley, however, was a tolerationist long before this time, and his memorial to Charles II a few years later deals with the subject, as we have seen[1], from a different standpoint.

Locke in Holland

Locke's political connection was destined eventually to get him into trouble. He fell under the displeasure aroused at Court by the later part of his patron's political career, and in 1683 retired into Holland where he remained till 1689. It was while he was in hiding in Amsterdam, during the winter

wrote the "Epistola de Tolerantia,"

of 1685–6 that he wrote the "Epistola de Tolerantia" in Latin to his friend Limborch, who published it, anonymously, and apparently without Locke's knowledge, in the spring of 1689 at Gouda in Holland.

published 1689.

Translations into Dutch and French were published almost immediately, and in the autumn (when the Toleration Act had been already passed) there

[1] p. 149.

appeared an English translation by one William Popple, a Unitarian merchant resident in London.

In the following April, "The Argument of the *Contro-* 'Letter concerning Toleration' briefly considered *versy with Proast.* and answered" by Jonas Proast was published at Oxford. To this Locke immediately replied under the pseudonym "Philanthropus" in "A Second Letter concerning Toleration." Proast rejoined with "A Third Letter concerning Toleration," and "Philanthropus" once more replied in "A Third Letter for Toleration"—an elaborate discussion three times as long as his two previous letters put together. This was in 1692, and Proast now retired from the conflict for several years, but reopened it in 1704 with "A Second Letter to the Author of the Three Letters for Toleration." In 1706 Locke died, leaving his answer—"A Fourth Letter for Toleration"— unfinished. It was in the codicil to his will that his authorship of the Letters was first distinctly acknowledged.

A good deal of the substance of the letters is *TheLetters* repeated from the Essay of 1667, but the subject *on Tolera- tion.* receives a much more elaborate treatment from a more comprehensive point of view. In the essay, as Fox Bourne points out[1], Locke considered primarily, but not exclusively, the duties of governments, and especially of the English government, towards Christians of various denominations; while in the "Epistola de Tolerantia" he considered primarily, but not exclusively, the duties of Christians of various denominations in all countries towards one

[1] *Life of John Locke*, ii. 35.

another. The second, third and fourth letters merely
defend, expand and supplement the first.

When men, says Locke, exhibit cruelty towards
those who hold different opinions, but indulgence
towards immoralities, their actions demonstrate that
their aim is not the advancement of the kingdom
of God, nor the composition of a truly Christian
Church (4)[1]: as a matter of fact Church and State
support one another for mutual profit (36). But
Christ did not arm his emissaries with force, nor
teach his followers to look for help to the great men
of the world (4, 335). Locke rightly lays emphasis
Distinction between spheres of civil government and religion. upon the necessity of distinguishing between the
respective spheres of civil government and of re-
ligion, and with a view to making the distinction
clear first considers the functions of the commonwealth[2]. "The commonwealth," he writes, "seems
to be a society of men constituted only for the
procuring, the preserving, and the advancing their
The care of souls not committed to the magistrate, for (1) he has no such commission from God or the people; own civil interests": the care of souls is not committed to the magistrate any more than to other
men; he has no such commission from God, nor has
he from the people, for no man has the power to
leave it to another man to choose his religion for
him (5, 6, 86), nor did any man enter into society to
save his soul—a purpose for which he did not need

[1] The numbers in brackets refer to the pages of Alexander
Murray's reprint of the Letters on Toleration, 1870. The first
letter occupies pp. 2–39; the second, pp. 39–93; the third, pp. 93–
379; the fourth, pp. 379–97.

[2] For a vivid and forceful reproduction of Locke's views on the
relation of the state to religion, see Macaulay's essay on *Gladstone
on Church and State*.

the force of society (80). Indeed, punishment for
religious opinions is an injury which everyone in a
state of nature would avoid; therefore protection
from such injury is one of the ends of the commonwealth, and everyone consequently has a right to
toleration (143). That the care of souls cannot *(2) force cannot*
belong to the civil magistrate is shown, secondly, *produce*
by the fact that, "his power consists only in out- *conviction;*
ward force; but true and saving religion consists
in the inward persuasion of the mind, without which
nothing can be acceptable to God. And such is the
nature of the understanding that it cannot be compelled to the belief of anything by outward force"
(6). If, therefore, the magistrate punishes the
Nonconformists "till they embrace, i.e. believe, he
punishes them for what is not in their power; if
till they embrace, i.e. barely profess, he punishes
them for what is not for their good; to neither of
which, can he be commissioned by the law of
nature" (343). A good life, Locke says, is the
proper way to seek salvation, and punishments for
this end are just and useful (43). In the third *(3) even if*
place, even supposing that penalties could produce *it could, its general*
conviction, the use of them would not help in the *applica-*
salvation of souls, for only one country would be in *tion would*
the right, and hence salvation would be dependent *be harm-*
upon the place of a man's birth (7), and more harm *ful;*
than good would be done to the true religion (144).
For if the magistrate has a right to promote the true
religion, he must also have a right to promote his
own (251); hence, "since there are more Pagan,
Mahometan, and erroneous princes in the world,
than orthodox; truth, and the Christian religion,

taking the world as we find it, is sure to be more punished and suppressed than error and falsehood" (77). To ensure the magistrate's acting rightly he must be gifted with infallibility (251); it is not enough that he should have assurance that he is right; the highest degree of assurance is not knowledge, and nothing can produce knowledge save what is capable of demonstration or self-evident (95). But even if the infliction of penalties were useful, it would not follow that the magistrate has the care of souls; mere usefulness does not make the infliction of penalties lawful without a commission to inflict them, for, if it does, then private men may use them as well as the magistrate (53).

(4) he has no special ability to discover the way to heaven. The magistrate cannot have the care of souls, fourthly, because he is no more able than anyone else to discover the way to heaven; indeed, if force is necessary to bring men to the true religion, the magistrate is destitute of the means of being brought to it (16, 390). But if it is contended that this objection is irrelevant because the magistrate does not himself judge, but enforces the decrees of the church, the question arises, of which church does he enforce the decrees? Clearly, of his own; so that it is a matter of his judgment, after all. But even if the magistrate be right, "no religion which I believe not to be true, can be either true or profitable unto me." "I may grow rich by an art that I take not delight in; I may be cured of some disease by remedies that I have not faith in; but I cannot be saved by a religion that I distrust, and by a worship that I abhor" (17–8).

So much for Locke's theory of the duties of the

civil power: let us pass on to consider his theory of the functions of the church. He defines a Church as "a voluntary society of men, joining themselves together of their own accord, in order to the public worshipping of God, in such a manner as they may judge acceptable to Him, and effectual to the salvation of their souls." Hence it follows that the right of making laws for it is only in the society and those authorized by it (7–8), and that no church has jurisdiction over another, for the civil government can give no new right to the church, nor the church to the civil government (11). No member of any church which does not claim infallibility can require anyone to take the testimony of any church as sufficient proof of the truth of her own doctrine[1] (60). Again, a church requiring for communion things which Christ does not require for life eternal—a church, that is, established on laws that are not his—cannot be the Church of Christ (9); for no man can have authority to shut any man out of the Church of Christ, for that for which Christ will not shut him out of heaven (162): this, however, does not prevent any particular church from excommunicating one who obstinately breaks its laws (10). The New Testament, Locke contends, gives no sanction to persecution; the authority of the clergy (force belonging wholly to the civil magistrate) should be

A church is a voluntary society

---

[1] In *A Defence of Nonconformity* written about 1682, Locke says, "All arguments used from the church or established church, amount to no more than this, that there are a certain set of men in the world upon whose credit I must without further examination venture my salvation." Quoted by Fox Bourne, *Life of John Locke*, I. 457.

confined within the bounds of the church, which is
absolutely absolutely distinct from the commonwealth, and
distinct should be exerted in favour of charity, meek-
from the ness, and toleration (9, 13).   In the matter of
common-
wealth. propagating the truth, a man must not make use
of any means save those which God has prescribed,
for no means can be effectual without the coöperation of grace (353).   The real remedy for Nonconformity Locke finds in " the discoursing with men
seriously and friendly about matters in religion, by
those whose profession is the care of souls" (298).
All church discipline should tend to the public
worship of God and by its means the acquisition of
eternal life : no force should be made use of; and
expulsion from the society should be the ultimate
ecclesiastical penalty (9–10).

Cere-   Since the question of ceremonies occupied so
monies prominent a place in the controversy between the
Church and the Nonconformists, it naturally re-'
ceives careful attention in the Letters.   As to the
imposition of ceremonies, Locke decides that they
may not be may not be imposed by the magistrate on unwilling
imposed on persons ; first, because ceremonies of human institu-
unwilling
persons, tion cannot be known to be necessary to salvation,
nor, being confessed (as in the preface to the Book
of Common Prayer) to be in their own nature
indifferent, so much as thought to be so (96, 225);
and secondly, " because whatsoever is practised in
the worship of God is only so far justifiable as it is
believed by those who practise it to be acceptable
unto him"; and it is a sin to force men to " compliance in an indifferent thing which in religious

worship may be a sin to them" (19, 225). Things
indifferent, certainly, are subjected to the legislative
power, but when brought into the worship of God
are beyond the magistrate's jurisdiction; and, besides, they cannot, for the very reason that they are
indifferent, be made by human authority part of the
worship of God, in which they are "not otherwise
lawful than as they are instituted by God himself"
(19–20).

As to the prohibition of ceremonies, such as are *nor pro-*
already practised must not be forbidden by the *hibited,*
unless un-
magistrate provided that they are not unlawful in *lawful in*
the ordinary course of life (22). "Is it permitted *ordinary*
life.
to speak Latin in the market place? Let those who
have a mind to do it, be permitted to do it also in
the church. Is it lawful for any man in his own
house to kneel, stand, sit, or use any other posture;
and to clothe himself in white or black, in short or
in long garments? Let it not be made unlawful to
eat bread, drink wine, or wash with water in the
church. In a word; whatsoever things are left free
by law in the common occasions of life, let them
remain free unto every church in divine worship"
(34).

Even an idolatrous church must be tolerated, *Idolatry*
for any power given to the magistrate for the sup- *to be*
tolerated.
pression of an idolatrous church may, in time and
place, be used for the ruin of an orthodox one (23).
What Locke means is that if we allow that the
magistrate has a right to suppress idolatry we
abandon the principle which denies his right to interfere with religion save upon purely civil grounds;

and that if that principle be abandoned orthodoxy
itself has no longer any guarantee against molestation.
If it be objected that idolatry is a sin, and therefore
not to be tolerated, Locke replies that it is not the
magistrate's business to punish sins which do not
disturb other men's rights or the public peace; and
he also sets aside the injunctions of the Mosaic law
to root out idolaters, as not being obligatory upon
Christians (24).

Articles of Religion: (1) speculative. Magistrate may not impose them,

Articles of Religion[1] Locke divides into two
classes, speculative, which "terminate simply in the
understanding," and practical, which "influence the
will and manners." With the former the magistrate
has no concern. He may not impose them because
our beliefs do not depend upon our will, and "it is
absurd that things should be enjoined by laws,
which are not in men's power to perform" (26).
Besides, it is useless to impose creeds on those who
own the Scriptures to be the Word of God and the
rule of faith; even the Apostles' Creed contains
more than is necessary to salvation, and it is unlawful to use force to bring men to a communion
to which anything is necessary which is not also
necessary to salvation (101–2, 223). Nor may the

or forbid their propagation.

magistrate forbid speculative opinions to be preached
or professed, for they have no relation to the civil
rights of the subjects. "If a Roman Catholic believes that to be really the body of Christ, which
another man calls bread, he does no injury thereby

---

[1] It may be noticed that a good deal under this head and the
next (*Exceptions from toleration*) is reproduced from the Essay
concerning Toleration, for which see pp. 237–42.

to his neighbour. If a Jew does not believe the New Testament to be the Word of God, he does not thereby alter anything in men's civil rights. If a heathen doubt of both Testaments, he is not therefore to be punished as a pernicious citizen. The power of the magistrate, and the estates of the people may be equally secure, whether any man believe these things or no" (26). With regard to *(2) practical.* practical opinions, Locke asserts that every man, in the *Every man* first place, has authority to judge for himself, because *has right* erroneous opinions do not violate another's rights, *to judge* and, in the second, is under an obligation to follow his *and act for* own judgment in practice, because obedience is due *himself.* first to God, and afterwards to the laws (27–9). In case the magistrate prescribes an action which a private person conscientiously considers unlawful (which, however, Locke says, will seldom happen "if government be faithfully administered and the counsels of the magistrate be indeed directed to the public good") then the latter must "abstain from the action that he judges unlawful, and undergo the punishment which it is not unlawful for him to bear" (29). The converse—the case of a magistrate forbidding what a private person feels bound in conscience to do—Locke does not consider, but he would presumably have given his decision on similar lines.

It should be noticed what stress Locke lays throughout on the necessity of complete individual conviction and sincerity in religion, in strong contrast to that school of divines which urged that scruples should be subordinated to the commands of authority. Indeed he emphasizes this to a fault

when he declares that " to conform to and outwardly
profess a religion which a man does not understand
and heartily believe, every one, I think, judges to be
a sin, and no fit means to procure the grace of God "
(273); for thus no place is left for those who, while
sceptical or even unbelieving, may not wish to sever
their connection with the church of which they are
members, or for those who may feel that two or
more forms of religion are of equal value[1].

*Exception
from toler-
ation of*

*opinions
contrary to
(1) human
society,*

*(2) civil
rights,*

*(3) re-
ligious
toleration,*

Locke next proceeds to lay down in what cases
toleration may be, or ought to be, withheld. The
magistrate's supreme care is the preservation of
society, therefore he must not tolerate " opinions
contrary to human society, or to those moral rules
which are necessary to the preservation of civil
society " (30). Secondly, men have no right to
toleration who " arrogate to themselves some peculiar prerogative opposite to the civil right of the
community," holding, for instance, such views as
that faith is not to be kept with heretics, that
kings, if excommunicated, forfeit their crowns and
kingdoms, or that " dominion is founded in grace "
(30). " These therefore, and the like, who attribute
unto the faithful, religious and orthodox, that is, in
plain terms, unto themselves, any peculiar privilege
or power above other mortals, in civil concernments...
have no right to be tolerated by the magistrate; as
neither those who will not own and teach the duty
of tolerating all men in matters of mere religion.
For what do all these and the like doctrines signify,
but that they may, and are ready upon any occasion

[1] Graham, *English Political Philosophy*, 74.

to seize the government, and possess themselves of
the estates and fortunes of their fellow subjects;
and that they only ask leave to be tolerated by the
magistrate so long, until they may find themselves
strong enough to effect it. Again, that church can *(4) civil
allegiance,*
have no right to be tolerated by the magistrate, *or*
which is constituted upon such a bottom that all
those who enter it, do thereby *ipso facto*, deliver
themselves up to the protection and service of
another prince" (31)—an obvious reflection upon
the Roman Catholics, though they are not mentioned by name. "Lastly, those are not at all to *(5) the
being*
be tolerated who deny the being of God. Promises, *of God.*
covenants, and oaths, which are the bonds of human
society, can have no hold upon an atheist. The
taking away of God, though even but in thought,
dissolves all. Besides also, those that by their
atheism undermine and destroy all religion, can
have no pretence of religion whereupon to challenge the privilege of a toleration" (31). Locke
has already laid it down that all men "are to enter
into some religious society that they may meet together, not only for mutual edification, but to own
to the world that they worship God" (19).

With the exception, however, of these cases the *Evil
effects of*
effects of persecution are bad. It acts mainly on *persecu-*
the irreligious and ignorant, and fills the church *tion.*
with hypocrites; upon the sincere it fails to act
(78, 260). Moreover it can at best only bring men
to conformity, and not to the mortification of their
lusts, which are, according to Locke's opponent, the
reason of their not embracing the true religion in

earnest (112). Again, it is more likely to make
men embrace error than truth, both "because men
out of the right way are as apt, I think I may say
apter, to use force than others," and also because not
one civil sovereign in ten, perhaps not one in a
hundred, is of the true religion (50). Intolerance,
too, is the real cause of immense evils that have
been ascribed to a different source. "It is not the
diversity of opinions, which cannot be avoided, but
the refusal of toleration to those that are of different
opinions, which might have been granted, that has
produced all the bustles and wars, that have been
in the Christian world, upon account of religion"
(36). Conventicles have been factious and seditious,
so far as they have been so, because they have been
oppressed. "Let us therefore deal plainly. The
magistrate is afraid of other churches, but not of his
own; because he is kind and favourable to the one,
but severe and cruel to the other" (32–3). Locke
here exposes a popular fallacy of which the consequences had been disastrous: if only the truth
for which he here contends had been recognized
earlier a great mass of suffering might have been
prevented. He further points out that the evil
effects of intolerance extend beyond the pale of
Christianity. "I ask, whether the magistrates in-
terposing in matters of religion, and establishing
national churches by the force and penalties of civil
laws, with their distinct, and at home reputed
necessary, confessions and ceremonies, do not by law
and power authorise and perpetuate sects among
Christians, to the great prejudice of Christianity,

and scandal to infidels, more than anything that
can arise from a mutual toleration, with charity and
a good life?" (163).

While persecution produces the serious results
just mentioned, tolerance would not have the *Advantages of toleration.*
disastrous consequences usually attributed to it,
but rather the reverse. "Truth certainly would do
well enough, if she were once left to shift for herself" (27): Christianity first grew up, and flourished
more than ever since without the use of force, "and
if it be a mark of the true religion, that it will prevail by its own light and strength, but that false
religions will not, but have need of force and foreign
helps to support them, nothing certainly can be
more for the advantage of the true religion, than
to take away compulsion everywhere" (41). Moreover toleration has this great advantage, that it
preserves charity. Even if it produces differences
in the ways of worship and in opinions, yet the
former, so long as they are not irreligious, will not
hinder sincere men from salvation: and as to the
latter, complete coincidence of opinions among thinking men is rare; while diversity of opinions will
very well consist with Christian unity, if there be
agreement in truths necessary to salvation, and
charity be maintained (255, 161).

Seeing the frequent use which Locke makes *The true religion.*
of the phrase "the true religion," it may be well
at this point to examine what exactly he implied
by it. In the third letter he says "that, and that
alone, is the one only true religion without which
nobody can be saved, and which is enough for the

salvation of everyone who embraces it " (291). In another work he expounds his views thus :—" 1. That there is a faith that makes men Christians. 2. That this faith is the believing ' Jesus of Nazareth to be the Messiah.' 3. That the believing Jesus to be the Messiah includes in it a receiving him for our Lord and King, promised and sent from God: and so lays upon all his subjects an absolute and indispensable necessity of assenting to all that they can attain the knowledge that he taught; and of a sincere obedience to all that he commanded[1]." This true religion the Church of England professes, but its religion is not the only true religion, if there is anything made part of it which is not necessary to salvation: indeed, possibly most, if not all, the differing churches contain the true religion (219). Even "the Romish religion " contains all that is necessary to salvation, but it is nevertheless not a true religion, because, so Locke implies, it contains things that are inconsistent with it (291).

Accusations of heresy and schism—especially of the latter—had been so bandied about in the toleration controversy, that in a postscript to his first letter, Locke deals with these questions. Heresy he defines as " a separation made in ecclesiastical communion between men of the same religion, for some opinions no way contained in the rule itself," and from this definition concludes that "amongst those who acknowledge nothing but the Holy Scriptures to be their rule of faith, heresy is a separation

Heresy, and

[1] *Second Vindication of the Reasonableness of Christianity.* Locke's Works (11th ed., 10 vols., London, 1812), vol. vii. p. 421.

made in their Christian communion, for opinions not
contained in the express words of Scripture." This
separation may be made in two ways: and the first
is, when the greater or stronger part of the church
excludes the rest for not professing belief in opinions
which are not found in the express words of Scripture;
" for it is not the paucity of those that are separated,
nor the authority of the magistrate, that can make
any man guilty of heresy." The second way of separation is exemplified when anyone separates himself
from the church because it does not profess some
opinions not expressly taught in Scripture (38).
Locke similarly defines schism as a separation made *schism.*
in the church because of some non-necessary part
of worship or discipline; and no part can be necessary
except such as have been expressly commanded by
Christ or the Apostles (39). By these definitions
Locke brings the charges of heresy and schism by
implication to bear on the Church of England: this
is made clearer in the third letter where he asks
" whether those are not most authors and promoters
of sects and divisions, who impose creeds and ceremonies and articles of men's making" (161). He
sums the matter up with the decision that " he that
denies not anything that the Holy Scriptures teach
in express words, nor makes a separation upon occasion of anything that is not manifestly contained in
the sacred text; however he may be nick-named by
any sect of Christians, and declared by some or all
of them to be utterly void of true Christianity: yet
in deed and truth this man cannot be either a heretic
or schismatic " (39).

Answers to Proast's arguments:
(1) in favour of moderate punishments to make men consider;

Locke's opponent, Proast, while disclaiming advocacy of "severities," yet urged that force, indirectly and at a distance, may do some service, that is, when it inflicts moderate punishments to bring men to consider those reasons and arguments which are proper and sufficient to convince them; and, further, that there is no other means than force to make them consider; therefore it is necessary (45-55)[1]. To this contention Locke has several replies which he elaborates at great length with many repetitions, especially in his third letter. In the first place, the "moderate penalties" must develop into "severities," for if they do not achieve their object nothing remains except to make them more heavy (47, 179), for to continue inefficacious penalties is unjustifiable cruelty (194). And there can be no end to them, for "if your punishments may not be inflicted on men to make them consider, who have or may have considered already for ought you know; then dissenters are never to be once punished, no more than any other sort of men. If dissenters are to be punished, to make them consider, whether they have considered or no; then their punishments, though they do consider, must never cease, as long as they are dissenters; which whether it be to punish them only to bring them to consider, let all men judge. Thus I am sure punishments, in your method, must either never begin upon dissenters or never cease.

---

[1] As everything important in *The Argument of the Letter concerning Toleration* is dealt with in Locke's *Second Letter*, and Proast's *Third Letter* introduces nothing new, the references are to the pages of the *Letters on Toleration* where Proast's arguments are quoted or stated by Locke.

And so pretend moderation as you please, the punishments which your method requires, must be either very immoderate, or none at all" (73). But, as a matter of fact, on this theory the penalties are inflicted on the dissenters not to make them consider, but because they are not of the national religion. "It is impracticable to punish dissenters, as dissenters, only to make them consider. For if you punish them as dissenters, as certainly you do, if you punish them alone, and them all without exception, you punish them for not being of the national religion. And to punish a man for not being of the national religion, is not to punish him only to make him consider, unless not to consider and not to be of the national religion be the same thing" (49). And this principle will promote Popery in France as Protestantism in England (50–1). Again, "to punish men out of the communion of the national church, to make them consider, is unjust. They are punished because out of the national church: and they are out of the national church because they are not yet convinced. Their standing out therefore in the state, whilst they are not convinced, not satisfied in their minds, is no fault; and therefore cannot justly be punished" (49). Further, if the object of penalties be to make men examine the grounds of their religion, penalties should be applied to the conformists as well: there is no reason for singling out the dissenters for punishment. "Have no dissenters considered of religion? Or have all conformists considered? That you yourself will not say. Your project is therefore just as reasonable, as if, a lethargy growing epidemical in England, you should propose to have a law made to blister and scarify and shave the heads of all who wear gowns : though it be certain that neither all who wear gowns are lethargic, nor all who are lethargic wear gowns.—'Men are generally negligent in examining the grounds of religion.' This I grant. But could there be a more wild and incoherent consequence drawn from it, than this ; 'therefore dissenters must be punished'?" (62–4).

(2) *that society was instituted for all attainable good ;* To Locke's assertion that the magistrate had no right to interfere with religion, because religion was excluded from his jurisdiction in the social contract, Proast replied that civil society was instituted for the benefits which it may any way yield[1]. If so, said Locke, then the same principle must apply to all societies, and it must be one of the ends of the family to preach the gospel and administer the sacraments ; "and one business of the army to teach languages and to propagate religion ; because these are benefits some way or other obtainable by these societies : unless you take want of commission and authority to be a sufficient impediment : and that will be so too in other cases " (79).

In this contention Locke is not justified : he supports the view that civil society was not instituted with a view to all the benefits attainable by it, on the ground that the magistrate has not com-

---

[1] Proast complained that Locke misrepresented him here. But as far as I can gather from his not very intelligible argument, he insisted on a distinction without a difference. See his *Third Letter concerning Toleration*, 57–8.

mission and authority to provide for all the benefits
attainable by civil society; but whether this is so
or not is the very point under discussion. And
Proast had just as much right to imagine a social
contract by which society was instituted with a
view to obtaining good in general, as Locke had to
imagine one by which it was confined to the pursuit
of civil good alone. Indeed, Proast's view is less
wildly unhistorical than Locke's. But Locke was
not trammelled by the facts of history, which he
reconstructed according to his view of what was
expedient under present conditions; hence he would
not allow that man emerging from the state of nature
instituted civil society, that is, put himself under
government, for any purpose for which government
was not, as a matter of fact, fitted; and in showing
its unfitness as a means for the propagation of truth
he was on firmer ground[1].

"It is a benefit," he continues, "to have true
knowledge and philosophy embraced and assented
to in any civil society or government. But will you
say therefore that it is a benefit to the society, or

[1] Compare Macaulay's criticism of Gladstone's claim that it is
one of the ends of the state to propagate religious truth. Essay
on *Gladstone on Church and State*, esp. pp. 475–7 (Longmans'
Silver Library ed. of Macaulay's *Essays and Lays*, 1903). Macaulay
closely follows Locke's line of reasoning, with the difference that
he bases his argument not upon historical but upon utilitarian
grounds. The seventeenth century had not sufficiently developed
the historical sense to distinguish between the two. The idea in
Locke's mind was no doubt at bottom the same as that in
Macaulay's: the difference in expression is a measure of the
difference in outlook of their respective ages. The fault of Locke's
thought is one of form rather than of essence.

one of the ends of government, that all who are not Peripatetics should be punished, to make men find out the truth, and profess it? This indeed might be a fit way to make some men embrace the Peripatetic philosophy, but not a proper way to find the truth. For perhaps the Peripatetic philosophy may not be true; perhaps a great many have not time, nor parts to study it; perhaps a great many who have studied it, cannot be convinced of the truth of it: and therefore it cannot be a benefit to the commonwealth, nor one of the ends of it, that these members of the society should be disturbed, and diseased to no purpose when they are guilty of no fault. For just the same reason, it cannot be a benefit to civil society, that men should be punished in Denmark for not being Lutherans; in Geneva, for not being Calvinists; and in Vienna for not being Papists; as a means to make them find out the true religion. For so upon your grounds, men must be treated in those places, as well as in England, for not being of the church of England" (79–80).

(3) *that the magistrate may promote the true, but not a false, religion.* This brings us to the consideration of a third important contention urged by Proast, that the civil magistrate has the right to use force for the promotion of the true religion, though not for the promotion of a false one. It is not absolutely fair to reply to this, as Locke does in his third letter, that if a magistrate has a right to use force to promote the true, he must have a right to use force to promote his own religion (250–1). It is conceivable that the magistrate should have a right, though it is impossible for a human mind infallibly

to distinguish between the legitimate use of it and illegitimate tyranny : it does not necessarily follow from this impossibility that the two operations are not distinct. But in such a case the right is, for all practical purposes, reduced to a nullity, and therein lies Locke's justification. He had, indeed, already dealt with the case more accurately and forcibly. " By what has already been said, I suppose it is evident, that if the magistrate be to use force only for promoting the true religion, he can have no other guide, but his own persuasion of what is the true religion, and must be led by that in his use of force, or else not use it at all in matters of religion. If you take the latter of these consequences, you and I are agreed : if the former, you must allow all magistrates, of whatsoever religion, the use of force to bring men to theirs, and so be involved in all those ill consequences which you cannot it seems admit, and hoped to decline by your useless distinction of force to be used, not for any, but for the true religion " (96). The distinction, in a word, even if theoretically sound, is for practical purposes valueless.

Such was Locke's theory of toleration. We need not feel surprise that it was by no means universally accepted. Sheer formless prejudice was no doubt, as usual, the driving power of intolerance, but other less irrational causes were at work. To those who hold that their particular religious body is in sole possession of the one truth, and that of this they have absolute certainty, many of the arguments for toleration, be they never so powerfully expressed,

Causes making against the acceptance of Locke's theory:

(1) *difficulty of realizing distinction between assurance and knowledge;*

are simply irrelevant; and even though this extreme of narrow-mindedness be left behind, yet a considerable liberalizing process must be undergone before the case for toleration can obtain a real hold on the intellect. The distinction between complete assurance and absolute knowledge is one which the unphilosophical mind, even if it admits it, may very well be incapable of entertaining as a realized belief. An assurance which is the central fact of a man's life, the truth of which, though he confess his own fallibility, he cannot really doubt, it is not unnatural for him to regard as absolute knowledge, and to scout the sceptical argument which asserts that this conviction, than which no other is more certain, is not knowledge. Knowledge in the metaphysician's sense it may not be, but knowledge in the sense in which he is accustomed to use the word it is: and if he may not take a serious step upon this assurance for fear of being mistaken, upon what assurance may he take any serious step at all?

(2) *conception of the true religion as a common factor;*

The High Churchman, too, could not be expected to approve very heartily of a theory containing such a conception of the true religion as that put forward by Locke, who treated it as a sort of common factor of most, if not all, of the Christian religious systems. This served its purpose as an argument for tolerating all who held this minimum, for if they held the true religion it was superfluous to persecute them for not holding additional and unnecessary beliefs: but in presenting an inadequate idea of the true religion Locke failed to bring forward the strong positive argument for toleration afforded by the conception of it rather as a common multiple than a common factor of religious systems, something more vast and comprehensive than any existing form, of which, indeed, "our little systems" " are but broken lights," presenting various component colours of the white radiance of truth.

On more purely ecclesiastical questions, too, he *(3) voluntary conception of the Church.* ran counter to widespread opinion. Visible churches seem to have been for Locke "accidents of religion, not parts of its essence, which lay in personal faith and conduct, and might flourish under any ecclesiastical organization or even apart from all organized religious societies[1]." With the additional obstacles to toleration raised by the conception of any religious organization as the one society divinely appointed for the inclusion of all men, he has nothing to do. Thus neither his definition of a church and the consequent complete separation of church and state, nor his principle of distinguishing between essentials and things indifferent, would particularly commend themselves to the contemporary High Church party.

And these things were at the very base of his theory. First in logical order is the conception of the church as a purely voluntary society, which finds its natural consequences in the sharply drawn distinction between church and state. It is a *The social contract.* characteristic of his age that having arrived at this theory from a sense of the fitness of things, Locke should proceed to manufacture an antecedent justification for it by basing it upon a particular reading of the social contract, according to which religion

[1] A. Campbell Fraser, *Locke*, 68.

was not included under the magistrate's control.
The social contract was merely a projection into the
mists of the past of any particular writer's conception
of the rules of social justice as applicable to his own
time. Mere abstract principles were thought to be
deficient in effective binding power. Hunger for the
concrete evoked out of the imagination a purely
fictitious contract which was supposed to give additional sanction to the moral code. It was a form
of expression which the dawning of the historic
sense rendered obsolete. From the historical point
of view it is of course the merest figment. It is
more than unhistorical as to fact; nothing short
of an almost total lack of the historic sense could
allow to pass unchallenged the absurdity of primitive
man appreciating the advantages of society before
it existed, and drawing up a contract for its constitution[1].

Especial falseness of Locke's conception of it.

But in nothing does Locke's theory of the social
contract find itself in more complete opposition to
ascertained fact than in that point upon which he
professes largely to base his theory of toleration—
the separation of religion from the civil government.
In primitive tribes and states in an early stage of
development such a separation would not have been

[1] The fact that the American colonists had actually founded
states by this method no doubt gave additional colour to the
theory. But the American colonists had the experience of civilization behind them. The text of the compact made by the Pilgrim
Fathers, the first of a series of "Plantation Covenants" (Jellinek,
Declaration of the Rights of Man and of Citizens, 64–5, trans. by
Max Farrand, published by Holt & Co., New York), will be found
in Arber, *Story of the Pilgrim Fathers*, 409–10.

conceivable, much less possible : and even if possible
could hardly have been other than disastrous.   The
whole conception is absurdly inapplicable to men in
that primitive condition in which they were supposed
to have formed the social contract, community of
custom and superstition being one of the strongest
ties in a rudimentary society.   Locke's mistake is
the converse of that of the anti-tolerationists : they
persisted too long in regarding the state as an
ecclesiastico-political community: he regarded it still
more falsely as never having been an ecclesiastico-
political community at all.   Both alike were blind
to the forces of social evolution by which the actual
character of the state was determined.   But Locke's
error was with regard to the past, their error was
with regard to the present ; hence for the practical
purposes of the controversy Locke was in the right.

But not only does Locke show a lack of the
historic sense—a common failing in the seventeenth
century ; he also shows a lack of insight into human *His exag-*
nature as it is. If he vastly overrates the intellectual *gerated estimate of*
capacity of the primitive man, he considerably over- *the human*
rates the intellectual capacity of civilized man. He *intellect as to*
is not ignorant of the fact that the average man
does not arrive at his religious views by a process
of independent reasoning, but he not infrequently
loses sight of it.   His idea, for instance, that people *(1) choos-*
join churches voluntarily, is, as a general rule, at *ing a form of religion,*
variance with facts[1].   For most men birth deter-

[1] Locke had no doubt in mind the history of the preceding
half-century, during the earlier part of which the idea of voluntary religious association had been perhaps more nearly realized
than in any period before or since.

mines to what church they shall belong: few leave that to which their birth has assigned them to join another. A similar failure to appreciate the real facts of the case—or at any rate to use them in his reasoning—is seen in his objection to persecution that, if universally applied, it will not help the salvation of souls, for "there being but one truth, one way to heaven," only one country would be in the right, and "men would owe their eternal happiness or their eternal misery to the place of their nativity" (7). But, if there is only one way to heaven, that is exactly what happens at present; for, as matters are, men usually adopt the religion of their country as far as they accept any religion at all; mental environment and social pressure in most cases checking the free exercise of their intellects, for all practical purposes, quite as effectually as the persecution which Locke deprecates[1]. Otherwise, why are Europeans born east of longitude 20° E. usually members of the Greek Church, and those born west of that meridian usually Roman Catholics or Protestants according as their birth takes place south or north of (roughly speaking) the 51st parallel of latitude?

(2) *inefficacy of penalties to convince.* Again, Locke, in common with many other writers on the same side, asserts that penalties cannot convince the mind. If all men were fearless or intellectually inflexible this would be true: as matters are, fear is a potent source of intellectual bias which may produce perfectly sincere conviction. And in

[1] Parts of this paragraph and the next are drawn from W. Graham, *English Political Philosophy*, 81, 73–4.

common with practically all the controversialists of
his time he seems to have completely overlooked the
very strong argument for persecution drawn from *The argu-*
the consideration that even if those to whom force is *ment from future*
applied become nothing more than conformists, their *genera-*
children, or at any rate their remoter descendants, *tions.*
are likely to be sincere believers. If Christianity
be beneficial, thirty generations of Germans must
have benefited from the mockery of the baptism in
crowds which their absolutely uninstructed ancestors
underwent as the pledge of submission to Charles
the Great[1]: if Roman Catholicism be beneficial,
seven generations of Frenchmen must have benefited
by the fact that multitudes of Huguenots (with
whatever degree of sincerity) were induced to re-
consider their religious position by the *dragonnades*
of Louis XIV.

It should be noticed that though Locke advocates *Exception*
the complete severance of church and state, he is *from toleration*
opposed to the severance of the state from religion. *of (1)*
Mohammedans are to be tolerated, but atheists are *atheists,*
not. It may seem regrettable that in this respect
Locke was unable to rise superior to the prejudices
of his time. The exception of atheists from toleration is a relic of theological domination in the moral
field. The belief that atheism connotes a repudiation
of all moral obligations, the belief that morality cannot stand by itself, but needs the support of theism,

---

[1] Even if we assume, as we probably may, that the nation
would ultimately have been converted in any case by less drastic
methods, the principle remains unaffected. What of the intervening generations who would have lived and died heathens?

betrays a deficient appreciation of the bases of morality[1]. It should be noticed, however, that in this belief Locke was only reflecting what was the practically universal opinion of his age[2]: and if atheism was generally regarded by both atheists and their opponents as a solvent of moral obligations it was quite natural that Locke should include it among his excepted opinions. His list begins with opinions "contrary to human society or to those moral rules which are necessary to the preservation of civil society[3]," and atheism is practically a special case of this class. It is difficult to see how Locke could satisfactorily reconcile the exception of any opinions, as such, from toleration with his own powerful arguments against the attempt to bring force to bear upon opinion; but the exception of atheism is a trifle less inconsistent than others, in that the general proposition which Locke proposes to establish is the right to toleration of all forms of religion, not of all forms of thought on the subject of religion.

(2) *the intolerant.* Another of Locke's exceptions from toleration deserves notice. It is the exception of those who do not own and teach the duty of religious toleration. Though perhaps Locke had the Roman Catholics

---

[1] The same exception was made by Grotius, who anticipated, if he did not inspire, several of Locke's views on toleration, and by Pufendorf. See E. E. Worcester, *The Religious Opinions of John Locke*, 101-9, published, (?) at Leipzig, 1889.

[2] For a vigorous modern assertion of the same opinion in connection with toleration, see Sir James Fitzjames Stephen, *Liberty, Equality, Fraternity*, 68-75.

[3] See p. 252.

mainly in his mind, the exception was one of wider
application, and certainly would have included the
Church of England, not only before the Revolution
but after it also. The principle of toleration was not
owned in the Toleration Act, nor the duty of toleration taught in the Church of England, save by the
latitudinarian minority.

As a tolerationist Locke cannot be regarded as *Locke's re-*
belonging to any particular school or representing *lation to his prede-*
any single tradition. We may see in him the *cessors.*
rationalism of the liberal Churchmen, the individualism of Independency, and the dispassionate
questioning spirit of the scientific revival : but whatever he adopted from previous writers he made his
own. It is useless to attempt to trace in him the
influence of particular writers upon the question
of toleration between the Restoration and the Toleration Act. We have no need to suppose that he
was appreciably indebted to any in particular of the
controversialists of intellectual calibre quite inferior
to his, who squabbled while he meditated in silence.
The controversy was a battle of pigmies in the twilight ; with the Letters on Toleration we pass into
the light of day.

Of his English predecessors he followed Chilling- *Chilling-*
worth in making the Bible, as interpreted by the *worth.*
individual reason, the sole authority for Protestants ;
and his dictum that no man can have authority to
shut any man out of the church of Christ for that
for which Christ will not shut him out of heaven is
drawn directly from Chillingworth. Taylor's "Liberty *Taylor.*

of Prophesying" also seems to have been drawn upon
considerably by Locke[1].

*Early
Puritan
environ-
ment.*

But probably Locke's opinions were due far less
to anything he read directly bearing upon the subject
of toleration than to the Puritan environment of his
youth. His father had been a captain in a regiment
of horse in the Parliamentary army; the Oxford of
Locke's undergraduate days was under the Independent influence of Owen. It is natural then, that
at the foundation of his theory of toleration should
be found the conception of the church as a voluntary
association of like-minded individuals.

*The
Letters a
summing
up.*

The importance of the Letters in the history
of the theory of toleration is not due to the fact that
they contain anything new. There is little in them
which had not been said before either by a writer
of repute or by some obscure pamphleteer. But
the Letters played the part of the judge's summing
up: they welded into a consistent whole, a closely
reasoned theory, the partial suggestions and dis-
connected speculations of a generation. Much of
the controversy on toleration of the preceding thirty
years had been carried on as a side issue in the
quarrel between the Church and the Dissenters:
the rights of conscience had been discussed side by
side with the testimony of the scriptures to the
theory of episcopal government: dissertations on
political philosophy had been written to provide
arguments for or against the use of the "nocent

[1] For a careful examination of the sources of Locke's views
see E. E. Worcester, *The Religious Opinions of John Locke*, ch. vi.

ceremonies." And the fact that the question of
toleration was one of pressing and practical importance meant that the writers on either side were
driven for the most part, into the position of mere
partisans. The Churchman had wrongs to avenge
and a revered institution to defend, as he supposed,
from imminent destruction; the Nonconformist
was groaning under oppression, and naturally his
main thought was to secure alleviation. Pains-
taking consideration of the facts in an unbiassed
spirit was not unknown, but it was, as usual, the
exception.

In Locke's Letters we ascend into a clearer atmo- *Their im-*
sphere where the heat and dust of mere contro- *partiality.*
versialism are left behind, and we can survey the
field from an elevated position of impartiality.
Locke writes primarily neither as a Churchman,
nor as a Nonconformist, but as a philosopher. His
treatment of the question is not biassed by a desire
to justify or to condemn certain articles or ceremonies; he argues it on its merits. And he shows
a powerful grip of the principles of his subject, in
nothing relaxed by extraneous interests. He deals
directly with the opposition between the Church
and the Nonconformists, but the Church and the
Nonconformists are types illustrative of his principle:
he has not discovered his principle with a view to
coming to a certain pre-arranged decision between
them.

Locke's ordered consistency of treatment, his
philosophical impartiality, and his grip of principle
enabled him to present the theory of toleration, not

s.   18

indeed in its final form, but in a form which settled some aspects of the question for all time; a form far above the grasp of the common intellect of his day, but towards the appreciation of which it might slowly rise.

CHAPTER V

FROM THE TOLERATION ACT TO THE
DEATH OF ANNE

FROM the Revolution onwards the toleration *New phase*
question presented a new phase. It became a far *of the question*
less prominent question in home politics, for the *after the*
Toleration Act, though not conceding the principle *Toleration Act.*
of religious liberty, conceded enough actual liberty
to satisfy for the present the vast majority of those
who had hitherto suffered under persecution, and by
whom or on whose behalf the controversy had been
conducted on the tolerant side. Thus while on the one
hand, a great step had been made towards religious
liberty, that step had gone beyond what a considerable section of the nation was willing to concede,
and there was a party prepared to recall even the
scanty measure of liberty just granted. Nothing
could make it more clear that the framers of the
Toleration Act were right in drafting the measure
upon unambitious lines, than that the act, even as
it was, fell into some danger of repeal. With the
passing of the Toleration Act, the storms of controversy were lulled into comparative quiet. Men

cared little for the principle of toleration; the question that had exercised them was the practical one whether the Dissenters should be tolerated or not. This question had been settled for the moment at any rate, and that formidable factor, the dead-weight of the *status quo*, was now upon the side of toleration. But since the act was but a partial measure, there remained certain problems unsettled. It was hardly likely that after the scare of James II's reign the Roman Catholics would be put on the same footing as the Nonconformists; and they were specially excepted from the Toleration Act. Those persons too, whether Unitarians, Deists or atheists, who did not believe the doctrine of the Trinity as set forth in the Thirty-nine Articles, were still exposed to persecution. Nor was the position of those who were included under the terms of the Toleration Act—apart from any question of the repeal of that measure—altogether settled. The problem of occasional conformity, though not new, rose into new prominence and became the subject of heated debate.

Problems still un-settled: position of (1) Roman Catholics,

(2) Non-Trini-tarians,

(3) Dis-senters.

Between the Restoration and the Revolution, the case of the Nonconformists was the main question under discussion; and by overshadowing that of the Roman Catholics[1] and non-Trinitarians gave to the controversy a unity which henceforward it lacks.

---

[1] The Roman Catholics do not seem to have ventured to any extent to plead for toleration through the press. No doubt during the considerable periods in which they enjoyed practical immunity they were glad enough not to draw any attention to themselves, but I do not remember finding any pamphlets of the reign of Charles II in favour of toleration written avowedly by Roman

The case of the Roman Catholics was complicated *ROMAN* by the Revolution and the formation of a Jacobite *CATHOLIC* *question* party. The mass of English Roman Catholics had *compli-* been perfectly willing to live their own lives without *cated by* *Jacobit-* disturbing the political settlement; but from the *ism.* Restoration onwards their position had been endangered by the intrigues of Jesuits and kings, ambitious to raise the Roman Catholic Church to power in England. Thus had been kept fresh a well grounded fear and hatred of Popery in the public mind, which neither wished nor was able to discriminate between the peaceable and the disturbers. The thorough-going measures of James II, which led to his expulsion, justified and renewed the feelings which had abated since the days of the Popish Plot; and now that the exiled king had taken refuge with his cousin and patron, the King of France, who was engaged in active measures to restore him to his throne, there was more reason than ever to suppose that Roman Catholics in general were disloyal to the existing government and leagued with a foreign power with which England was actually at war. *Quidquid delirant reges plectuntur Achivi.* The net result of the conspiracy of James II to raise the Roman Catholics to power was the indefinite postponement of the day of their emancipation, and the ultimate enactment of additional penal laws. It was not unnatural

Catholics, even in times of anti-Romanist excitement. Presumably a good proportion of the literature attacking the Test and supporting James II's Declaration of Indulgence proceeded from Roman Catholic sources.

that the opinion, however untrue, should be expressed that the Roman Catholics had ever since the Reformation tried to ruin the Church by promoting toleration and had made the Dissenters their instruments for above six-score years[1]. After all, this had actually been the policy of the last two Stuarts, and might well have made, as indeed it did, the whole question of toleration, of Dissenters and Roman Catholics alike, odious in some quarters.

"Method for the Extirpation of Popery." 1690.   An illustration of the strength of feeling against the Roman Catholics at this time is given by "A Short and Easy Method for the Extirpation of Popery, in the space of a few years[2]" published in 1690. "I can see," says the author, writing under the popular pseudonym of "A Person of Quality," "but one possible method to quiet the nation; and that is once for all to clear it of these monsters, and force them to transport themselves, not out of the English dominions, but out of this island."

William secured the Roman Catholics practical toleration.   But in spite of the serious provocation which had been given, the nation's bark proved a good deal worse than its bite. William had been unable to secure legal toleration for the Roman Catholics; but he used his influence, and used it effectively, to secure them "a connivance." Persecution of the Roman Catholics since Elizabeth's days had been defended upon purely political grounds, religious

[1] See a pamphlet published in 1690 entitled, *Brethren in Iniquity or, the Confederacy of the Papists with the Sectaries, for the Destroying of the True Religion as by Law Established, plainly detected.*

[2] To be found in the *Somers Tracts*, vol. IX. pp. 463–8.

grounds being explicitly disavowed; and it was now upon purely political grounds (whatever his own sentiments may have been) that William managed to bring about its practical suspension. According to Burnet, "He in his own opinion always thought that conscience was God's province, and that it ought not to be imposed on; and his experience in Holland made him look on toleration as one of the wisest measures of Government. He was much troubled to see so much ill-humour spreading among the clergy, and by their means over a great part of the nation. He was so true to his principle herein that he restrained the heat of some who were proposing severe acts against the Papists. He made them apprehend the advantage which that would give the French to alienate all the Papists of Europe from us, who from thence might hope to set on foot a new Catholic League, and make the war a quarrel of religion, which might have very bad effects. Nor could he pretend to protect the Protestants in many places of Germany, and in Hungary, unless he could cover the Papists in England from all severities on account of their religion. This was so carefully infused into many and so well understood by them, that the Papists here have enjoyed the real effects of the toleration, though they were not comprehended within the statute that enacted it[1]." New persecuting acts were carried in the reigns of William, Anne, and George I, but these either were never executed at all or fell into disuse almost immediately. The Revolution, which brought toleration

[1] *History of My Own Time*, IV. 21–2, Oxford, 1823.

by law to the Nonconformists, brought toleration in effect to the Roman Catholics also[1].

"Apology for Roman Catholics." 1703.

In 1703 a Roman Catholic published "An Apology for Roman Catholics[2]" which pleaded not merely for toleration, but for the removal of political disqualifications. He laid down two propositions, first, that the only end and design of a government is to preserve the rights and liberties of a people—the view for which Locke had so strenuously contended; and secondly, that the liberty of a people does not stand upon a true foundation, unless all the subjects are equally capacitated by law to discharge the greatest trusts, and enjoy the greatest honours and profits which belong to the nation. "I could not discern," he continued, "by what means the English Common Prayer Book did qualify any man for a public trust, any more than the presbyterian directory or the Popish mass-book; for there are honest men and knaves of all persuasions....If I am a native of

[1] Tallard, the French ambassador, who came to England after the Peace of Ryswick, says that the Catholic religion "is here tolerated more openly than it was even in the time of King Charles II, and it seems evident that the King of England has determined to leave it in peace in order to secure his own": see Stoughton, *The Church of the Revolution*, 244 and note. According to Lecky, during the greater part of the reigns of Anne, George I, and George II, Roman Catholic worship in private houses and chapels was undisturbed, estates were regularly inherited, and no serious difficulty was found in education. In 1700 it was complained that there were few parishes in London where mass was not celebrated, and three Roman Catholic bishops were exercising their functions in England. *England in the Eighteenth Century*, I. 304–5 (8 vols., 1878).

[2] *Somers Tracts*, vol. XII. pp. 241 f.

England, and am both as able and willing to serve
the government as you are, I have thereby as much
natural right to serve the public as you have....
I confess I know but one policy whereby to establish any government, of what sort soever it be;
which is to take away all causes of complaint, and
make all the subjects easy under it; for then the
government will have the whole strength of the
people in its defence, whenever it shall want it....
'Tis true that transubstantiation is a proper test
whereby to find out a Roman Catholic: but in my
opinion it will not be a sufficient test whereby to
discover whether that Roman Catholic be a lover
of his country or not. Make us therefore a test
whereby an honest Catholic may distinguish himself, by owning the Queen's rightful title to the
crown of England, and all its dependencies, and by
disowning the Pope's pretended authority upon any
account in this realm." The ostentatious loyalty
of the writer becomes distinctly amusing when, referring to the rising of the Camisards, he asserts
that "none but a traitor could say that there was
any rebellion in the kingdom of France, sith that
the rightful sovereignty over France is lodged in
the Queen's majesty, whose Protestant French subjects arose in their own defence against the lawless
usurpation and tyranny of Lewis XIV[1]."

But notwithstanding such protestations the public
mind remained unconvinced. In "A Letter from a
Country Gentleman to his Friend in London," the
principle of persecution on religious grounds is

" Letter from a Country Gentle- man." 1711.

[1] *Ibid.* 247.

openly advocated.   The doctrine that princes should not interfere in religion is described as "extravagant" and "culpable" (3), for everyone must promote the true religion according to that character wherewith God has endowed him (4).   If princes ought not to interfere when it is corrupted through the abuses made by the authority of "another ill prince," "the true religion would be quite lost for ever, and that without remedy" (6).   Princes, the author holds, may suppress idolatry, superstition, and heresy (13)—possibly a rather comprehensive commission if it is left to the individual prince to determine the meaning of the words.   It is right to suppress Roman Catholicism (to which the author refers by quoting texts about the Beast); but this does not imply that Popish princes have a right to suppress Protestantism, any more than the right to punish malefactors implies that a tyrant has a right to punish the innocent (17–9).   The contrary idea rests upon the absurd theory that an erroneous conscience has the same privileges as one that is orthodox (21).   Proast is clearly not the only controversialist impervious to Locke's logic.   No direct reference is made to the Nonconformists; but it is clear that the writer repudiates the idea of persecuting them.   It is merely to justify the oppression of the Roman Catholics that he urges the duty of everyone to promote the true religion according to his station—a root-doctrine of persecution which might be used to justify any extreme of atrocity.

But even those who whole-heartedly supported the principle of toleration continued to regard the

Roman Catholics as politically dangerous, and there- *Sherlock's*
fore to be excepted.   Dr Thomas Sherlock[1], Master *sermon,*
of the Temple, preached a sermon upon the subject *Nov. 5th,*
(afterwards published in pamphlet form) before *1712.*
the Lord Mayor of London on Guy Fawkes' day,
1712.   The propagation of religion by destroying,
injuring, or abusing our fellow-creatures, he stigma-
tized as an indignity to God, a contempt of Christ
and a blemish cast upon religion.   Even the object
of benefiting offenders does not justify the use of
temporal punishments by the Church, for "the
Kingdom of Christ is not of this world; nor is it
to be erected or supported by worldly power" (6–7).
But the magistrate has the right to use the sword
to preserve peace and order, whether men act from
conscience or not.   And this is the reason for laws
against Popery, for "whenever a man's conscience
leads him to be a Papist, it leads him to be an
enemy to the constitution of this government" (10).
"The Church has no right to impose penal laws
upon any account in matters purely of a religious
nature, the State has no right neither; but of such
matters perhaps there may be a great scarcity in
the world; for the passions of men work themselves
into their religious concerns; and the controversy...
often breeds convulsions that shake the very constitution of the civil government....The magistrate

---

[1] Eldest son of William Sherlock (the author of *A Discourse
about Church Unity*, for which see p. 202) and his successor in the
Mastership of the Temple. According to. *The Dictionary of
National Biography* he did not take the degree of D.D. till 1714,
when he became Master of Catharine Hall, Cambridge; but the
initials D.D. follow his name on the title-page of the sermon.

has nothing to do with conscience; and therefore on the one hand *he* has no right to bring conscience to his bar, to punish the errors and mistakes of it; or to censure even the actions which proceed from it, unless they affect that which is his immediate care, the public good, or the private peace and property of his subjects; and on the other hand, no one else can bring conscience before him, or by the pleas of it supersede his authority in any case proper for his cognizance " (12–14). Sherlock proceeds to draw the conclusions that the methods of conversion pursued by the Roman Catholics are unjustifiable, and that the civil power has a right to punish their practices, which are seasonably reflected upon by a reference to Gunpowder Plot (16). "There is nothing," the sermon continues, " an Englishman has more to fear than the prevailing power of Popery....To design the advancement of Popery is to design the ruin of the state, and the destruction of the Church; 'tis to sacrifice the nation to a double slavery, to prepare chains both for their bodies and their minds " (17).

Increased prominence of the NON-TRINI-TARIANS: The second class of persons specially excepted from the Toleration Act was that of disbelievers in the doctrine of the Trinity. In 1698 was carried another act[1] imposing penalties on such as " shall by writing, printing, teaching or advised speaking, deny any one of the Persons in the Holy Trinity to be God, or shall assert or maintain that there are more gods than one, or shall deny the Christian religion to be true, or the holy Scripture of the Old and New Testament to be of divine authority." This

[1] 9 Will. III, c. 35. See Appendix III.

class of persons engaged a good deal more attention
after the Revolution than before it. "There has
probably been no period in which liberty of thought
on religious subjects has been debated in this
country so anxiously, so vehemently, so generally,
as in the earlier part of the eighteenth century.
The Reformation had hinged upon it; but general
principles were then greatly obscured in the excitement of change, and amid the multiplicity of
questions of more immediate practical interest. For
150 years after the first breach with Rome, it may
be said that private judgment was most frequently
considered in connection with a power of option
between different Church communions. A man had
to choose whether he would adhere to the old, or
adopt the new form of faith—whether he would
remain staunch to the reformed Anglican Church,
or cast in his lot with the Puritans or with one or
other of the rising sects—whether Episcopacy or
Presbyterianism most conformed to his ideas of
Church government. When at last these controversies had abated, the full importance of the
principles involved in this new liberty of thought
began to be fully felt. Their real scope and nature
apart from any transient applications, engaged great
attention, first among the studious and thoughtful,
among philosophers and theologians, but before long
throughout the country generally. Locke among
philosophers, Tillotson and Chillingworth among
divines, addressed their reasonings not to the few,
but to the many. Their arguments however would
not have been so widely and actively discussed, had

it not been for the Deists. Freethought in reference
to certain ecclesiastical topics had been for several
generations familiar to every Englishman; but just
at a time when reflecting persons of every class were
beginning to inquire what was implied in this liberty
of thought and choice, the term was unhappily appropriated by the opponents of revelation, and as if
by common consent, conceded to them[1]."

a natural develop-ment of the appeal to reason.
This extension of the field of freethought from
ecclesiastical questions to questions of the truth of
orthodox Christianity was but a natural development of movements which we have already noticed.
Before the Revolution the problems mainly discussed were those which had exercised the minds
of Chillingworth and Hales; it was chiefly after the
Revolution that the problems which the Platonists
had faced came into general discussion. They and
other seventeenth-century theologians had attempted
to base religion on philosophy, and boldly appealed
to reason. Glanvill, for instance, in his sermon Λόγου
Θρησκεία, asserted that "reason is certain and infallible, and in a sense the word of God" (23-4) and
further that the essentials of religion are so plainly
revealed that no man can fail to understand who
has not some bias of will or affections (28).
These contentions were a dangerous foundation,
for they promptly overturn the edifice they were
designed to bear, for anyone to whom the clear-
ness with which the distinctive doctrines essential to Christianity are revealed is questionable;

[1] Abbey and Overton, *The English Church in the Eighteenth
Century*, I. 294-5.

and, generally, the philosophical foundations to
which our theologians appealed, proved capable of
supporting unorthodox superstructures.   This was
a development scarcely contemplated, in spite of
the warning, clear for those who had eyes to see,
given in Lord Herbert's writings many years before;
and it was met by the most ungenerous accusations *Survival*
of dishonesty.   These imputations show the survival *of the*
intolerant
of that spirit of intolerance, which ascribes to the *spirit.*
alleged moral error of one party differences of
opinion really due to the fact that both parties
share in the general intellectual fallibility of mankind.   This latter was now largely recognized as
the cause of differences on minor matters; but
men were reluctant to make the same concession
when the essentials of Christianity, as they were
then held, were called in question.

   But the reason for persecuting the "freethinkers" *" Free-*
was not that they were supposed to have reached *thinking"*
supposed
their conclusions by a disingenuous process, but that *inimical to*
society,
their opinions were held to be inimical to society.
The more enlightened minds of the age had passed
from the old idea that intellectual error is identical
with, or stands on the same level with, moral error,
to the idea that certain intellectual opinions (pre-
supposed erroneous) are solvents of morality.   Persecution of the Dissenters had been carried on until
the Toleration Act, because in the general mind
theology had not yet been separated from politics;
persecution of the "freethinkers" survived it because
theology had not yet been separated from morals.
It was not yet perceived "that there was an adequate

basis for the maintenance of political society in those
principles of right and wrong which were universally
recognized by its citizens apart from their position
or belief as members of a religious organization[1]."
We have already seen that in this matter, as far
as atheism was concerned, Locke was in agreement
with the general feeling of his age[2].

but not really persecuted. The persecution, however, was, like that of the
Roman Catholics, theoretical. The act against the
unorthodox seems not to have been actively endorsed
by public opinion, for in spite of the Deistic controversy no instance of prosecution under it is known.
Character of the act of 1698. Though the opinions proscribed are spoken of in
the preamble as "greatly tending to the dishonour
of Almighty God"—a survival of the religious motive
for persecution—the main reason for the act is no
doubt the next alleged, that they prove destructive
to the peace and welfare of this kingdom—the
politico-social motive. Now, as we have remarked
already, the soundness or unsoundness of this motive
in any given case is likely to be more or less capable
of practical demonstration; and the fact that the
freethought of the eighteenth century inflicted no

[1] J. O. Bevan, *Birth and Growth of Toleration and Other
Essays*, 23.

[2] pp. 226, 243. This view of morality is further illustrated by
the assertions of contemporary preachers that virtue is dependent
on the expectation of a reward beyond the grave. Similarly consideration of the disastrous consequences of unbelief, should
Christianity prove true, was put forward as a reason for belief.
This deplorable argument (not unknown in some quarters even at
the present day) implies, in direct contradiction to Locke, that not
only punishment, but fear of punishment, is a source of rational
conviction.

obvious damage on the social structure is no doubt responsible alike for the absence of prosecutions under the act and for its subsequent repeal in 1813. It should be noticed that the act makes no attempt to extirpate the proscribed opinions except in so far as prevention of their promulgation may contribute to that end; no one is brought within its reach by the mere holding of them, but only by "writing, printing, teaching or advised speaking." As the act is intended to protect the peace and welfare of the kingdom and not the souls of the citizens, so it makes no attempt to rescue the misbeliever from error: with spiritual affairs it has no concern[1].

In 1697 had appeared "An Essay concerning the Power of the Magistrate and the Rights of Mankind in Matters of Religion," by Matthew Tindal, fellow of All Souls College, Oxford, and a sufficiently considerable authority on international law to be consulted on occasion by the Government. For a short time under the second James he was a Roman Catholic, but before the Revolution he returned to the Church of England, and afterwards became one of the most prominent of the Deists. Tindal speaks of his subject as "in a manner wholly exhausted by the three incomparable Letters on Toleration" (2), and certainly the influence of "that great and good man, the author of the Letters concerning Tolera-

Tindal: "Essay concerning the Power of the Magistrate." 1697.

---

[1] Sir F. Pollock, *The Theory of Persecution*, in *Essays in Jurisprudence and Ethics*, 160–2, from which the substance of the paragraph is mainly drawn. There is, of course, the additional explanation that it is only by explicit avowal that "freethought" reveals itself: it does not involve attendance at proscribed services or necessarily even absence from the established worship.

tion" (113), is very apparent in his essay. His argument begins, as did Locke's, with the com-

Magis-trate com-missioned by the people. hence has no right to punish for religion. mission of the magistrate. The magistrate, says Tindal, is commissioned not by God, but by the people (3–4), who could not give him the right to use force in religious matters, because the law of nature gives no right to deprive of life, liberty, or property, except in defence of one's own. Hence the magistrate's power extends, in the first place, to the duties of man to man, and conscience is no valid plea against the magistrate in such matters; and in the second place, even to such duties to God as influence human life and conduce to the welfare of human societies—belief in God, for instance, without which no society can subsist (5, 6): but it does not extend to "those opinions and actions which relate to God alone, in which no third person has an interest" (6, 7). Indeed, members of civil society have a right to be protected in their religious worship as in any other matter (9); and the magistrate cannot have the right to disturb society, as by persecution he does (11). The duties which social existence lays upon men are reciprocal, and if the magistrate uses force against one party, that party may disobey the magistrate, and use force against him and his party (14, 15).

Even if commis-sioned by God, not commis-sioned to punish for religion. But even if the magistrate receives his commission from God, yet he receives no commission to use force in matters of mere religion (17). For such a power in the first place tends to men's eternal ruin by making them act contrary to their consciences (27); secondly it is inconsistent with

those duties, such as charity, forbearance and justice,
which God for the sake of men's temporal happiness
requires of them (30, 36), in fact it is directly contrary to the main design of God's laws as to matters
wherein men are concerned one with another, which
is their mutual good (42). Thirdly, it is directly
contrary to the honour of God, partly because it
prevents men from worshipping Him according as
they think most agreeable to His will (47); and
also because it makes the honour of God and the
good of mankind clash (50), and imputes to the Holy
Ghost "a doctrine which destroys the end and in-
tent of all natural as well as revealed religion" (52);
and supposes that God delights in man's blood (53).

In the second part Tindal considers some of the *Objections*
objections brought against toleration. To the ob- *to toleration*
jection that the imposition of penalties makes men *answered.*
consider, he replies that men ought indeed to use   (1)
their reason upon matters of religion, but they
ought to do it impartially, which is just what
penalties prevent: the imposition of them is consequently a great crime (87–8), and promotes
ignorance and superstition (108–9). To the ob-   (2)
jection that the magistrate has the right to use
force to prevent the spread of erroneous opinions,
his answer is, "If force prevents men from running
into errors it must be because it hinders men from
freely and impartially examining matters of religion....And as error where impartial diligence is
used is wholly innocent; so where it's neglected,
the accidental stumbling on truth will not justify
or excuse the neglect of it: therefore if it should

tend to hinder error by preventing men from impartially considering, it would not give the magistrate a right to use force" (108). "As to merely religious or speculative points of the true religion, men's lusts or passions, since these are in no way concerned how those are held, do not incline them to prefer falsehood before truth. And as for those parts of religion wherein men's lusts and passions may be supposed to sway them, those I own (as far forth as my adversaries) do belong to the magistrate's jurisdiction, and all men for the sake of their common good are obliged to get them believed and practised; for it's equally the interest of governors and governed to embrace the true religion, contrived by the infinite wisdom of God (3) for the benefit of mankind" (108). To the objection that the good of the society obliges the magistrate to hinder different professions of religion, Tindal again follows Locke in replying that differences in religion only cause disturbances because men are persecuted for them (144–5); and that in consequence of the persecution the persecuted sects combine against the common enemy the government (149). But persecution is inconsistent with Protestantism: "Protestants, while they persecute any, condemn themselves" (117). He further urges the exemption of the Dissenters from the test (Part II, chapter VIII[1]).

[1] Tindal dealt with the question of toleration also in the introduction to his *Rights of the Christian Church*, the object of which was to show that the ecclesiastical power is not independent of the civil power; repeating, with no important additions, some of the arguments of the *Essay concerning the power of the magistrate*.

Atheists, as we have seen, Tindal excepted from *Shaftes-*
toleration, but even the cause of the atheists found *bury.*
a partial defender in the third Earl of Shaftesbury,
the grandson of the first Earl, the organizer of the
Whig party. He had been the pupil of Locke, and,
like Tindal, was generally regarded as a Deist. In
" The Moralists," published in 1709, he pointed out
that "if reason be needful, force in the meanwhile *Atheists,*
must be laid aside; for there is no enforcement of *and how*
to deal
reason but by reason. And therefore if atheists are *with them.*
to be reasoned with at all they are to be reasoned
with like other men, since there is no other way in
Nature to convince them." He proceeded to divide
atheists into two kinds, those who doubt, and those
who deny. The latter "set up an opinion against
the interest of mankind and being of society" and
(in spite of what he has just said about reason),
being obnoxious to the magistrate and the laws, are
punishable. The former would not be punishable
"unless the magistrate had dominion over minds as
well as over actions and behaviour" (Part II, § 3).
Shaftesbury seems to be guilty not only of a misuse
of language—for a man who merely doubts is not
an atheist—but· also of a confusion of thought, for
his classification does not account for all the possibilities. Those who doubt and keep their doubts
to themselves are sheep: those who disbelieve and
promulgate their disbelief are goats. But the man
who doubts and promulgates his doubts is a hybrid
monster for whom no provision is made[1]. In any

[1] The fourth possible combination—that of disbelief and
silence—is also ignored. This is not very serious, for such cases

case Shaftesbury's concessions do not amount to very much, since he bans the publication of definitely atheistic opinions, which it was at least plausible, in view of the current ideas as to moral sanctions, to regard as dangerous. Thus Shaftesbury, even though he asserted the existence of an innate moral sense, and that morality was not dependent even on the Supreme Will itself, held, naturally enough, that theism with a belief in future rewards and punishments was useful to reinforce the claims of right conduct.

Toleration necessary to rational belief. In the "Miscellaneous Reflections," published two years after "The Moralists," Shaftesbury makes some further remarks on toleration. "There can be no rational belief but where comparison is allowed, examination permitted, and a sincere toleration established." He followed Locke in protesting against the idea of persecution by means of moderate penalties. "There is nothing so ridiculous in respect of policy, or so wrong and odious in respect of common humanity, as a moderate and half-way persecution.... If there be on earth a proper way to render the most sacred truth suspected, 'tis by supporting it with threats, and pretending to terrify people into the belief of it " (II, ch. III). But, it might well be asked, if this were so, how was the belief in the existence of God, the preservation of which Shaftesbury regarded as so important, to escape suspicion? In fact, he was not prepared to allow that method, by

could never (since silence is maintained) raise a practical difficulty. But the case of combined doubt and speech is a thoroughly practical one.

which alone, he asserted, rational belief could be attained, to be applied to the very cardinal point of his creed. It is well worthy of remark how very slowly toleration, applied first to "non-fundamental" and "indifferent" matters, later to questions of greater importance, was extended to the fundamental articles of Christianity, though it was already justified in cases of less importance on grounds which in consistency demanded its application to all.

Passing on from the two classes excepted from the Toleration Act—Roman Catholics and "freethinkers" of various sorts—we come to the consideration of the position of the Nonconformists, now that the toleration which had been so long withheld had been at last extorted by the pressure of circumstances. A vexed question which came into new prominence was that of occasional conformity. With that question we are not now concerned; suffice it to say that it clearly brought out the irreconcilable hostility of an influential section of the Church to the Nonconformists, and showed that not only would there have been overwhelming opposition to the grant of any further measure of liberty, but that the Toleration Act itself was in serious danger. Notwithstanding the attempt of the anonymous author of a pamphlet published in 1689, entitled "The Conformists' Charity to Dissenters," to prove that the divines of the English Church concurred in the act and were friendly towards the Nonconformists, it was disliked by the mass of the clergy. "The clergy," says Burnet, "began now to show an implacable hatred

Position of the NONCON- FORMISTS.

Hostility of the High Church party.

to the Nonconformists, and seemed to wish for an occasion to renew old severities against them[1]." This disposition was not unnaturally intensified by the persecution to which the Scotch Episcopalians were subjected by the now triumphant Presbyterians, the episcopal clergy being violently expelled from their benefices in even more summary fashion than the English Nonconformists in 1662. According to Burnet, "All these things were published up and down England, and much aggravated, and raised the aversion that the Church had to the Presbyterians so high, that they began to repent their having granted a toleration to a party that, where they prevailed, showed so much fury against those of the Episcopal persuasion[2]."

The controversy over the toleration of the Dissenters had received two serious blows in the passing of the Toleration Act, and the publication of Locke's letters, and it languished in consequence. Pamphlets on the subject were, compared with those of the last two reigns, few and far between, and the writers could do little but reproduce arguments already sadly threadbare. It behoves us nevertheless to examine them, and to try to catch a glimpse, if it may be, of what was passing in men's minds.

We have already noticed the suspicion with which toleration in general was in some quarters regarded; as a device for the ruin of the Church, promoted by her enemies[3]. In those quarters it was

[1] *History of My Own Time*, iv. 21, 6 vols., Oxford, 1823.

[2] *Ibid.* iv. 52.

[3] p. 278.

not likely that peaceable counsels would prevail. The logical extreme of the High Church principles of the day was given in bitter satire in Daniel Defoe's "The Shortest Way with the Dissenters[1]," published in 1702, which he wrote in the assumed character of a High Churchman. "How many millions of future souls," he wrote, "shall we save from infection and delusion, if the present race of poisoned spirits were purged from the face of the land !...If one severe law were made, and punctually executed that *whosoever was found at a conventicle should be banished the nation and the preacher hanged*; we should soon see the end of the tale! They would all come to church again, and one age would make us all one again!"

Defoe: "The Shortest Way with the Dissenters.' 1702.

Incidentally, as we have pointed out elsewhere, this argument from the protection of posterity, though receiving practically no attention in the period to which this essay is devoted and very little at the present day, is one of the strongest that can be advanced in favour of persecution. The satire was accepted by the High Church party as a serious exposition of their views. Defoe's own account of it appears in his "Dissenters' Answer to the High Church Challenge." "I'll prove by the preachings, printings, and declared judgment of several of the most zealous High Party, that however the practice was disowned by the party upon the unreasonable exposing it, by the book called 'The Shortest Way'; yet that it has all along been

[1] Recently reprinted in Aitken's *Later Stuart Tracts*, pp. 191–204.

their desire and very often their design. And I appeal for the truth of it among many instances, to a letter of a known Churchman, whose original I have by me, it being written to a person who sent him the book for a present.—' Sir, I received yours, and, enclosed, the book called "The Shortest Way with the Dissenters," for which I thank you: and, next to the Holy Bible and Sacred Comments, I place it as the most valuable thing I can have. I look upon it as the Only Method! and I pray God to put it into the heart of our most gracious Queen, to put what is there proposed in execution[1].'" The discovery of the real nature of the tract roused them to fury; and Defoe was fined, pilloried and imprisoned in expiation of the success of his practical joke.

"Memorial of the Church of England." 1704.   "The Memorial of the Church of England," an anonymous pamphlet[2] which created a great stir upon its publication in 1704, is illiberal in tone. The sectaries, it was said, hold the same principles as those of the preceding generation, who overturned Church and State, and the same principles naturally lead to the same designs; and it is manifestly the design of the Dissenters to pull down the Church (1-2, 14). "There is no High Churchman (as they abusively call us[3]) of us all, who would break in upon the toleration, if it were in their power, provided that the ambition of the Dissenters

[1] Aitken, 189.

[2] Attributed to James Drake, a physician, and one Poley, M.P. for Ipswich, jointly.

[3] The terms "High Church" and "Low Church" were now coming into fashion.

would stop there" (25). In spite, however, of this limit, and of strong opposition to occasional conformity, no definite proposal is made in the pamphlet for the withdrawal of toleration.

The views of the Tories on Church and King were *Public feeling more tolerant since the Revolution.* so closely bound up together that the severe blow which the Revolution dealt their creed in the one respect, could not fail to act as a severe shock to it in the other. In addition to this the accomplished fact of the Toleration Act, and no doubt also the powerful exposition of the theory of toleration by Locke, had done much to make the general feeling of the nation more tolerant. We have seen that the author of the "Letter from a Country Gentleman," who held firmly to the very root-principle of persecution, repudiated the idea of persecuting the Nonconformists, as well as Thomas Sherlock, who gave his adherence to the principle of toleration[1].

As "The Memorial of the Church of England" *"Memorial of the State of England." 1705.* was much less truculent than the pre-Revolution tracts, so "The Memorial of the State of England[2]" which replied to it was extremely liberal in tone, declaring religious diversity to be positively advantageous. We cannot, it was urged, be of the same mind in all things, and since the articles of a man's creed hurt nobody besides himself, the magistrate has nothing to do with them (546). "The question is not if men's opinions be true, or their ceremonies the best, but if they be hurtful or not" (547). Nor can a plea be justly made in favour

[1] pp. 281–4.
[2] *Somers Tracts*, xii. 526–74.

of moderate punishments: "there's no punishment so small but it justifies a greater" (547). Persecution obstructs all progress in knowledge, and begets prejudice, slavishness and barbarity: and "putting a man to death for a religion by which you think salvation is not to be had is no better nor worse than the action of that Italian, who made his enemy blaspheme God, and then stabbed him that he might be damned" (548). It is "not the difference of opinions but using men ill for this difference" which gives colour to the idea that diversity of religion in a state is inconsistent with good government. "Diversity of religion is so far from being dangerous that it ought rather to be counted beneficial, as it creates a noble emulation in manners, learning, industry and loyalty" (549). The author further advocated the repeal of the test, and justified occasional conformity (550–3).

"The Memorial of the Church of England" had protested that the High Church party would not "break in upon the toleration" but for fear that the Dissenters would use it as a preliminary to greater things. Correspondingly it was protested from the other side that the Dissenters accepted the public welfare as the criterion of legislation, and demanded nothing inconsistent with it. This was asserted in *Humfrey:* the "Free Thoughts" of John Humfrey, whom we *"Free Thoughts."* have already met as joint-author of "The Peaceable 1710. Design," and who was "aged now past 89 years" as the title-page informs the reader[1]. We are obliged

[1] This pamphlet—alone, as far as I remember, among those I have examined—bears the price upon the title-page. In this case

to obey, he wrote, if what the magistrate command
is for the people's good; otherwise we may obey but
are not obliged to do so. As to judging whether a
law is for the people's good or not, the magistrate
must judge as to the making the law, and we must
judge as to our obedience to it (51–2). "There is
no toleration," he added, "to be desired, or is desired
of the sober Nonconformist, but one stated and so
far agreed to in the general, that the articles of our
Christian faith, a good life, and the government of
the nation be secured" (56).

As before the Revolution, toleration was the *Positions of Whigs and Tories.*
principle of the Whigs, while persecution was the
natural outcome in that age of the tenets of the
Tories; but the tendency to political inactivity—
the instinct to let things be—had changed sides
with the passing of the Toleration Act, and was an
impediment in the Tories' path. And it was well
for the Dissenters that it was so, for with the
accession of Anne came a High Church Tory reaction which threatened to sweep away the Toleration Act itself. But Toryism had lost much ground
at the Revolution, and this, in spite of the oft-raised

---

sixty-four pages were to be had for a shilling. Humfrey (born
1621) received Presbyterian ordination in 1649, but afterwards
was an open royalist. At the Restoration he submitted reluctantly
to reordination; but subsequently, becoming uneasy in mind,
read a renunciation to the bishop's registrar, and in August 1662
threw in his lot with the ejected. Though in his ninetieth year
at the time of publishing his *Free Thoughts*, he still had a considerable period of active life before him, for he continued his
ministry into his ninety-ninth year, in which he died (1719),
having lived under the government of six kings, one queen, two
Protectors, a parliamentary oligarchy, and an army.

cry of "The Church in danger," it was not strong enough altogether to recover.

Swift on the views of the Whigs.

Of the views of the Whigs Jonathan Swift has left us an interesting sketch in number 36 of "The Examiner[1]." "As to religion; their universal undisputed maxim is, that it ought to make no distinction at all among Protestants; and in the word Protestant they include everybody who is not a Papist, and who will, by an oath, give security to the government. Union in discipline and doctrine, the offensive sin of schism, the notion of a Church and a hierarchy, they laugh at as foppery, cant, and priestcraft. They see no necessity at all that there should be a national faith; and what we usually call by that name, they only style the religion of the magistrate. Since the Dissenters and we agree in the main, why should the difference of a few speculative points, or modes of dress incapacitate them from serving their prince and country in a juncture when we ought to have all hands up against the common enemy? And why should they be forced to take the Sacrament from our clergy's hands, and in our posture, or indeed why compelled to receive it at all, when they take an employment which has nothing to do with religion?"

His own intolerant views.

In the following number of "The Examiner," setting forth the views of his own party, Swift was not ashamed to bring up against the Dissenters the

---

[1] I take the number from the original *Examiner*. In the 1772 edition of Swift's works, 20 vols., Dublin, the number is given as 35. The date is Thursday, March 29th to Thursday, April 5th, 1711.

hoary accusation of having rebelled against and murdered Charles I, and, needless to say, supposed that they were devising the ruin of the Church. Had Mr Dick, of David Copperfield fame, been alive under the later Stuarts, he would have found himself by no means alone in his inability to get rid of King Charles. In "The Presbyterians' Plea of Merit" Swift brought up the expulsion of the bishops from the House of Lords against the Presbyterians (154), and further stated "I am at a loss to know what arts the Presbyterian sect intends to use in convincing the world of their loyalty to kingly government....From the first time that these sectaries appeared in the world it hath been always found, by their whole proceeding, that they professed an utter hatred to kingly government" (156, 160). It is true, of course, that Presbyterianism is not calculated to fit in well with autocracy. Such was the experience of James I, who declared that "The Presbytery agreeth as well with monarchy as God with the devil," making, no doubt, a slight slip as to the order of the second pair of nouns. But as a weapon against the English Presbyterians Swift's accusation was most unfair. Seeing, however, that the "kingly government" had almost invariably oppressed them when able to do so, it would not have been surprising had it been true. The Dissenters generally in fact were accused of the inexpiable crime of the rhinoceros:

> "Cet animal est tres mechant ;
> Quand on l'attaque, il se défend."

Intolerant Tory reaction.

Such being the feelings of the Tory party, the Tory reaction under Anne was fraught with considerable danger to the Dissenters. The Occasional Conformity Act[1] after a long struggle was carried in 1711; henceforward any man, who, having qualified for state or municipal office by taking the sacrament in church, afterwards attended a Nonconformist meeting, was to be fined, and disabled from holding office thereafter. More serious was the Schism Act[2] of 1714, which prohibited any person from acting as tutor or schoolmaster who should not have received the sacrament according to the usage of the Church of England, and have obtained a license from the bishop[3]. It was more or less a renewal of the educational provisions of the Act of Uniformity and might well seem the first instalment of a new Clarendon Code[4]. From a return of the evil days of fifty years before, how-

[1] 10 Anne, cap. 6 : see Appendix III.

[2] 13 Anne, cap. 7 : see Appendix III.

[3] § XII. contains an interesting and important exception. " Provided always, That this act shall not extend...to any person who...shall instruct youth in reading, writing, arithmetic, or any part of mathematical learning only, so far as such mathematical learning relates to navigation, or any mechanical art only, and so far as such reading, writing, arithmetic or mathematical learning shall be taught in the English tongue only."

[4] Bolingbroke, indeed, in 1717 wrote, '' I verily think that the persecution of dissenters entered into no man's head." But this was when he was expiating in exile the failure of his plans. And he admits that, though the existing generation of Dissenters was not to be persecuted, the next was to be prevented from being brought up in error : in other words Dissent was to be extirpated. See his *Letter to Sir W. Windham*, Works, I. 115-6 (4 vols., Philadelphia, 1841).

ever, the Dissenters were saved by the death of
Anne, on the very day on which the Schism Act
came into operation[1]. Thereupon followed the pro- *Tolerant*
clamation of George Lewis, Elector of Hanover, by *Whig pre-*
dominance
whose Whig ministers the work of the Tory reaction *under the*
was undone.   Toleration for Roman Catholics and *Hanover-*
ians.
Unitarians, and religious equality for any who dissented from the Church of England were slow in
coming, and the first grant of relief to Roman (1778)
Catholics was followed by the outburst of fanaticism
known as the Gordon riots; but the desire to main- (1780)
tain existing acts of Parliament is a very different
thing from the desire to make new ones, and even
the revival of Toryism under George III did not
renew the danger to religious liberty which had
resulted from the revival under Anne.   During the
intervening half-century of Whig rule the idea of
active persecution for religion had practically evapo-
rated from the minds of men.

[1] Neal, *History of the Puritans*, v. 89, 5 vols. 1822. Its provisions, however, seem not to have been enforced; perhaps this
was due to the opportune change of government, but the same is
true, as we have seen, of other persecuting acts of the period.
It was repealed together with the Occasional Conformity Act in
1718.

CHAPTER VI

GENERAL REVIEW

WE have now traced the history of the theory of toleration from the Restoration to the passing of the Stuart dynasty; but, lest the main thread of that history should be lost amid the mass of detailed quotation from contemporary writers which we have thought the best indication of the real feelings of the age, it may be well briefly to summarize and comment upon the main tendencies which we have seen at work.

Character of period. 1660–88. The reigns of the two sons of Charles I form a period to themselves—a period of comparative but decreasing calm between two storms. To say that the Restoration brought modern England into being would imply that there is some sort of fairly general agreement as to what institutions and ideas are characteristic of modern England ; but at least it may be said that it marks a momentous step in the process of its creation. Constitutionally the Restoration inaugurated a period of transition (through a system ostensibly of coöperation, but really of rivalry, between Crown and Parliament) from prerogative government by the monarchy towards parliamentary govern-

ment by the landed aristocracy.   Intellectually it is
characterized by an uprising of secularity, or—if the
word be allowed—of lay-mindedness.   It might have
been prophesied that the continuance of this growth
would ultimately prove fatal to religious persecution,
but its first unconscious aims were far less ambitious :
it merely sapped the foundations of those motives to *Seculariz-*
persecution which had regard to another world.   The *ation of*
persecu-
religious motive is not greatly insisted on : the theo- *tion.*
logical motive is all but absent from the controversy :
the doctrinal motive is of secondary importance : the
ecclesiastical motive derives its main strength from
the idea that the Church is a pillar of society : it is
the politico-social motive that is the ultimate resort
and the most prominent feature of the case for
persecution.   The principle of not persecuting save
for secular reasons was recognized in the Declaration
of Breda, and as time went on persecution became
more generally the outcome of merely political considerations.

It is the business of the politician to look both *Mutual*
back and forwards that he may apply the lessons *animosity,*
political
of the past to the problems of the present.   But *stability,*
this procedure requires for its correct performance *and per-*
secution.
a freedom from prejudice and a calmness of judgment to which few men attain, and which were sadly
to seek in the latter half of the seventeenth century.
Otherwise memory may generate an animosity which
masquerades as zeal for the welfare of the state.
Particularly is this likely to arise in religious matters
where passion tends to run high ; and thus, in
the case of religious persecution, animosity may

be ostensibly dictated by the interests of political stability ; whereas in reality the latter is imperilled only because violent animosity between the two parties already exists. Thus animosity, if mutual and sufficiently strong to imperil political stability, does in a sense provide for persecution, if not a justification, at least a rational basis. For while passion runs high on both sides, and both parties are, or appear to be, strong, that which has for the time the upper hand dare not lay its weapons down for fear of overthrow. Thus subjective emotional reasons grounded on political or religious animosity tend to create and to cloak themselves with objective rational reasons—if the phrase be allowed—dictated by the interests of political stability.

This is what happened in the period we have been considering. In the twenty years preceding the Restoration had been sown seeds of passion that would bear fruit for many a year—which indeed is *Triple* not yet wholly exhausted. Looking back to the year *division* 1640 in the light of what followed, we may divide *of the* *nation in* the Englishmen of that date into three classes. The *1640.* first is that section which soon developed into the Royalist party, including both the High Churchmen who followed Laud, and the Liberal Churchmen such as Falkland and Chillingworth. The second comprises the Puritan party in the Church of England of which Pym and Hampden were prominent spokesmen in Parliament and Baxter a representative among the clergy. Thirdly, there were the separatists, at present few and persecuted, soon to be numerous and tyrannical. The main line of eccle-

siastical cleavage cut off these last from both the *Lines of ecclesiastical and political cleavage.*
parties which were within the Church of England;
for the Puritan Churchmen at least had this in
common with the Laudians, that they were all alike
members of one ecclesiastical body, which the separatists stood definitely outside.   And this line of
ecclesiastical cleavage which parted the Puritan
Churchmen from the separatists was soon to become, as the Independents rose to power, a line
of political cleavage, parting the Independent army
from the Presbyterian Parliament; but those days
were not yet.   More important for the present was
a secondary line of ecclesiastical cleavage, that which
within the Church separated Anglican from Puritan ;
for this coincided with the main line of political
cleavage which in the latter half of 1641 parted
Royalist from Parliamentarian.   War is the great *The Civil War opened a gulf between Puritans and Anglicans,*
divider, and compared with the gulf that now
appeared between those who stood for Charles and
those who stood for the Parliament, all other divisions were minor matters.   Hence it came about
that the Puritan Churchmen were flung temporarily
into the arms of the Scots (and so Presbyterianized),
and associated with the Independents and sectaries.
But soon the line of cleavage between them and their
new associates, developing a political, in addition to
its original ecclesiastical, character, became in its
turn a yawning gulf; and the Puritan Churchmen
began to think of healing the breach between themselves and their old associates—the now oppressed
Episcopalian party.   The renewed outbreak of the
Civil War in 1648 marked the narrowing of this

breach; the Restoration its all but actual closure through fear of anarchy. But the negotiations ending in the Savoy Conference, which should have brought about a permanent reconciliation, were a dismal failure; and the gulf which they failed to *which the* close the Act of Uniformity widened once more and *Act of Uni-* fixed. That is to say, political reasons were tempo-*formity* *fixed.* rarily strong enough to unite Presbyterian and *Political* Episcopalian for purposes of the Restoration, that *considera-* *tions* chaos might be reduced to order, but not strong enough to keep them united when order had been restored. The Presbyterian alliance was the ladder by which the Episcopalians climbed back to power; and, this once regained, like others before and after them, they scorned the base degrees by which they did ascend. A man is judged by the company he keeps, and the Presbyterians had kept such bad company of late that men of unstained loyalty could have nothing to do with them.

An alliance between the Church and the Dissenters in general, contracted in fear of Romanism, brought toleration for the latter in 1689: the alliance between the Episcopalians and the Presbyterians, contracted in fear of the sectaries, should have brought reunion at the Restoration, when as yet no Clarendon Code had intervened further to intensify their estrangement[1]. But at the Restoration the causes making for union

[1] But the retention of the Presbyterians within the Church would possibly have been a catastrophe for the rest of the Nonconformists, and have delayed the coming of toleration, for the Church would have been numerically stronger and no less intolerant. The Presbyterians disliked toleration at least as much as the Episcopalians did.

were the outcome of a merely temporary situation, to which the Restoration itself put an end, and with it to the causes making for union. The political reasons for disunion, on the other hand,—the memory *exagge-* of the Civil War and of the subsequent oppression *rated the religious* of the Episcopalians—were deeper set in men's *cleavage* consciousness by reason of longer standing and *between Episco-* intenser feeling; and these were so far from being *palians and Pres-* abolished by the Restoration that they received *byterians.* from it a new access of vigour. The breath of returning power fanned smouldering passion into flame. It was not because ecclesiastical differences had altered, but because this fire was no longer blazing with its first fury, and had for the moment been almost quenched by the Roman danger, that toleration was possible in 1689. At the Restoration the ecclesiastical differences between the parties were largely a mask for political antipathy. The great question was, on which side had a man borne arms or on which side were his sympathies enlisted? Had he been for or against the King? This rough and ready method of ecclesiastical classification ignored the differences between the various sections of Puritans, and by classing them all together made the religious cleavage between the Episcopalians and the Presbyterians at once apparently much wider, and actually much more keenly felt, than would otherwise have been the case. War was the great divider.

Hence political considerations took the place of *prac-* first importance in the arguments against toleration. *tical con-* Stillingfleet's "Irenicum," for instance, and Parker's *sidera-* *tions,*

(1) Politi-
cal con-
sidera-
tions were
prominent
in the case
for perse-
cution:

(a) false
ideas as to
duty of
obedience,

(b) sup-
posed in-
compati-
bility of
religious
diversity
with peace,

"Discourse of Ecclesiastical Polity" alike reproduce to a considerable extent the political intolerance of Hobbes, though stopping short of his crowning achievement, the discovery of the source of morality in the will of the ruler. The "late troubles" had impressed upon men's minds to a preposterous extent the duty of obedience to the civil power, and most men seemed incapable of distinguishing between a desire to reform the law and a desire to break it, as though the whole legal system were like a piece of china which cannot be modified in shape, but is in imminent danger of being broken by the effort to modify it. Such drastic changes had recently been carried out with such profoundly unsatisfactory results that all change was anathema. "Fear God, and honour the King," wrote the worthy Evelyn, "but meddle not with them who are given to change![1]" Moreover men were unable to understand how two or more distinct religious organizations could coexist in the same state and yet remain at peace with one another. Religious differences had played a prominent part in the recent civil war, which had been contemporary with the final stages of that more fearful struggle of religions in Germany which had lasted for a generation. What was more natural than that men should fight if they differed about religion? Indeed, supposing the parties to be at all equal in strength, how could they help fighting about it? The weaker party then must not be allowed to gather sufficient strength to have the least chance of success in an appeal to arms.

[1] Diary, Jan. 30, 1661.

A kingdom in which more than one religion was allowed was necessarily a kingdom divided against itself and likely to suffer the fate assigned to such kingdoms.

The worst of it was that these uncompromising political views were actually supported by the incontestable evidence of recent experience: the men who held them were only doing what men are always doing—generalizing from a single instance. They thought that they possessed irrefutable evidence in favour of the ecclesiastico-political theory of the state, which reinforced persecuting tendencies by providing them with a theoretical basis suited to the growing secularity of the time. Hence the popularity of the views, held by such men as Thorndike, Stillingfleet and Saywell, that the Church would be destroyed or nearly so by the loss of exclusive State support, and that the State would be convulsed by the loss of the bond of union which membership of a common religious organization supplied. These views, it should be noticed, were diametrically opposed to the ecclesiastical theory of the Independents, and blocked the approach to toleration along the lines they had marked out. *which recent events seemed to confirm.*

The case of the Nonconformists was complicated by the case of the Roman Catholics. For the latter, indeed, legal toleration was out of the question, with such general fear and detestation was their Church regarded; but this horror of Romanism bore upon the Nonconformist question in two distinct, and, curiously enough, antagonistic, ways. On the one hand the supposed seditious tendencies of Noncon- *(Bearing of the Roman Catholic question upon the Nonconformist question.)*

formity were appealed to as proof of affinity with the Papists who held the monstrous doctrine that kings might be deposed. On the other hand, among both Conformists and Nonconformists warning voices were raised against the danger of division in face of the common enemy, and urging the Roman peril as a spur to reconciliation. Thus the Nonconformist controversy was soon entangled with the Roman Catholic question, which was intermittently to supersede it and eventually to play a great part in settling it. Popery scares came periodically. In the intervals Protestants had leisure to persecute one another.

(2) *Economic considerations.* Among forces making for toleration economic considerations must be given a prominent place. The period was one of conscious commercial expansion and vividly realized commercial rivalry. One war with the Dutch had already been fought under the Protectorate; in the very year before the next broke out the Conventicle Act brought persecution to bear upon a large section of the trading classes[1]. Men asked themselves, as well they might, whether such a measure was economically sound, and whether Englishmen might not do better in taking a leaf out of the Dutchmen's book and practising religious toleration. This point of view was insisted upon, amongst others, by John Owen, and found favour in high places. Ashley specially brought it before the attention of the King, who

[1] Officiating ministers were liable to punishment under the Act of Uniformity: the Conventicle Act provided for the punishment of their hearers.

alleged it, probably quite sincerely[1], as a reason for his Declaration of Indulgence in 1672.

Thus purely practical and mundane reasons appeared to be ambiguous. They could be alleged with some show of reason on either side. Care for the stability of the state seemed to point to persecution: care for commercial prosperity seemed to point to toleration. But as time went on the balance tended to incline in the latter direction, for while economic considerations remained where they were and maintained their importance, political considerations, or what men took for such, showed a tendency to be found of no weight or even to change sides.

If the verdict of practical considerations was ambiguous, that of the intellectual tendencies of the age was not. The political philosophy of Hobbes, indeed, gave full scope for the exercise of intolerance, but was not itself necessarily intolerant. Hobbes himself advocated a wide latitude in religious affairs, and was, no doubt with justice, accused of actually promoting tolerance in that his philosophy could easily be appealed to in support of the indifference of all religions. And all the other main currents of thought were making for toleration. With the Quakers toleration was the natural outcome of their religious views, and the sect produced, about a decade after the Restoration, a powerful advocate of it in William Penn. The

INTELLEC-TUAL TEN-DENCIES.

---

[1] Charles seems to have been genuinely desirous of the expansion of English commerce, especially as he saw that national prosperity was beneficial to the Crown. See Cunningham, *Growth of English Industry and Commerce*, II. 194–5 (1903).

influence of the Cambridge Platonists made in the
Latitudi-
narianism
same direction, because of their appeal to reason,
and their insistence upon the eternity of morality
and its importance in religion, in which respects
they at once represented and stimulated a widespread movement of the age. Their influence was
brought to bear upon practical politics mainly
through the latitudinarian school of which they
were the centre and the inspiration. For the
latitudinarians the main thing was that a man
should be morally good; not that he should be
intellectually sound on the details of party controversy. This concentration of attention upon a
question on which there was little difference of
opinion (except as to the relative ethical importance
of obedience to the civil power as such) was a
serious solvent of the case for persecution. Just as
Hobbes's theory that morality was dependent upon
the command of the civil power was largely made
(irrespective of his own personal preference) to
serve the cause of intolerance, so the assertion of
a morality independent of all external considerations
made for toleration.

But the latitudinarianism which the Cambridge
men inspired did not reach the height of its influence for some time after the Restoration: as we
approach the Revolution we find it an increasingly
practical force, becoming at once more widely felt
and less lofty in tone, as it passed from the academic
atmosphere in which it was nurtured to the more
practical atmosphere in which they move who have
their business amidst the everyday affairs of the

outside world. Thinkers are for the most part as
it were but corks on the waves of thought in the
general consciousness; and the wave that had raised
up the Cambridge Platonists was gathering strength
and volume. In exalting reason and morality in *appealed*
religion the latitudinarians reflected the dominant *to reason,*
tendency in the spirit of the age. In religious
matters the High Churchmen of the Laudian type
appealed to church authority; the sectaries and
Quakers appealed to the Spirit or the inner light;
but, in opposition to both of these alike, the keynote
of the coming eighteenth century was sounding
more and more insistently—the appeal to reason[1].

Akin to latitudinarianism especially in this respect was Naturalism, a movement destined to *as also did*
diverge further from narrow orthodoxy than did *Natural-*
latitudinarianism. The latter raised up the divines *ism:*
who in the next century defended Christianity, as
it was then interpreted, against the Deists; the
Deists themselves were the intellectual offspring of
Naturalism. As yet however Naturalism mainly
appeared as a background of thought which it did
not dominate: instances of this phase are afforded
by Stillingfleet, Savage, and Wolseley. Its tolerant
tendency lay, as we have seen, in the fact that it
assumed and discovered an actual community in
fundamentals between divergent parties.

But behind and including these intellectual *behind*
currents towards toleration was the growth of the *both of*
these was
inquiring or sceptical spirit characteristic of the *the growth*
of the

[1] *Essays and Reviews* (7th ed. 1861), p. 328. (Pattison on *spirit of*
Religious Thought in England, 1688–1750.) *inquiry,*

age—a spirit working itself out in scientific progress, religious indifference, and unbelief. The scientific spirit, whatever be its ultimate bearing upon religious belief, is certainly unfavourable to religious belief credulously held. The challenge, whether answerable or not, is still a challenge that demands an answer. And this spirit was spreading. In 1662 the King granted a charter of incorporation to the already existent Royal Society, the aim of which was to promote " Physico-Mathematical Experimental Learning[1]." The advance of such learning inevitably involves the retreat of theology from a field over which it unjustly usurps dominion in absence of the rightful possessor, science. Phenomena previously interpreted as divine interferences with nature are discovered instead to be the inevitable outcome of the laws of nature ; the most obvious manifestations of the existence of the Deity, by which men were cheered or rewarded, warned, thwarted, or catastrophically destroyed, are discovered to be links in unbroken, concurrent, and interacting sequences of causes and effects. This necessitates a recasting of conceptions widely entertained as to the relation of nature to the Creator, and opens the door to scepticism and unbelief. Thus the first vague *which* stirrings of the sceptical spirit rouse men to investi- *further* gate, and investigation produces definite scepticism *makes for* *toleration* on particular questions, and therefore a tolerant *through* *the pro-* attitude in regard to them. *duction of* Positive unbelief, indeed, which is generally *(a) unbe-* *lief,* produced in some minds by the same causes as

[1] *Social England*, IV. 286. Evelyn's Diary, Aug. 13, 1662.

those producing scepticism in others (but from which scepticism must be clearly distinguished), is by no means itself necessarily tolerant: there are not wanting indications that the vice of persecution even for religion is far from being monopolized by the religions. But in the case under consideration the unbelievers were not strong enough even to dream of persecuting Christianity in general, and would naturally be indifferent, as far as religious considerations went, to the points at issue between the Church and the Dissenters. And unbelief from one cause or another was on the increase.

While tolerance was promoted by unbelief, not *(b) scepti-cism,* because of the nature of unbelief, but because of the circumstances of the time, it was promoted by scepticism because scepticism is by nature tolerant For it is the negation of conviction, and conviction is a necessary antecedent to persecution. And though scepticism may go only so far as to substitute for un-compromising conviction the recognition of a view as a satisfactory and highly probable working hypo-thesis, yet even so it produces a state of mind that is not prone to persecute. In many cases it goes further and takes the form of religious indifference. It is in the light of this great movement of the inquiring spirit that we must view the Hobbism which could reduce national religion to little more than the creature of a tyrant's caprice. Hobbism was at once the offspring and the parent of religious indifference. Whatever were Hobbes's personal be-liefs, no man even moderately conscious of the importance of religion could have propounded his philosophy: nor could his philosophy ever have attained to such influence and popularity as was attributed to it save in an age in which religious indifference was common: nor in any age could it have attained to such influence and popularity without intensifying and spreading such religious indifference as existed.

(c) *a dispassionate attitude,* But, even in minds where no form of unbelief or scepticism is generated, scientific research is yet, in general, a foe to intolerance. Men not only learn from science to substitute the idea of physical laws for the idea of arbitrary divine interference, but also unlearn the enlistment of passion in support of an intellectual position. Religion is so largely an affair of the emotions, that vehement emotional support is immediately forthcoming for the theories upon which it rests or is supposed to rest. But science is comparatively unemotional, and its problems admit more easily of calm discussion. And as an acrimony more natural to religious differences has sometimes been displayed by opposing scientists, so the habit of dispassionate consideration of scientific questions must have done an incalculable amount to still the tempests of religious bigotry.

(d) *diversion from religious topics.* Moreover new interests naturally turn men's attention away from old controversies, and in our period experiments with diving bells and " Prince Rupert's drops " were refreshing pursuits to which to turn from such subjects as infant baptism and the possibility of salvation for a Papist.

To sum up our review of the general tendencies at work in our period we may say that among practical considerations it was mainly on political grounds that the persecution was supported, while toleration was advocated on economic grounds: the intellectual tendencies of the day were on the tolerant side, and of these we have especially noticed the growing appreciation of morality, naturalism, and, behind and informing both of these, the growth of the sceptical or rationalistic spirit. In reaction from the religious ebullitions of recent years secularism was strongly influential, and the secularization of the question of persecution was the preliminary to toleration.

In his Declaration of Indulgence, as in his *The Declaration* Declaration of Breda, Charles took a purely secular *claration* and practical view of the situation: whatever may *of Indulgence,* have been at the back of his mind, political and *1672.* economic considerations alone are mentioned. Its effects were permanent. Dissent had reached its lowest point when it was almost extinguished by the vigorous execution of the Second Conventicle Act: it now received a new lease of life. An instructive point with regard to the Declaration is the opposition with which it was met by many of the Dissenters themselves, in spite of the relief which it gave them and the very substantial advantages they took of it. The intensity of passion with which the Roman Catholics were regarded could hardly be more strikingly proved than by the fact that the Dissenters preferred that the Papists should be persecuted rather than that they themselves should have liberty. Though the lion's share of the "indulgence" fell to them, yet so swayed were they by religious passion and fear for the constitution, that they gave up their own claims to spiritual food rather than allow the members of the hated Church to be fed.

Drift of popular feeling towards toleration. The upshot of the whole affair—the Declaration, its compulsory withdrawal, and Charles's alliance with the Church of England—was a renewed enforcement of the penal laws against the Dissenters; but, though the tide of persecution ebbed and flowed, the ocean-current of popular feeling set towards toleration. As we have noticed, the persecution was mainly inspired by the memory of the rebellion and the interregnum; but the Dissenters were gradually living down their dreadful past. To an increasing proportion of Conformists they must have appeared less as men who had cut off the royal martyr's head and oppressed the Episcopalian party, than as men who were now being imprisoned, not for any real fault, but only for what had been arbitrarily made one in a domineering and vindictive spirit deeply tinged with fear. Men's attitude towards them was largely determined according as they laid more stress on what was or on what had been; and while for all men the memory of "the late troubles"—however capable of rousing passion—was a receding memory, a new generation was growing up which knew the Dissenters not as oppressors but as oppressed. Memory was giving way to sight, and consequently passion was being slowly allayed and was leaving room for the growth of respect.

Gradual recognition of the permanence of Dissent. Moreover, Dissent had taken firm root; or rather it was merely the expression of a permanent type of religious feeling which from the Reformation to the

Civil War had found quarters (latterly increasingly uncomfortable) in the Church of England[1]. The Act of Uniformity did not create a new religious party, it merely added to Nonconformity the characteristic of Dissent[2]. This permanence of Dissent—prophesied in 1660 by John Corbet for his own party, the Presbyterians—was gradually coming to be recognized. The Declaration of Indulgence of 1672 and "The Naked Truth," published three years later, alike drew attention to the ineffectiveness of the repressive measures. Disturbance was being caused to no purpose: as far as the Dissenters were concerned the public estimation of political expediency was beginning to change sides. The actual course of this change perhaps it is hardly possible to trace with any exactness upon the surface of affairs. What it is important to notice is that it did take place, and had been completed by 1689.

The change that was passing over the public mind resulted mainly from the mere pressure of events, and not from an intelligent grasp of principle. Hence it was hampered by the fact that no rational scheme of toleration could be put forward to render it articulate. Its irrational and yet practical character is well shown in its eventual outcome, the Toleration Act—a typical specimen of English legislation, in that, untrammelled by abstract

[1] Except, of course, the comparatively small number of separatists.

[2] The Puritan malcontents in the Church of England before the Civil War were called Nonconformists. After the Restoration the terms Nonconformists and Dissenters were used to all intents and purposes interchangeably for the ejected party.

principle, it devised such remedies as were expected to be practically adequate in the then state of affairs.

The Popish Plot scare and the reaction.

But before that end could be reached, times of storm and stress must be passed through. In the first fear at the revelation of the Popish Plot Churchman and Dissenter were once more drawn together in defence of their common Protestantism. But the temporary alliance was followed by a disastrous reaction. The threatening appearance of the Whigs at Oxford in 1681, the Rye House Plot, and lastly Monmouth's rebellion, made it seem to many that the return of the days of 1641 and 1642, long prophesied, had actually come to pass; and the Nonconformists suffered in consequence.

The Declaration of Indulgence, 1687.

But, by the irony of fate, as the Popish Plot scare, raised with the intention of ruining the Roman Catholics, eventually brought evil days upon the Dissenters, so a measure devised for the relief of the Roman Catholics brought the Dissenters freedom. The King offered them a precarious freedom for the present: the Church in eager competition held out hopes of a stable freedom in the future. The Dissenters took both. On the one hand, though they for the most part repeated the refusal of 1672 to applaud a benefit which the Papists shared with them and which was unconstitutionally conferred, they naturally took advantage of James's declaration. On the other, by ranging themselves upon the side of constitutional liberty and religious intolerance, they bought the permanence of their own religious liberty. " By bringing into prominence the essential agreement of the nation on the fundamental issue of Protestantism, the restored Stuarts promoted the victory of so much toleration as the circumstances of the country admitted[1]."

Hence came the Toleration Act, which did not concede the principle of religious liberty, but did concede the individual's right to choose his religion within narrow limits with impunity. It should be noticed that it was granted as a matter of expediency by those who had hitherto opposed toleration. It came, not from the Independency which forty years before was practically identified with the spirit of toleration, but from the descendants of the Cavaliers and Presbyterians who had withstood it[2]. The moral and intellectual position of the persecutors had been weakened during the reigns of Charles II and James II; and James had added the crowning argument. Unless the Church would guarantee the toleration of Dissent, his "indulgence" bade fair to be a stepping-stone to the re-establishment of the Roman supremacy. The toleration which the Church had withheld became in the King's hands a weapon for her overthrow, and the Church was compelled to meet him with his own weapon. In this rough and ready way the opponents of toleration were partially converted without the theory of the Independents, save in so far as it had coöperated with other pleas for toleration in previously weakening their position.

The Toleration Act.

[1] Henson, *English Religion in the Seventeenth Century*, 262.
[2] Gardiner, *Cromwell's Place in History*, 30–1, 109–10.

Locke's Letters.

Meanwhile, without taking part in the controversy, John Locke had been quietly elaborating his theory. The unpublished "Essay concerning Toleration" contained the nucleus of the views set forth—too late to influence the Toleration Act—at such inordinate length in the Letters. In these the tolerant stream of Independent thought comes again in full vigour to the surface in union with other streams flowing in the same direction. Locke supported the complete separation, not indeed of religion, but of all religious organizations, from the state: church and state were for him distinct organizations with distinct ends: the care of souls was no business of the civil magistrate, and the infliction of civil penalties was no business of the church: religion itself was connected with the state mainly as a necessity for the maintenance of civil rights and public order.

After Locke's letters little that was new could be said in favour of toleration, at any rate by anybody of that age. Since the Restoration there had proceeded an irregular and largely ill-directed but lively fire from both sides: then came the deadly volley of Locke's letters, and thereafter but the bickering of the tolerationist outposts with the few survivors of the defeated army who still had stomach for the fight. The cause of toleration had gained a victory in the field of theory more signal than that which it had gained a short time before in the field of practice.

The Roman Catholics,

Thus immediately after the Revolution the pressing question of the position of the Noncon-

formists was in its main aspects settled. The
Roman Catholics on the other hand stood where
they had been: the Revolution had done nothing
to make them less than before in the eyes of the
nation idolaters and traitors. On the contrary, the *in spite of*
recent danger from a Romanizing king, from which *recent events,*
the nation had just escaped, and the present danger
from the Roman Catholic power of France which
had enlisted itself in support of the exiled king, and
the possibility of the former danger being renewed
by the intrigues of the Jacobite party at home might
well have brought upon the unhappy Romanists—
the mass of whom were in no way responsible for
the dangers and misfortunes of the nation—an
enmity more vindictive and implacable than ever.
As a matter of fact more stringent laws were in
course of time added to the penal code, but this
was little or nothing more than empty threatening.
Under Charles II the Roman Catholics had been
practically tolerated, except in times of excitement,
in respect of private worship: after the Revolution
they seem to have been tolerated more openly. This *enjoyed*
was no doubt largely due to the influence of William, *practical toleration;*
but would seem to indicate also a considerable de-
cline of the persecuting spirit in the people at large.
The terrific enactments of Parliament were the sur-
vivals of a custom already out of date.

The spirit of the age, which was favourable to *as also*
toleration, also produced, or rather now brought into *did the unortho-*
prominence, another class which stood in need of *dox,*
toleration. The growth of the rational and scientific
spirit had led men to seek for a fusion of religion

and philosophy, as the Platonism of the Cambridge school and the growth of the idea of Natural Religion testified. Many minds were thus satisfied in giving a liberalizing turn to orthodoxy; but the orthodoxy of those days was too narrow, and too little capable of expansion for all inquiring minds to find rest so. And variations from orthodoxy were met in a most intolerant and undiscriminating spirit by the orthodox, the more zealous of whom denounced the slightest unorthodoxy as atheism : and atheism, it was then held, struck away the very foundations of society. And even if all unorthodoxy was not actually atheistic it was at any rate blasphemous, and might be confidently expected in one way or another to militate against the nation's welfare. So in this case also penalties must be enacted; but in this case also they were left unenforced. The act was a sign of disapproval, expressed in the customary manner, and no doubt strongly felt, but not felt strongly enough and generally enough to find practical expression in persecution.

whose existence testifies to the strength of the rationalistic movement. The existence of this comparatively prominent body of unorthodox thinkers has another bearing upon our subject, besides the fact that they were the objects of theoretical persecution and actual toleration. They constitute in themselves an explanation of the fact that the persecution was only theoretical. A widespread intellectual movement is often most convincingly illustrated by its extremest products, and the post-Revolution Unitarians and Deists testify by their existence to the strength of the tendency which we may describe as scientific, sceptical, or rationalistic, and which, as we have already noticed, is essentially a tolerant force, apart from its liability to produce unbelief in previously accepted or even unchallenged propositions.

For the Nonconformists, the battle for mere *The Non-* toleration was already won. All that at present *conform-* *ists were* could reasonably be hoped for was theirs, and the *now on the* task before them was not to gain fresh concessions, *defensive.* but to keep what they had already gained. And it was by no means obvious that it could be kept. Political considerations had been the main driving power of the persecution before the Revolution, and political considerations raised its ghost after the Revolution in the question of occasional conformity, culminating in the Occasional Conformity Act. The Schism Act carried matters further and seemed to hold out a likelihood of the revival of the Clarendon Code. But the days for this were past. Even early in Anne's reign, when the danger first took shape, the only men still alive who had taken an active part in the Civil War were a few aged veterans already past their threescore years and ten ; and none but men well advanced in the latter half of life could recall even as their earliest childish memory the sight of Cromwell's regiments marching by.

The evolution of the Puritan party in the Church *Stages in* of England into a group of religious bodies organized *the evolu-* *tion of the* apart from that church on a footing of equality *Noncon-* before the law may perhaps be most conveniently *formists:* divided into five stages. First comes the stage of

(1) *to 1642 : differentiation.* increasing differentiation, culminating in the *régime* of Laud, under which the government of the Church came to be definitely and aggressively associated (2) *1642– 62 : separation.* with one of the parties within it. The second stage is that of the Civil War and the Interregnum, which latter ended for ecclesiastical purposes not in 1660, but in 1662. In this the two parties became separated by the clearest possible line of demarcation, that of actual armed collision followed by the oppression of one by the other; and it was only in the natural course of things that it should end in the expulsion of the weaker party by the stronger. The war had thrust the Puritan Churchmen into the arms of the hitherto small body, or rather aggregate of bodies, which stood altogether outside the Church; and into the company which they had chosen when the Episcopalians would have been glad to keep them in union with themselves, now, when they desired union with the Episcopalians, they were driven against their will. The second stage, then, culminated in definite separation. The Puritans, expelled from the Church by the Act of (3) *1662– 89 : persecution.* Uniformity, became Dissenters. But the Church which had refused to allow that they had a right to remain within its communion, further refused to allow that they had a right to exist outside it; and its refusal took the practical form of persecution, (4) *1689– 1828 : toleration.* the characteristic of the third stage. The fourth was inaugurated by the recognition in the Toleration Act of this right of the Dissenters to exist: what had originally been an opposing party within the establishment, was now a legalized system of alter-

native religious organizations. The fifth—that in which the Dissenters have attained equality before the law—came only after a long interval and by slow degrees. The repeal of the Test and Corporation Acts may be taken as marking the solid beginnings of the new advance[1]; but its full development is still comparatively recent. At the date which marks the limit of this essay that stage was still in the distant future; but under the first two kings of the House of Hanover the rule of the Whigs, giving the nation a tranquillity in which might be generated mutual confidence and respect, at least made permanent, in religious as in constitutional affairs, the gains of the Revolution[2].

(5) *from* 1828: *equality.*

[1] It had been, however, customary for a century to pass an annual act of indemnity for transgressors of these statutes.

[2] Lecky doubts whether religious liberty owes anything to the Revolution, on the ground that James II saw the necessity of including the Dissenters with the Roman Catholics, while the Church would have been driven by competition to large concessions. *History of England in the Eighteenth Century*, I. 203 (8 vols., 1878). It is possible that toleration might soon have come without the Revolution; the fact remains however that it was by the Revolution that it came.

Mutual relations of motives	*Motives to persecution*

Concerned with the salvation of souls. (12–18)

1. Of misbelievers: A. directly. (12–13)

Unsoundness incapable of demonstration. (14) Relate to the unseen world. (12)

wholly. (12)

I. RELIGIOUS. Desire to vindicate the honour of God. (9–10)

Supposed injunctions of Scripture. (10)

primarily.

II. THEOLOGICAL. Belief in exclusive salvation. (10)

2. Of believers: B. indirectly. (12–18)

III. DOCTRINAL. Desire to protect the church from infection with false doctrine. (10–11)

C. remotely. (13)

Unsoundness capable of demonstration. (30) Relate to this world. (12)

Arise from conservatism. (10)

primarily.

IV. ECCLESIASTICAL. Desire to protect the structure of the church. (11)

wholly. (12)

V. POLITICO-SOCIAL. Desire to protect the structure of the state and of society. (11)

N.B. This table does not profess to give an exhaustive statement of the cases for and against toleration, or, necessarily, the views of the present writer. It is designed merely to help the reader more easily to

---

Opposing considerations

Higher conception of God.   (15)

Disclaimers of infallibility.   (16)

Tolerance of New Testament.   (15–16)

Higher conception of God.   (16)

Human fallibility (and consequent distinction between intellectual and moral error).   (17–19)

Man's right and duty to follow his own judgment.   (22)

That truth prevails by its own strength.   (22)

That persecution does not and cannot achieve its object.   (23–24)

Evil moral effects of persecution.   (24)

That persecution checks further discovery of truth.   (26–27)

That unanimity is impossible.   (27)

That church and state are not necessarily merely different aspects of the same social organism : hence
  1. that the cohesion of the church is independent of the civil power.   (32–33)

  2. that the cohesion of the state and of society are independent of ecclesiastical unity.   (32–33)

---

follow or to recollect the argument of pp. 9—33, in reference to which alone it should be read.

II. TABLE OF EVENTS, 1660–1714.

1660.   Declaration of Breda.
         The Restoration.
1661.   Savoy Conference.
         Corporation Act.
1662.   Act of Uniformity.
             Expulsion of the Dissenting clergy.
             Charles's proposal for the mitigation of the Act of
1663.   Uniformity by the dispensing power rejected
             by the House of Commons.
1664.   Conventicle Act.
1665–7. War with the Dutch.
1665.   The Plague.
         Five Mile Act.
1666.   The Fire of London.
1667.   Fall of Clarendon : rise of the Cabal.
1668.   Failure of Wilkins' scheme.
         Expiration of Conventicle Act.
1668–9 (?). Ashley's memorial to Charles II.
1670.   Second Conventicle Act.
         Treaty of Dover.
1672–4. Renewed war with the Dutch.
1672.   Declaration of Indulgence
1673.   withdrawn.
         Test Act.
             [Shaftesbury now organizes the Whig party ;
             and Charles, abandoning his Romanizing
             and tolerant policy, turns to the Church
             of England.]
1678.   Popish Plot scare raised by Titus Oates.
         Parliamentary Test Act.
1679–81. Exclusion Bill controversy.
1681.   Tory reaction.
1685.   Death of Charles II : accession of James II.
         Monmouth's rebellion.
1687–8. Declarations of Indulgence.
1688–9. The Revolution.

1689 (spring). Locke's *Epistola de Tolerantia* published in
           Holland.
    (May). Toleration Act receives royal assent.
    (autumn). English version of Locke's Letter published.
1698.   Blasphemy Act.
1702.   Death of William III : accession of Anne.
           High Church reaction.
1711.   Occasional Conformity Act.
1714.   Schism Act.
           Death of Anne : accession of George I.

III. SUMMARY OF THE PRINCIPAL PENAL AND TEST ACTS, 1660–1714.

Corporation Act, 1661 : 13 *Cha. II, St. II, c.* 1.

Persons bearing office in cities, corporations and boroughs required

    (1) to take the oaths of allegiance and supremacy,
    (2) to take an oath that it is not lawful, upon any
           pretence whatsoever, to take arms against the
           King,
    (3) to subscribe a declaration that the Solemn League
           and Covenant carried no obligation and that it
           was an unlawful oath. §§ IV, V, VI.

No persons henceforward to be appointed to such offices who should not have taken the sacrament according to the rites of the Church of England within one year before. § XII.

[For text see Grant Robertson, *Select Statutes etc.*, 10–12.]

Act of Uniformity, 1662 : 14 *Cha. II, c.* 4.

Services to be said by all ministers in all places of public worship in such order and form as was mentioned in the book annexed. § III.

Every minister holding benefice or promotion publicly to read Morning and Evening Prayer according to the said book, and to declare his "unfeigned assent and consent to all and every thing contained and prescribed in and by the book[1]," upon some Lord's day before the feast of S. Bartholomew, 1662, on pain of deprivation of all spiritual promotions. §§ III, IV, V.

Every person thereafter receiving any benefice or promotion to read Morning and Evening Prayer and publicly to make the prescribed declaration of unfeigned assent and consent to the Prayer Book upon some Lord's day within two months after being in actual possession, on pain of deprivation. § VI.

All clergy, fellows etc. of colleges, schoolmasters and tutors to subscribe a declaration that

> (1) it is not lawful upon any pretence whatsoever to take arms against the King,
>
> (2) they would conform to the liturgy of the Church of England,
>
> (3) the Solemn League and Covenant carried no obligation to endeavour any change of government in church or state and was in itself an unlawful oath,

on pain of deprivation.   §§ VIII, IX, X.

No minister not episcopally ordained to retain or be admitted to any benefice, or to consecrate and administer the sacrament.   §§ XIII, XIV.

Preachers of lectures or sermons to be licensed by archbishop or bishop, to declare unfeigned assent to the 39 articles, and to make the prescribed declaration of unfeigned assent and consent to the Prayer Book, on pain, in case of

---

[1] The Act runs as follows :—" shall...declare his unfeigned assent and consent to *the use of* all things in the said book...in these words, and no other: 'I, A.B., do here declare my unfeigned assent and consent to all and every thing contained and prescribed in and by the book....'" The omission from the actual declaration of the words "the use of" made a vital difference. Whether the declaration should be interpreted in the light of the requisition, or the requisition in the light of the declaration, was a nice point for a casuist, and some men's benefices depended upon their decision of it. See Abbey and Overton, *The English Church in the Eighteenth Century*, I. 386–7.

preaching after disablement by the act, of imprisonment for three months in the common gaol. §§ XIX, XXI.

[For text see Grant Robertson, 12–26.]

Conventicle Act, 1664 : 16 *Cha. II, c.* 4.

Persons of 16 years of age and upwards, present at a conventicle attended by five or more persons in addition to the household, for first offence to be imprisoned for not more than three months, or to be fined not more than £5 ; for third offence to be transported for seven years or fined £100 ; further offences to be punished at the rate of £100 increment each time. §§ I, II, III, V, VI.

Quakers and others refusing to take the oaths to be transported. §§ XVI, XVIII.

Act to be continued for three years after end of present session of Parliament, and thence forward to end of next session of Parliament after the said three years and no longer. § XX.

Five Mile Act, 1665 : 17 *Cha. II, c.* 2.

Persons in holy orders or pretending to holy orders, who

(1) had not declared unfeigned assent and consent to the use of all things in the Prayer Book, and
(2) had not subscribed the declaration in the Act of Uniformity, and
(3) should not take and subscribe an oath that
   (*a*) it is not lawful, upon any pretence whatsoever, to take arms against the King,
   (*b*) they would not at any time endeavour any alteration of government either in church or state, §§ I, II,

and all such persons as should preach in any conventicle, should not come within five miles of any city, corporate town, or borough, or of any place where (since the Act of Oblivion[1]) they had been vicars, curates, lecturers, etc., or preached in a conventicle, until they should have taken and subscribed the oath aforesaid ; on pain of a fine of £40 for each offence. § III.

---

[1] 12 Cha. II, c. 11, 1660.

No person so restrained, and not frequenting the established service, might teach in any school or take boarders for purposes of instruction, on pain of a fine of £40 for each offence. § IV.

Any two J.P.'s, upon oath to them of any offence against the act, might commit the offender for six months without bail, unless he should before them swear and subscribe the aforesaid oath and declaration. § V.

[For text see Grant Robertson, 33–35.]

Second Conventicle Act, 1670: 22 *Cha. II*, c. 1.

Persons of 16 years of age and upwards, present at a conventicle attended by five or more persons in addition to the household, to be fined five shillings for the first, and ten shillings for each subsequent offence. §§ I, II.

Preachers in such conventicles to be fined £20 for the first and £40 for each subsequent offence; and the owner of the premises to be fined £20. §§ III, IV.

All the clauses in the act to "be construed most largely and beneficially for the suppressing of conventicles, and for the justification and encouragement of all persons to be employed in the execution thereof[1]." § VII.

[For text see Grant Robertson, 35–38.]

Test Act, 1673: 25 *Cha. II*, c. 2.

Persons holding office or receiving pay from the King, or serving in the King's or the Duke of York's household (and such as should subsequently do so), resident in, or within thirty miles of, London or Westminster, to take the oaths of supremacy and allegiance, to make a declaration against transubstantiation, and to receive the sacrament according to the usage of the Church of England, on pain of being incapacitated for the post. §§ I, II, IV, IX.

Persons who should "refuse to take the said oaths or the sacrament as aforesaid," and yet should "execute any of the said offices," to be "disabled from thenceforth to sue or use any action, bill, plaint or information in course of law, or to

---

[1] These latter were further encouraged by a clause (v) imposing fines upon them for neglecting to enforce the act.

prosecute any suit in any court of equity, or to be guardian of any child, or executor or administrator of any person, or capable of any legacy or deed of gift, or to bear any office "; and to be fined £500.   § v.

[For text see Grant Robertson, 39–42.]

Parliamentary Test Act, 1678: 30 *Cha. II, St. II, c.* 1.

All members of either house to make a declaration against

    (1) transubstantiation,

    (2) invocation of saints and the sacrifice of the mass,

    (3) the Pope's power to dispense with or annul their declaration, §§ II, III,

on pain of

    (1) exclusion from the Royal Presence,

    (2) exclusion from Parliament,

    (3) forfeiting and suffering as popish recusants convict, and

    (4) incurring the disabilities and fine prescribed in § v of Test Act (see above).   §§ v, vi.

Blasphemy Act, 1698: 9 *Will. III, c.* 35 (*otherwise* 9 *and* 10 *Will. III, c.* 32).

Persons having been educated in or having at any time made profession of the Christian religion in England, who should, by writing, printing, teaching or advised speaking,

    (1) deny any one of the Persons of the Holy Trinity to be God,

    (2) assert or maintain that there are more gods than one,

    (3) deny the Christian religion to be true, or

    (4) deny the Holy Scriptures of the Old and New Testament (*sic*) to be of divine authority,

to be for the first offence disabled to hold any office ecclesiastical, civil, or military ; in case of second conviction to incur the disabilities (but not the fine) prescribed in § v of the Test Act (see above) and to be imprisoned for three years.

Occasional Conformity Act, 1711 : 10 *Anne, c.* 6 (*otherwise c.* 2).

Persons obliged by the Corporation Act (1661) and the Test Act (1673) to receive the sacrament according to the usage of the Church of England, attending a conventicle after admission to their respective offices, to forfeit £40, and to be disabled thenceforth to hold any office or employment, unless they should subsequently conform for a year without attending any conventicle, and receive the sacrament according to the usage of the Church of England at least three times in the year. §§ I, II, III.

[For text see Grant Robertson, 107–110.]

Schism Act, 1714 : 13 *Anne, c.* 7 (*otherwise* 12 *Anne, St. II, c.* 7).

Persons acting as schoolmasters or tutors before

(1) subscribing a declaration that they would conform to the liturgy of the Church of England, and
(2) obtaining a licence from the bishop only to be granted to persons who should
   (*a*) produce a certificate of having received the sacrament according to the usage of the Church of England within one year before,
   (*b*) have taken or subscribed the oaths of allegiance, supremacy, and abjuration, and
   (*c*) have subscribed the declaration against transubstantiation prescribed by the Test Act (1673),

to be imprisoned for three months in the common gaol. §§ I, II.

Schoolmasters and tutors resorting to a conventicle after complying with the preceding regulations to be liable to the penalties prescribed in this act, and incapacitated thenceforth to act as schoolmasters and tutors unless they should subsequently conform for a year and receive the sacrament at least three times in that year. §§ III, X.

The act not to extend to persons giving instruction only in reading, writing, arithmetic, such mathematics as relate to navigation, or in any mechanical art, all such teaching being in English only. § XII.

[For text see Grant Robertson, 110–113.]

IV. THE DATE OF STILLINGFLEET'S "IRENICUM."

The date of the publication of Stillingfleet's "Irenicum" is frequently given as 1659. This assertion seems to be based upon a statement in the Life prefixed to the 1710 edition of Stillingfleet's Works. On page 4 the author, after recording Stillingfleet's appointment as Rector of Sutton in 1657, goes on to say, "and here he published his Irenicum before mentioned in the year 1659, and when he was not above twenty-four years of age, which he also reprinted in 1662." The last statement is confirmed by the existence of an edition of the "Irenicum" described upon the title-page as the second edition and bearing the date 1662. But the alleged edition of 1659 I have not found. The University Library at Cambridge, the Bodleian Library at Oxford, and the British Museum all contain copies dated 1661 and 1662, but in none of them is there a copy dated 1659. In one of the British Museum copies there is a MS alteration of the date from 1661 to November 21, 1660.

The supposition that the 1661 edition is merely a reissue of a 1659 edition which has been completely lost is negatived by internal evidence. In the preface (on the eleventh page) we find the following passage: "in the mean time what cause have we to rejoice that the Almighty hath been pleased to restore us a prince of that excellent prudence and moderation, who hath so lately given assurance to the world of his great indulgence towards all that have any pretence from conscience to differ with their brethren!" The preface, then, clearly did not take its present form till 1660 or later.

The internal evidence of the body of the work is less conclusive, but points the same way. On page 64 we find among the "bounds to be set in restraint of Christian liberty," "that no sanctions be made, nor mulcts or penalties be inflicted on such who only dissent from the use of such things whose lawfulness they at present scruple, till sufficient time and means be used for their information of the nature and indifferency of the things, that it may be seen whether it be out of wilful contempt and obstinacy of spirit, or only weakness of conscience and dissatisfaction concerning the things themselves that they disobey." This passage surely points to a definite expectation of a speedy settlement on Anglican lines.

On pages 110 and 111 the question is proposed, "Supposing a Church then to remain true, as to its constitution and essentials, but there be many corruptions crept into that Church; whether is it the duty of a Christian to withdraw from that Church because of those corruptions, and to gather new Churches only for purer administration, or to join with them only for that end? This as far as I understand it, is the state of the controversy between our parochial Churches and the Congregational—For parochial Churches are not denied to have the essentials of true Churches by any sober Congregational men—All that is pleaded then is corruption and defect in the exercise and administration of Church order and discipline." Again, on page 123, "And it cannot but be looked upon as a token of God's severe displeasure against us, if any, though unreasonable, proposals of peace between us and the Papists should meet with such entertainment among many; and yet any fair offers of union and accommodation among ourselves be so coldly embraced and entertained." The context makes it clear that Stillingfleet regarded the Churchmen as in a position to receive proposals from those who dissented from them. As in the previous passage, the Church is supposed to be in the stronger position.

Another interesting passage occurs on page 415 (wrongly numbered 417). "That proposal of his late most excellent Majesty of glorious memory is most highly reasonable. 'His Majesty thinketh it well worthy the studies and endeavours of Divines of both opinions, laying aside emulations and private interests, to reduce Episcopacy and Presbytery in such a well-proportioned form of superiority and subordination, as may best resemble the Apostolical and Primitive times, so far forth as the different condition of the times and the exigences of all considerable circumstances will admit.' If this proposal be embraced, as there is no reason why it should not; then all such things must be retrieved which were unquestionably of the primitive practice, but have grown out of use through the length and corruption of the times. Such are the restoring of the Presbyteries of the several churches, as the senate to the Bishop, with whose counsel and advice all things were done in the Primitive Church. The contracting of dioceses into such a compass as may be fitted for the personal inspection of the Bishop, and care of himself and the Senate ; the placing of Bishops in all great towns of resort, especially county towns ; that according to the ancient course of the Church its government may be proportioned to the civil government. The constant preaching of the Bishop in some churches of his charge, and residence in his diocese ; the solemnity of ordinations with the consent of the people ; the observing of provincial synods twice a year. The employing of none in judging of church matters but the clergy. These things are unquestionably of the primitive practice, and no argument can be drawn from the present state of things, why they are not as much, if not more necessary than ever." This passage, both in its actual proposals and in its general tone, certainly seems more in keeping with the state of affairs following the Restoration when Archbishop Usher's scheme of " modified episcopacy " was much in the air, than with that preceding it. There is no suggestion that Episcopacy is under the ban of the law, and while there is talk of restoring the presbyteries, there is none of restoring the bishops. The most natural inference is that they were already restored. The uncompromising terms in which reference is made to King Charles I seem to point in the same direction.

To sum up the positive internal evidence, we may say that it would seem to favour a date not earlier than the Restoration : as regards the body of the book the evidence is not quite conclusive ; but even if that retains the form in which it was written in 1659 (supposing that to be the date of publication), the preface certainly does not.

Hence if we accept the statement in the " Life " that the book was first published in 1659, we must suppose that the edition of 1661 was not a mere reprint with a different date, but a second edition, and therefore that that of 1662 was the third edition. But the " Life " implies that the edition of 1662 was the second, and in this implication it is supported by the conclusive evidence of the title-page of that edition.

It remains for us to infer that the statement that the first edition appeared in 1659 is probably false. This inference is supported not only by the fact that there is no copy of the alleged edition of 1659 in the libraries mentioned, and the positive internal evidence of the book itself, but by the negative internal evidence that no reference (so far as I know) is made in the 1661 edition to any change of circumstances having taken place since the first publication of the book—a strange omission if the Restoration had intervened. Stillingfleet would hardly have failed in such a case to have called attention to the increased facilities for putting his theory into practice since that theory had first been broached.

Stillingfleet's other writings do not, as far as I am aware, give us any clear evidence on the question. The references to the " Irenicum " in " Several Conferences between a Popish Priest, a Fanatick Chaplain etc." (pp. 148–9) are quite indecisive. In the preface to his " Unreasonableness of Separation " (this is itself dated 1681, but John Owen's " Answer " is dated 1680) he speaks of the interval which had elapsed since the publication of the " Irenicum" as "twenty years time " (lxxii), but there is no reason to suppose he was making an exact computation. In his " Epistle Dedicatory before the ordination sermon at S. Peter's, Cornhill, March 15, 168$\frac{4}{5}$ " he speaks of the " Irenicum " as published "above twenty years since," and says that the systematic study which resulted in it was begun "about 25 years since." These passages, like the preceding one, are, no doubt, not meant for strict interpretation ; but perhaps it is just worth noticing that in none of the three cases would a strict interpretation force the date of publication back beyond 1660. In the same Epistle he says that the book was written " before the Church was reestablished," and that he wrote "to bring over those to a compliance with the Church of England (then like to be reestablished) who stood off upon the supposition that Christ had appointed a Presbyterian government to be always continued in his Church." These passages might be taken as referring to the period when the Restoration, though not yet an accomplished fact, was regarded as imminent, with the re-establishment of the Church as a probable consequence ; but I am inclined to think that they would refer still better to the period between the Restoration and the Act of Uniformity, in which it became clearer that Presbyterianism could have no place in the Church of England.

There is, then, a good deal of evidence to controvert, and none that I know of to support, the authority of the Life. And that authority is less than is in some quarters supposed. It is sometimes attributed to Richard Bentley, who, having been closely associated with Stillingfleet, first as tutor to his second son, and afterwards as chaplain, was in a position to know the facts accurately. But I understand from Mr A. T. Bartholomew, of Peterhouse and the University Library, Cambridge, who has recently compiled a bibliography of Bentley's works ("Richard Bentley: a bibliography of his works and of all the literature called forth by his acts or his writings," 1908), that this ascription is certainly a mistake. We need not feel, then, so much compunction in setting aside the authority of the anonymous biographer. There is even an explanation to hand of the cause of his error, as it seems to be. My attention has been called by Mr T. G. Crippen, of the Congregational Library (Memorial Hall, Farringdon Street, E.C.) to a pamphlet entitled "Irenicum: or an Essay toward a brotherly peace and union between those of the Congregational and Presbyterian Way." This was published in 1659, and the similarity of title possibly accounts for the assignation of that date to Stillingfleet's work.

Though I am aware that none of the evidence brought forward is final, yet I venture to think that its accumulated force lends considerable probability to the view that the "Irenicum" was published not in 1659, but in 1661, or, if we regard the MS correction in the British Museum copy as the work of a contemporary hand, perhaps in the latter part of 1660. To the practice of dating books with the year following that of their publication I have referred in the preface to this essay, and it is perhaps worth noticing that it seems to have been followed in the case of another of Stillingfleet's works—"The Unreasonableness of Separation," as we have seen above.

BIBLIOGRAPHY

This bibliography is primarily a list of the books, articles, etc., referred to in the text or the footnotes. Thus while it includes some books which bear but very slightly on the subject owing to the accident of reference or quotation, it makes, on the other hand, no pretence to completeness. References to the subject mainly occur in stray chapters, essays or passages in books dealing either with broader aspects of the history of the period or with the subject of toleration in general ; and probably widely differing lists of equal value could be compiled. Very few books give much attention to our subject : a list of those which throw at least some appreciable light upon it would rapidly swell to inordinate dimensions. It is hoped, however, that the list here given may be useful as a guide to such as may wish to study the subject for themselves. In most cases only a small portion of or a few passages in the book are strictly relevant. In cases where doubt is likely to arise the edition referred to is specified. I have not thought it necessary to give a list of contemporary contributions to the controversy, as the chief of these are easily discoverable from the marginal notes of Chapters III and V.

In books marked thus, *, the relevant portions are of especial value. Books enclosed in square brackets have little bearing on the subject. The numbers denote the pages of this essay on which the references in footnotes occur.

*Abbey and Overton : *The English Church in the Eighteenth Century.* 2 vols. 1878. 72, 108, 286.

Airy, O.: *The English Restoration and Louis XIV.* 108.

Aitken (ed.): *Later Stuart Tracts.* 150–1, 297–8.

[Arber : *Story of the Pilgrim Fathers.*] 266.

Bate, Frank: *The Declaration of Indulgence, 1672.* 98, 107–8, 113, 172, 181, 183.

Bevan, J. O.: *Birth and Growth of Toleration, and Other Essays.* 4, 41, 288.

Bolingbroke: *Letter to Sir W. Windham* in vol. I. of Works. 4 vols. Philadelphia, 1841. 304.

Bourne, H. R. Fox: *Life of John Locke.* 2 vols. 1876. 237–8, 243, 247.

Brown, Louise F.: *Religious Factors in the Convention Parliament.* (In *Eng. Hist. Rev.* XXII. 51, Jan. 1907.) 93.

Buckle: *History of Civilization in England.* 3 vols. Longmans' Silver Library, 1908. 3, 9, 70.

Burnet, Gilbert: *History of My Own Time.* 6 vols. Oxford, 1823. 67–8, 170, 214, 279, 296.

Calamy, Edmund: *The Nonconformist's Memorial,* ed. Samuel Palmer. 3 vols. 1802. 107.

Chillingworth, William: Works. 3 vols. Oxford, 1838. 51–5.

Christie, W. D.: *Life of the First Earl of Shaftesbury.* 2 vols. 149, 150.

Clarke and Foxcroft: *Life of Gilbert Burnet, Bishop of Salisbury.* 211.

Creighton, M.: *Persecution and Tolerance.* 20, 26, 36, 125.

[Cunningham, W.: *Growth of English Industry and Commerce,* vol. II. 1903.] 177, 315.

Debary: *History of the Church of England, 1685–1714.* 210.

Des Maizeaux: *Historical and Critical Account of the Life and Writings of William Chillingworth.* 51.

[Dicey, A. V.: *The Law of the Constitution.* 6th ed. 1902.] 36.

Dictionary of National Biography. 73, 210, 219, 225, 283.

Evelyn's Diary. 66, 183, 191, 312, 318.

Figgis: *The Divine Right of Kings.* 127, 221.

Fowler, T.: *Locke.*

—— *Shaftesbury.*

Fraser, A. Campbell: *Locke.* 265.

Gardiner, S. R.: *Cromwell's Place in History.* 64, 115, 325.

Gardiner and Mullinger: *Introduction to English History.* 110.

Gooch: *English Democratic Ideas in the Seventeenth Century.* 141.

Graham, W.: *English Political Philosophy.*   252, 268.

Greenslet: *Joseph Glanvill.*   125.

*Gwatkin, H. M.: *Toleration in England (Cambridge Modern History,* vol. v. ch. xi.).   73, 109, 233.

—— *The Knowledge of God.*   2 vols.

Hallam: *Constitutional History of England.*   3 vols.   1897.   157.

—— *Literature of Europe.*   3 vols.   1854.

Harrington: Works, ed. Toland.   1746.   78–9.

Henson, Hensley: *English Religion in the Seventeenth Century.*   64, 108, 235.

*Hunt, J.: *Religious Thought in England from the Reformation to the End of the Last Century.*   3 vols.   Ch. ii *passim,* 187, 197.

Hutton, W. H.: *History of the English Church, 1625–1714.*

Jellinek: *The Declaration of the Rights of Men and of Citizens:* trans. by Max Farrand.   Holt and Co., New York.   266.

Journals of the House of Commons.   85.

*Lecky: *History of Rise and Influence of Rationalism.*   2 vols.   1877–8.   39, 70.

—— *History of England in the Eighteenth Century.*   8 vols.   1878.   280, 331.

Locke: *Letters on Toleration.*   Alexander Murray's reprint, 1870.   244.

[—— *Second Vindication of the Reasonableness of Christianity,* in vol. vii of Works.   10 vols.   London, 1812.]   256.

Macaulay: Essay on *Gladstone on Church and State.*   244, 261.

Masson: *State of the Toleration Controversy, 1644,* being pp. 98–159 of vol. iii. of *Life of Milton.*   6 vols.   1859–80.   59, 60, 63.

Milton: Works.   8 vols.   London, 1851.   61–4, 105.

[Moore: *The Christian Doctrine of God.*   (In *Lux Mundi,* 3rd ed., 1890.)]   15.

Mozley, J. K.: *Ritschlianism.*   47.

Neal: *History of the Puritans.*   5 vols.   London, 1822.   171–2, 305.

Overton, J. H.: *Life in the English Church, 1660–1714.*

Owen, John: Works, ed. Russell. 21 vols. 1826. 126-37, 148, 171.

*Pattison, Mark: *Tendencies of Religious Thought in England, 1688–1750.* (In *Essays and Reviews*, 7th ed., 1861.) 64, 317.

Pepys' Diary. 148, 170.

Perry, G. G.: *Student's English Church History.* 1878. 93.

Pollard: *Factors in Modern History.* 234.

Pollock, Sir F.: *Theory of Persecution.* (In *Essays in Jurisprudence and Ethics.*) 10, 17, 32, 37–8, 165, 289.

—— *Locke's Theory of the State.* (In *Proceedings of the British Academy*, 1903–4.)

Pollock, J.: *The Popish Plot.*

Ritchie, D. G.: *Natural Rights.* 38, 163.

Robertson, Grant: *Select Statutes, Cases, and Documents.* 179, 232.

Scherger: *Evolution of Modern Liberty.* 59, 60.

Smith, A. L.: *English Political Philosophy in the 17th and 18th Centuries.* (*Cambridge Modern History*, VI. ch. XXIII.)

Social England, vol. IV (non-illustrated edition). 318.

Stephen, Sir James Fitzjames: *Liberty, Equality, Fraternity.* 42, 270.

—— *Horae Sabbaticae.* 3 vols. 57.

Stephen, Sir Leslie: *English Thought in the Eighteenth Century.*

—— *Prefatory Essay to Encyclopædia Britannica*, vol. XXVIII. 28–9, 42.

Stoughton: *The Church of the Restoration.*

—— *The Church of the Revolution.* 280.

—— *Religion under Queen Anne.*

Taylor, Alex.: Preface to his ed. of Patrick's Works. 71.

Taylor, Jeremy: *Liberty of Prophesying*, in Works, ed. Heber. 15 vols. London, 1822. 57.

Tillotson: Works. 12 vols. London, 1756. 28, 210.

Trevelyan, G. M.: *England under the Stuarts.* 173, 181, 235.

*Tulloch: *Rational Theology and Christian Philosophy in England in the Seventeenth Century.* 2 vols. Ch. II *passim*, 108, 122–3, 206.

Underhill, E. B. (ed.): *Tracts on Liberty of Conscience and Persecution, 1614–1661.* 60, 98–104.

Whately: *Errors of Romanism.* 1830.   24.

—— *Essays on some of the Dangers to Christian Faith.* 1839.

Whewell: *Lectures on the History of Moral Philosophy in England.* 1852.   80.

Wilkins, W. W. (ed.): *Political Ballads.* 2 vols. 1860.   117, 128, 203.

Worcester, E. E. *The Religious Opinions of John Locke.* [A treatise submitted for the degree of Ph.D. Leipzig : printed (? at Leipzig) 1889.]   270, 272.

INDEX

N.B. An asterisk marks the principal reference to a subject: references of minor importance are bracketed.

Liberalism in the Church of England: 48-51. See also Latitudinarians, Rational Theologians.

Liberty of Conscience asserted and vindicated (anon.): 215-6.

Liberty of Conscience...asserted and vindicated (Wolseley): (139 n.), 141-3, 167.

Liberty of Conscience in its order to Universal Peace, 215.

Liberty of Conscience the Magistrate's interest: (141), 144-7.

Liberty of Prophesying: 56, 271.

Licensing Act, 1662: 115.

Limborch: *Epistola de Tolerantia* addressed to, and published by, 242.

Lob, Stephen: *Peaceable Design Renewed:* 195.

Locke: (54), (70), (236), and the Independents, 237 and n., 272; connection with Shaftesbury, and retirement to Holland, 242; controversy with Proast, 243; death, 243; theory of the civil power, 244-6, of the church, 247-8, 265; on ceremonies, 248-9; on idolatry, 249-50; on Articles of Religion, 250-1; on sincerity, 251-2; exceptions from toleration, 252-3, 269-71; on effects of persecution, 253-5; on advantages of toleration, 255; on strength of truth, 255; on the true religion, 255-6, 264, 265; on heresy and schism, 256-7; answers to Proast's arguments, 258-63; view of the social contract, 244, 260-1, 265-7*; obstacles to acceptance of his theory, 263-5; his exaggerated estimate of the human intellect, 267-8; relation to his predecessors, 271-2; 285; tutor of third Earl of Shaftesbury, 293.

Essay concerning Toleration: 237-42, (326).

Defence of Nonconformity: 237 n., 247 n.

Letters on Toleration: history of *Epistola de Tolerantia,* 242-3, of the other letters, 243; compared with *Essay,* 243; substance of, 244-63, 326; estimate of, 272-4; effect of, 296, 299, 326.

Louis XIV: religious bigotry of, 111; Charles II's agreement with, 181; effect of his treatment of the Huguenots, 234; 269, 277; alleged usurpation of Anne's sovereignty over France by, 281.

Mackenzie, Sir George: 121-2. *Religio Stoici,* 121.

Magistrate, authority of: Stillingfleet on, 89-90, 198; Savage on, 101-3; L'Estrange on, 118-121; Wolseley on, 142-3; 143-4; Parker on, 154-65; 167-70; growing importance of question, 198; Locke on, 238-40, 244-6; T. Sherlock on, 283-4; Tindal's essay on, 289-92.

Marsiglio of Padua: 36.

Mary, Queen of Scots: 30.

Memorial of the Church of England: 298, 299, 300.

Memorial of the State of England: 299-300.

Method for the Extirpation of Popery: 278.

Milton: on religious liberty, 61-3.

Mischief of Separation: 193-4, 195, 237 n.

Moderator," "An Humble: 184.

Modern Pleas etc.: 139-41.

Mohammedans: (99), (133), (245), included by Locke in toleration, 269.

Monmouth's rebellion: 220, 324.

For EU product safety concerns, contact us at Calle de José Abascal, 56–1°, 28003 Madrid, Spain or eugpsr@cambridge.org.

www.ingramcontent.com/pod-product-compliance
Ingram Content Group UK Ltd.
Pitfield, Milton Keynes, MK11 3LW, UK
UKHW012329130625
459647UK00009B/155